PARIS AND HER
CATHEDRALS

PARIS AND HER CATHEDRALS

R. HOWARD BLOCH

LIVERIGHT PUBLISHING CORPORATION

A Division of W. W. NORTON & COMPANY

INDEPENDENT PUBLISHERS SINCE 1923

For information about permission to reproduce selections from this book,
write to Permissions, Liveright Publishing Corporation, a division of
W. W. Norton & Company, Inc., 500 Fifth Avenue, New York, NY 10110

For information about special discounts for bulk purchases, please contact
W. W. Norton Special Sales at specialsales@wwnorton.com or 800-233-4830

Manufacturing by Lakeside Book Company
Book design by Barbara M. Bachman
Production manager: Anna Oler

ISBN 978-1-63149-392-8

Liveright Publishing Corporation, 500 Fifth Avenue, New York, N.Y. 10110
www.wwnorton.com

W. W. Norton & Company Ltd., 15 Carlisle Street, London W1D 3BS

1 2 3 4 5 6 7 8 9 0

To Ellen Joan Handler, whose love of beauty and knowledge of beautiful things has been a source of inspiration and of counsel from the grandest understanding of how art makes meaning to what it means to live a loving life of the mind.

CONTENTS

———————

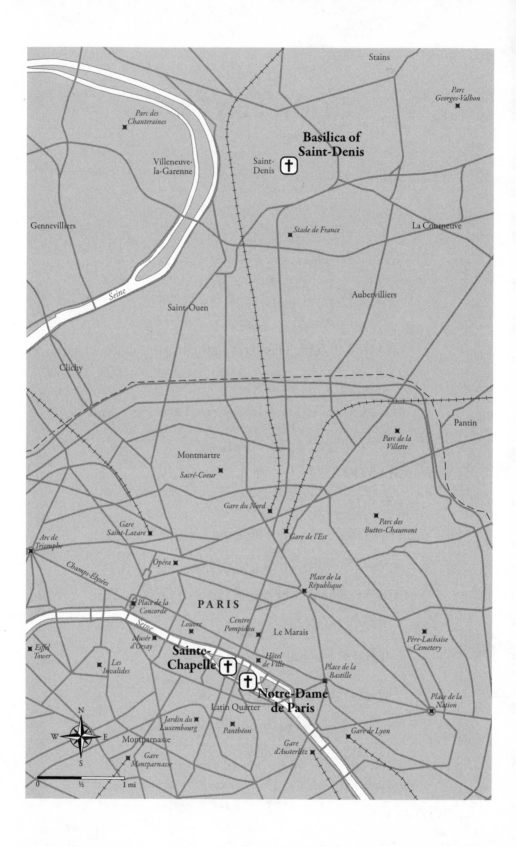

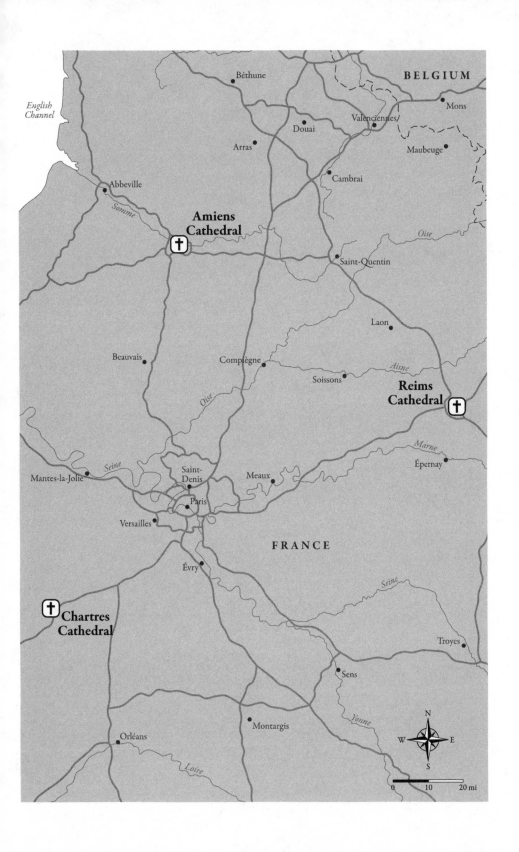

PREFACE

FOR SEVERAL DECADES I HAVE VISITED, STUDIED, AND ENGAGED with students about the cathedrals in the orbit of Paris. Such long experience has taught me that standing before or inside a monumental Gothic church may spark wonder at its size or beauty, but knowing something about it makes for a closeness that borders on love. What more can one ask from any work of art, even a total work of art like a cathedral, which bears witness to prodigious changes in worldview between the Middle Ages and the Renaissance of the sixteenth century when art came to occupy some of the psychic and social space that once belonged to religion.

Much of what one finds in scholarly writings about cathedrals is inaccessible to readers without a deep knowledge of medieval architecture or culture. On the other hand, guidebooks for tourists show insufficient interest in what went into the making of the Gothic structures of northern France, or how they have changed over time. *Paris and Her Cathedrals* bridges the gap between scholarly and popular literature. If you know nothing about the history of art or architecture, you will find here an introduction to the construction of some of the most astonishing buildings the world has ever known. If, however, you are versed in medieval history, you may discover new ways of looking at familiar things. The chapters of this little book can be read separately in preparation for an enlightened visit. Read as a whole, they open a window upon the High Middle Ages in France, one of the great moments of turning in the West.

My aim is that you experience as well as understand the glorious churches of Saint-Denis just north of Paris, of Notre-Dame and the

Sainte-Chapelle in Paris proper, and of Chartres, Amiens, and Reims in the cities of those names. Each chapter is organized along the lines of a walk around and then through the space of the cathedral such that the actual or virtual visitor feels the rich sweep of the church. That experience is, of course, visual, and I focus primarily on what can still be seen, and not, as do many historians of art, on what was first there or what the original builders had in mind. The underlying premise of what follows is that seeing is enhanced by knowing, the cathedrals themselves being part of the teaching and preaching culture of the twelfth and thirteenth centuries. And so the images of the buildings are framed first by descriptions of what they look like, and then by considerations—religious, social, economic, cultural—of how they came to be: how they were made and who made them; how they were used and who used them; how they changed the world around them; and how they have fared between the Middle Ages and the present—all keys to what a particular cathedral might mean today.

Nature has not been kind to these exquisite high buildings, subject over centuries to damage visited by rain, strong winds, and lightning strikes, even now called "acts of God." Storms and lightning took down the north tower of Saint-Denis in the 1840s; hail badly damaged the west rose window of Reims in 1886. History was especially cruel to religious monuments in France, symbols of the alliance between altar and crown, after the Revolution of 1789 and before the extensive restorations of the nineteenth century. Wars, too, have taken their toll: Amiens was caught in the midst of the Hundred Years' War, Reims was shelled throughout World War I. Cathedrals have suffered as a result of accidents and human error. In the seventeenth century, the explosion of a powder mill in the city of Amiens blew out stained glass on the proximate side of the church. The spectacular fire that destroyed the roof of Notre-Dame Paris in April 2019 was caused either by a faulty electrical circuit or a discarded cigarette. Thus, we shall follow the fate of cathedrals not only as they rose to full height in the Age of Cathedrals, but as evolving masterworks of stone, glass, wood, and metal in the post-medieval world.

There are ways of knowing cathedrals apart from historical or technical understanding. These lie in the realm of the imagination and of feelings, which may be subjective, different for each of us, but not without overlap or limits. We can no longer see the past, but we can imagine it, and we can still feel the emotional pull of what is left of it. I have tried to account—then and now—for the "cathedral effect," what one might have felt or imagined when they were covered inside and out by the bright colors of painted stone, visible at present only in traces, as by the deeply saturated glazings that in some places have been replaced by transparent glass. Cathedrals were once filled with gleaming liturgical objects, rich clerical vestments, tapestries, and rugs, and with the protracted sounds of organ and chant which made the vast volume of the medieval church as powerful a total work of art as anything ever produced in a large public festival, modern theater, or opera house. Though less visually vivid now and less acoustically rich, the wonder of Gothic churches continues to move and impress, and to inspire delight, ecstasy, terror, awe, and even pathos at what they have lost alongside admiration for what they have kept.

Part of acquainting ourselves with Gothic cathedrals has to do with vocabulary. The word "cathedral" comes from the Latin *cathedra*, meaning an "easy chair," and came to refer to the "church" or "seat of a bishop," or "the site of a bishop's seat." The cathedral functioned as the central church of a diocese, which derives from the Greek word for "administration." The diocese or bishopric may be divided into smaller units or parishes under the care of a priest. Not all the monuments we shall consider are, strictly speaking, cathedrals, nor have they always enjoyed that title. For centuries Saint-Denis was known as an abbey church attached to the monastery on its southern flank. After the Revolution of 1789 and the dispersal of religious institutions associated with monarchy, it became the Basilica of Saint-Denis; and only after 1966, when the diocese of Saint-Denis became a bishopric, did the old abbey church officially become a cathedral. Similarly, the Sainte-Chapelle was originally built as the private chapel of King Louis IX, and has never been associated with a bishop, though most visitors today think of it, alongside of Notre-Dame Paris or Chartres, as one of the cathedrals of France. The status of religious buildings has blurred in the wake of the state appropriation of church property, now managed by the French Ministry of Culture.

The terms used to describe the basic components of a cathedral, from the portals and porches of the west facade to the ambulatory chapels of its easternmost flank, from the crypt below to the towers and spires above, are familiar to medieval specialists, but not to the general public. This poses a dilemma: what to call the elements of their design so as to include the reader without losing the hallowed flavor of time-tested terms? Some of what makes a Gothic cathedral different from, say, a Greek temple, the entrance to an apartment building in Paris of the 1880s, a Hindu temple, or a modernist house of steel and glass, all of which have lintels, are the names drawn from the singular discipline of medieval architecture and that have lodged deep in that associative zone where words summon the essence of things. So, I have not steered clear of designations like "tympanum," "trumeau," "transept crossing," "triforium," "clerestory," "apse," and "nave," but have provided definitions upon their first use and, toward the end of the book, a glossary for this venture into a world that may seem strange because of the words used to describe it but is still recognizably our own.

The cathedral has famously been characterized as a Bible for the poor or for the illiterate, which is true to a degree. The biblical figures and narratives with which Gothic buildings are covered stem from a time when even the largest landholders and most powerful rulers could neither read nor write, and those who could had of necessity received a clerical education. In putting chapter and verse to what we see, I have used the Douay-Rheims Bible, whose particular wordings may seem offbeat to readers of the King James or the New Standard Revised editions. This, however, is the English translation of Saint Jerome's (d. 420 CE) Latin rendering from the original Hebrew, Aramaic, and Greek, which was the bible known to those who designed the cathedrals of the High Middle Ages as well as to those who prayed there.

Our travels in and around Paris, to the West toward Normandy, and to the North and East into the regions of Picardie and Champagne, might have been organized geographically, with journeys on foot in Paris's fourth and first arrondissements between Notre-Dame and the Sainte-Chapelle, and via subway or RER (express railway) to the northern suburb of Saint-Denis. Chartres and Amiens are both accessible by a standard train ride of between an hour and an hour and a half, and Reims via an express train (TGV) in less than sixty minutes. However, since all three are in different directions and the French railroad system is organized radially from Paris, a combined visit via public transportation is a difficult matter and is best undertaken by car.

I could have organized the chapters that follow according to the chronological order in which each cathedral was begun, though the historical window is relatively narrow between the beginning of Saint-Denis in the 1140s and the laying of the first courses of stone at Amiens in 1220 or the papal blessing of 1244 for construction of the Sainte-Chapelle, which was already underway. But medieval cathedrals were never actually begun. They were rebuilt on the foundations of previous structures, often as a result of devastating fire, or were simply rebuilt in the Gothic style as per the start date at the beginning of each chapter.

A completion date is hardly more meaningful for the understanding of medieval churches. Some, like Amiens, were completed in the astonishingly short period of around fifty years; others, like Notre-Dame Paris, took over a century and a half, construction ending after Amiens, though it was begun almost sixty years earlier. Still others, like Beauvais, were never fully realized. And the Sainte-Chapelle, built on a smaller scale than any of the grand cathedrals, was ready in a decade to receive the holy relics King Louis IX had amassed before his departure for the seventh crusade in 1248. In any case, "completion" is an inexact term. Gothic cathedrals are, in the phrase of the great restorer of church buildings in the nineteenth century, Eugène Emmanuel Viollet-le-Duc, "living organisms" and are never really finished, requiring as they do constant building and rebuilding, renovation and structural maintenance, which is why they are still standing—still "living"—eight centuries after they were "begun."

I have, then, arranged our travels to the major cathedrals in the vicinity of Paris according to the order in which I have visited them with my students. This rhythm, leaving and returning to the city at intervals that conform nicely to the discrete character of the cathedrals and to the means of public transportation at our disposal, has over the years yielded a thick appreciation of the ways in which they articulate with each other. What is more, this time-tested order allows me to share with you the pleasures of teaching and research, what the Renaissance writer François Rabelais termed the "substantive marrow" of learning.

A word to the reader on the use of *Paris and Her Cathedrals*. The chapters are meant to be read sequentially, and the cathedral-effect is richer for the cumulative comparative layering of examples. However, each chapter is devoted to one of the paramount churches, and though it may contain references to others, it can be read on its own. The map inserted at the outset orients the reader in terms of the geography of northern France; a synoptic survey at the head of each chapter contains essential

coordinates and facts, including how to get there; and the Glossary clari-
fies terms used throughout.

Finally, a word about illustrations. One of the notable phenomena
connected to Gothic cathedrals is the similarity of visual motifs as one
moves from place to place. Representations of the signs of the zodiac
along with what was known as the Works of the Months, the Parable
of the Wise and Foolish Virgins, life-size sculptures of Mary with the
infant Jesus on her hip, the Last Judgment and the redemption of souls at
the end of time are to be found everywhere, in keeping with a deep principle of cathedral-making: though travelers or pilgrims may wander,
the universal truth of the Church is there to greet them wherever they
go. I have, therefore, tried to strike a balance between distance shots of
encompassing swaths of architecture and close-ups of detail which are
not reproduced to show every example, but may be visually inferred
from one building to the next. I also concentrate on drawing the reader's
attention to objects and motifs that he or she might not ordinarily notice
and not to the well-known pictures on postcards that add little to the
appreciation of the thing itself. At the back of the book, a list of websites
for those interested in more images accompanies suggestions for further
reading along with the Glossary and Index. If you are planning to visit
the vast and high Gothic churches of northern France with this little
book in hand, I would suggest bringing along a pair of binoculars. The
cathedrals are decorated so exquisitely inside and out, often with details
not visible to the naked eye, that your visit will be enhanced by access
to the beauty that some in the Middle Ages believed was reserved only
for the eyes of God.

Now let's board the Paris metro anywhere along the number 13 line
to the station—Basilique de Saint-Denis—just behind the city hall of
the northern suburban commune, less than a minute's walk from the
birthplace of the Gothic style in France.

PARIS AND HER
CATHEDRALS

SAINT-DENIS
The First Cathedral

BASILICA OF SAINT-DENIS.
I RUE DE LA LÉGION D'HONNEUR,
SAINT-DENIS, SIX MILES NORTH OF PARIS.

Access via rapid train (RER) from Châtelet or the Gare du Nord or number 13 metro line which splits at La Fourchette. Be sure to take direction Saint-Denis-Université and get off at the next-to-last stop. Begun ca. 1137 CE by Abbot Suger, who left a stunning record of construction, historic burial place of royalty, central church of France until the thirteenth century, heavily damaged at the time of the French Revolution, restored in the nineteenth century, and cleaned 2012–15.

···   ···

H AVING ARRIVED AT SAINT-DENIS, WE SHALL EXAMINE THE cathedral from the outside before entering the haunting, light-filled space of the burial place of kings. But first, let's take a little historical journey into how, why, and by whom the first Gothic cathedral came into being.

Theologians, clergymen, statesmen, great feudal princes, the knights in their service, and the common people had been convinced that the world would end around the year 1000. This belief in the "process of the Last Days" in the phrase of the Norman monk Raoul Glaber (d. 1047) may have discouraged building in the century preceding the end of the first millennium. When the world did not end, it was as if the survivors of the cataclysm that never came were forced to recognize that the present was here to stay, and they began to build for the future. Raoul noted that "the earth became clothed in a white robe of churches." First among these was the abbey church of Saint-Denis, whose enterprising abbot acknowledged that history was no longer end-stopped, but is open-ended. "Study of the past is the promise of the future," Abbot Suger declared, in undertaking to build a new church upon the old Romanesque abbey some six miles north of the center of Paris and less than a mile from the Seine as it loops northeast in the first of three great zigzags across the Parisian basin.

We know a lot about Saint-Denis because Abbot Suger, who was dedicated to the abbey by his parents at the age of ten and who was its head between 1122 and his death in 1151, left an extraordinary account of its construction, beginning in 1140. Suger was an exceptional figure. Born to humble circumstances, he attended school with the future King Louis VI (d. 1137), who ruled as king of the Franks in the first third of the twelfth century. Suger served as the king's spiritual and political advisor, his ambassador, and eventually his biographer in a work entitled *The Deeds of Louis the Fat*. Abbot Suger made four trips to Rome on behalf of the French king. He served as regent in the absence of Louis VI's successor, Louis VII (d. 1180), during the Second Crusade (1147–49). And, in the winter of 1122, returning from a royal mission to Pope Calixtus II in southern France, Suger learned of his predecessor Abbot Adam's death and of his own election to head the monastic community of Saint-Denis. I was "elevated from this dung heap," he wrote, "to sit among princes."

For the four preceding centuries, Saint-Denis had been the burial place of French kings, beginning with the Frankish leader Dagobert, who died in 639. However, Abbot Suger, a man of exceeding ambition, more for the French king and the state than for himself, thought the old abbey church too small, its entrance too narrow, and the space around the main altar too cramped. Dagobert had made his "basilica of the Saints" magnificent, rich and full of treasure. "Only one thing was wanting in him," Suger wrote: "that he did not allow for the size that was necessary."

The old building presented what we call today a "security issue," the danger of controlling the crowds that came to worship on special holidays. "Often on feast days, completely filled, it disgorged through all its doors the excess of the crowds as they moved in opposite directions, . . .

no one . . . could move a foot; no one . . . could [do] anything but stand like a marble statue, stay benumbed or, as a last resort, scream." This mid-twelfth-century security issue was also a feminist one. "The distress of the women," Suger continued, "was so great . . . that you could see with horror how they, squeezed in by the mass of strong men as in a wine press . . . , cried out horribly as though in labor." His greatest fear, however, was that, in all the commotion, the abbey's holy treasure would be stolen by visitors who, "having no place to turn, might escape with the relics through the windows."

THE WEST FACADE

STANDING ON THE PLACE Victor Hugo before Saint-Denis, you might be overwhelmed by the size of the cathedral, surrounded, as it was in the Middle Ages, by low-lying buildings: on the right, where the former monastery attached to the cathedral once stood, a school for the daughters, granddaughters, and great-granddaughters of recipients of the medal of the Légion d'honneur; and, on the left, city hall. The western facade or frontispiece of the cathedral was restored between 2012 and 2015, its surfaces cleaned by microabrasion, the clock with its snake arms and blue numerals, repaired and regilded.

You might also wonder why Saint-Denis is missing one of the two towers associated with the frontal presentation of both Romanesque and Gothic churches. Lightning hit the northern (left) spire in the first half of the nineteenth century, and violent storms ravaged it in the 1840s. The man hired to rebuild the spire, the pointed structure on top of the tower, was a specialist in the construction of Parisian theaters. He quarried stone that was too heavy for the job. When the structure below began to crack, the rebuilt spire was removed. Beginning in 1987, the mayors of Saint-Denis have expressed interest in rebuilding with the very stones that originally collapsed and that had been numbered, catalogued, and stored in a nearby warehouse. Documents in the National Archives, including some of the earliest architectural photography, outline the work in detail—this project along the lines of the rebuilding in 1912 of the campanile of Saint Mark's Basilica in Venice, which collapsed in 1902, or the Basilica of Saint Francis of Assisi, destroyed by an earthquake in 1997.

Nothing in today's world of the arts or religion can match the multi-

West Facade

sensorial experience of what it must have felt like to stand outside or inside a church like Saint-Denis in the twelfth or thirteenth centuries— the Age of Cathedrals. Combining as it does the concert hall, the museum, the library, the theater, the university, and a sacred shrine, cathedrals came as close as any institution anywhere and at any time to a total work of art. Though they are now for the most part silent, the great high churches of the Middle Ages were once filled with the chanting of prayers both day and night and with the sound of pipe organs, the "king of instruments" in the phrase of the fourteenth-century poet and composer Guillaume de Mauchaut, a canon of the cathedral of Amiens. Medieval churches were from the outset even more resonant treats for the eye than they are today, the sculpture on the outside of the building covered in vivid colors that have been lost to the elements over time or destroyed in the devastations of the French Revolution and replaced with unpainted reproductions. The nighttime *son et lumière* or light shows available in the summer at some cathedrals—Amiens, Chartres, Reims, and Rouen, for example—harness the technology of precisely projected light to give some impression of the kaleidoscopic beauty of the Gothic church. Many of the walls inside of the cathedral were painted as well, and the spaces between the masonry supporting the arches were filled with vibrant stained glass windows that have been lost to decay, damage, or a desire among clerics at the time of the Enlightenment for more light. They were replaced by transparent or lightly patterned or monochrome—grisaille—glass. Over the centuries, cathedrals have been stripped of the rich decorative and liturgical objects with which they were filled—the rugs, clerical robes, tapestries, and other hangings, painted sculpture and paintings, crosses, reliquaries, monstrances, and chalices made of precious metals and jewels that made them a delight for the eye. As they were for the mind. The extraordinary wealth of local, historical, and biblical stories displayed in sculpture, paint, and glass across the length and breadth, inside and out, of the great Gothic monuments made them a reservoir of knowledge, both scientific and spiritual, of the known world—a teaching and preaching tool whose intricacy, height, and size bear witness to the technical and mechanical arts.

Suger began his rebuilding of the old Carolingian church in the new Gothic style on the western facade, which is the strongest angle by which to understand his achievement. This frontispiece is a multimedia monument, consisting as it does of stone, wood, glass, and metal, and showing traces of figural sculpture, decorative columns and arches, fortress-like crenelation and towers, flat masonry surfaces, and written plaques. Suger was not shy in placing his name or his image on the innovative church whose construction he supervised. Just above the central doorway or portal and to the right of the outside of a stained glass window rounded at the top, a Latin inscription is his signature piece: "In honor of the Church which nurtured and exalted him, Suger worked, rendering back to you your due, Saint Denis, martyr. He prays that your prayers will obtain for him a place in Paradise. In the year of the Word eleven hundred and forty the consecration took place." To the left of the window is an inscription commemorating Napoleon Bonaparte's visit in 1806 to reconsecrate the church after the French Revolution. The Emperor had originally picked Saint-Denis as his final resting place. He would have been in good company. On either side of the upper half of the clock you will see full-length bas reliefs (sculpture in low relief) of crowned scepter-wielding kings of France, an architectural feature that will blossom in later buildings into the free-standing royal phalanx of sculptures known as the gallery of kings, here topped by a crenellated battlement reminiscent of defensive stone castles.

Suger included his name in the written inscription on the front of the cathedral which he is credited with building, and there can be little doubt that by today's standards, it took some degree of self-advocacy, which by medieval standards might have passed for the sin of pride or "superbia." Yet, some consider him one of the greatest builders of all time. On the frieze of the Albert Memorial in London (1875), Suger stands between William of Sens, the master mason responsible for the rebuilding of Canterbury cathedral in the Gothic style about thirty years after Saint-Denis, and Anthemius of Tralles, the architect of Hagia Sophia in Constantinople.

There were no architects as such in the Middle Ages. The closest thing to an architect was the master mason—a *magister cementarius* or cement master—who supervised the choice of suitable stone from the quarry, its rough cutting and transportation to the building site, carving and laying in aligned courses and other patterns as the building went up. The master mason might make drawings upon the floor of the mason's lodge or hut, a shed-like structure erected at the building site, though few such drawings have survived. At the outset of construction, he laid out the piers, or vertical supports, and columns that would support the structure by means of a rope of fixed length rotated around a stake driven into the ground. Consulting with the canons, clerics responsible for maintaining the divine office of prayers inside the church as well as for the upkeep of the "fabric" or physical plant of the cathedral, the master mason orchestrated the carvings of sculptures, both large and small. He supervised the chiseling of ornate columns and the decorative friezes or capitals atop columns, the manufacture of moldings, mullions (or bars between glass in a window), and window frames. Working with carpenters, he orchestrated the erection of wooden frames beneath high arches, vaults, and flying buttresses, as well as their removal when the mortar, whose mixing he also managed, had dried.

The master mason was someone who knew a lot about stone, and there is a lot to know in terms of weight, grain, and color, especially when one sees some of the delicate designs of great Gothic rose windows, with their wheel-like designs and finely turned spokes, and similarly elegant arches. Suger was neither an architect nor a master mason, but something on the order of the producer of the first Gothic cathedral, much like today's movie producer who gathers the resources for making a film, but who hires a director to supervise the actual work. The director might then hire actors, camera operators, costumers, and makeup artists. Suger claims he assembled an international team of bronze founders, jewelers, and enamel workers from the valleys of the Rhine and Meuse, masons and stone carvers from Normandy, Burgundy, and southwestern France, mosaicists from Italy, and "many masters" of stained glass from "different regions."

In addition to being a multimedia monument, the west facade of Saint-Denis is a multicultural mélange. The three-portal arrangement characteristic of both earlier Romanesque and Gothic cathedrals harks back to Rome and the three-bay arches of Septimius Severus (203 CE) or of Constantine (312) with detached columns, bas relief, and writing on their faces. The inscription on the latter, "To the Emperor Caesar Flavius Constantinus, . . . inspired by the divine," is significant, as Constantine was the first Roman emperor to espouse the Christian religion. Passing through the arch on his way to assume divine power, the emperor foretells the liminal space of the cathedral's western portals, a threshold between secular and sacred worlds. The visual connection to Roman imperial authority serves as a reminder of the intimacy between ecclesiastical and secular power, in the case of Suger, his closeness to kings Louis VI and VII and his status as a powerful feudal lord within his diocese and further afield.

Suger had been to Rome, which was very much in his mind throughout the construction of his new, more spacious and secure church. When it came time to locate suitable marble columns and none could be found locally, the adventuresome abbot contemplated obtaining them from the

Eternal City, "for in Rome we had often seen wonderful ones in the Palace of Diocletian and other Baths." He plots transportation "by safe ships through the Mediterranean, thence through the English Sea and the tortuous windings of the River Seine." Miraculously, however, suitable columns were found in a quarry near Pontoise, a distance of less than fifteen miles. With the help of God and prayers to the saints, the shafts were "conveyed to the site of the church on a cart."

In building and furnishing Saint-Denis, Suger had his eyes on the East. Constantine may have marched triumphant into Rome, but he would later move the capital of the Empire to Constantinople, the city of relics amassed by Constantine's mother Helena, and Suger was obsessed by the rivalry with Hagia Sophia. Crusaders returning from the First Crusade had seen the great Byzantine church, and there is plausible evidence that the impetus to enlarge the old Romanesque churches of France came from those who were impressed by the broad pendentive arches, like the triangular surface covering the spherical corner of a room, in the sixth-century cathedral of the imperial city. Suger admits that he used "to converse with travelers from Jerusalem." He was delighted to learn that "the things here" might compare favorably with "the treasures and ornaments of Constantinople and the ornaments of Hagia Sophia." It can be no accident, then, that the first Gothic cathedral was built some thirty to forty years after the crusaders who had fought in the First Crusade (1096–99) returned from the Middle East.

FOLLOWING THE ZODIAC
AND WORKS OF THE MONTHS

Saint-denis looks, somewhat mysteriously, to the pagan past. Signs of the zodiac, which originated in Babylonian astrology, line the north jambs, the vertical decorative framed reliefs that flank each side of the left door. The upper part of the left jamb displays the image of Virgo, the maiden under whose sign, according to the ancient zodiac calendar, the year begins; below Virgo, Taurus, the bull; and just below Taurus, Aries, the ram; still lower, the astrological sign Pisces, represented as two fish, and below Pisces, the figure of a man pouring water out of a jug, Aquarius. On the upper part of the right jamb, lies Gemini or the Twins, then Libra with her scales, and below Libra, Cancer. Below Cancer sits Sagittarius, half horse and half human, the centaur which is also

Signs of the Zodiac on the North Portal, West Facade

an archer placed just above Capricorn, the horned goat with a sea creature's tail, which ends the astrological cycle as it ends the current calendar year. Only Scorpio and Leo are missing.

Between the astrological signs and the actual doors stand two ornamented columns, the one on the left featuring a scroll-and-vine pattern in which human figures are entwined, and the one on the left overlapping perforated tongue-like ovals. Below the base of each column a figure draped in a flowing three-quarter smock seems, like a female caryatid, to support effortlessly the decorated shaft. At the round base of the columns two pairs of figures, each depicting a man and a woman crouching, like doodles of the kind found in medieval manuscripts, appear to inspect each other's legs or feet. This kind of drolerie is sometimes a complete mystery, and I hazard a guess that these images of familiar scenes of everyday life speak to pilgrims who have walked a long distance to visit the relics at Saint-Denis and who suffer discomfort in their lower limbs. The tops of the columns display acanthus leaves on the left and, on the right, a pair of addorsed griffons, mythological creatures with the body of a lion, the wings of an eagle, and the heads of a man and a woman, which, again, glances toward the Orient.

Before we leave the signs of the zodiac at Saint-Denis, let me draw your attention to a set of parallel figures on the south portal jambs that also involve the natural cycle of the seasons. Unlike the signs of the zodiac around the north portal, the Labors of the Months are arranged more or less in order according to an annual cycle. They are worth a close look for the light they shine upon the domestic life of the High Middle Ages. Beginning on the lower right, the figure of January presents as a man with two faces, one looking forward and the other back, *Janus* being the etymological root for both "January" and "door." Above January, the image of February features a couple shut in by the cold weather, the man with a pair of tongs in his hands tending the fire while his wife reads a book to him. March shows two men involved in early spring agricultural activity, one turning the earth with a spade while the other prunes a leafless tree; and, for April, a man stands between two flowering plants. May depicts a knight holding a banner in front of a saddled horse. He is setting out for war, which in the Middle Ages was a seasonal activity beginning with the thawing of roads in May. The pennant in the knight's hand may be a reference to the "oriflamme," the rallying military banner of France kept at Saint-Denis, which was, until the middle of the thirteenth century, the spiritual center of France. June is represented by a bare-chested man hoeing the earth, his shirt hanging on a nearby tree because of the heat.

Continuing the cycle of the year, at the top of the left door jamb a man with a sickle in his hand stands before a field of partially reaped grain, signifying July, while below him, for August, a reaper with a scythe pauses before harvested sheaves of grain. September features two men pouring the fruit of the vine into a barrel for the making of wine, an image also found inside the cathedral. October shows a man picking what appear to be chestnuts from a tree, with a wild boar in the foreground. November's seasonal task consists of the butchering of the rear-quarters of a pig, the rest of the animal hanging on a rack behind the knife-wielding butcher. The year ends with feasting in December and the image of a couple before a table full of good things to eat, a roaring fire in the background.

If the signs of the zodiac and the seasonal tasks of the year appear around the entryways to Saint-Denis, it is because the abbey depended upon the agricultural production of the surrounding countryside and more distant landholdings for its daily comestibles and annual income. Abbot Suger was at the center of an unprecedented demographic and economic takeoff in the region around Saint-Denis, the Parisian basin, and the valley of the Oise. He claims to have tripled the revenue of the abbey during his tenure. Part of the income came from the pilgrims who flocked there for bodily cures through contact with the relics—the bodies of saints and what were delicately referred to as the "instruments" of the Passion, a nail from the cross and a part of the crown of thorns. You may question—O skeptical reader!—a belief in such miracles, but I am here to assure you that those who left home for Saint-Denis in the twelfth and thirteenth centuries, some for extended periods of time, firmly believed in the efficacy of their prayers before the relics of saints. We know about such belief not only via historical and literary accounts but also because of the official records, sometimes illustrated, of inquests conducted at the time pious individuals were canonized, or considered for sainthood. In our own time, the shrines of Lourdes in southern France or Sainte-Anne-de-Beaupré outside of Quebec City are both heavily draped inside with the discarded canes, crutches, braces, and other prosthetic devices that once belonged to recovered invalids. So, while I, too, find some stories difficult to believe, it is nonetheless my role as an historian to help you to imagine other worlds and other systems of belief, which is one of the benefits of studying history in the first place.

Part of the income of Saint-Denis was derived from pious dona-tions, "the kings, princes, and many outstanding men," in Suger's phrase, "who took the rings off of their hands." Income accrued from three annual fairs held at Saint-Denis, including the well-known Fair of Lendit. The abbey received a percentage of the sales of tools, food, cloth and expensive textiles, skins, leather, fur, shoes, and parchment brought to what was a center of trade in the early twelfth century. Most of the abbey's annual revenue came, however, from the vast estates it owned as far away as Berneval on the Norman coast or in the region of Beauce, between the Seine and Loire Rivers. Much of the land that had come to Saint-Denis from Merovingian and Carolingian rulers had been alienated in the period preceding Suger's tenure as abbot. Aided by the king, however, he fought aggressively to recover lost holdings, and he was a superb manager of the estates which provided the wine and grain depicted on the door jambs of the south portal of the west facade as well as income to feed, house, and clothe the monks, provide alms for the poor, and build a new church.

THE SAINT IN SAINT-DENIS

THE SOUTH AND NORTH PORTALS of the west facade of Saint-Denis are joined by their depictions of astrological and monthly cycles of the year. They are also united by their depiction of the martyrdom of Saint Denis, at once a local saint and the patron saint of France, through whom the first Gothic cathedral is tied to Greece and Rome of the first centuries of Christianity. The Saint Denis in Saint-Denis is a composite figure whose multiple identities were intentionally conflated in order to add to an aura of mystery surrounding the relics of the abbey. The first candidate is Dionysius the Areopagite, a first-century Athenian judge portrayed in the Acts of the Apostles (17:22–34) as having been converted to Christianity by Saint Paul and who then served as the Bishop of Athens. The second is a fifth-century eastern neoplatonic philosopher and mystical writer known as Pseudo-Dionysius who claimed to have witnessed the eclipse of the sun at Christ's death, to have been present at the dormition of the Virgin, to have known Saint John the Evangelist, and, further, to be the very Areopagite converted by Paul. As unlikely as all this is, the Pseudo-Dionysius is credited with having written a work known as *The Celestial Hierarchies* which was a fulcrum between the world of Late Antiquity and the High Middle Ages as well as between East and West (see pp. 21, 36). *The Celestial Hierarchies* came to the West through a diplomatic exchange between Byzantium and the Carolingian court. Emperor Michael the Stammerer bestowed a Greek manuscript containing the works of the Pseudo-Dionysius upon Charlemagne's son Louis the Pious at Compiègne in 827 CE. From there, the book, which can be said to have inspired the first Gothic cathedral the way that certain works have the capacity to define a culture and to affect world historical change, came to the treasury of the royal abbey at Saint-Denis.

The third potential Saint Denis was a Christian martyr who was sent with two companions—Rusticus and Eleutherius—to proselitize in France in the early centuries of Christianity. They were executed by the Roman authorities on what is now the hill of Montmartre.

The beheadings of Saints Denis, Rusticus, and Eleutherius in the middle of the third century CE are depicted over the doorways of the south and north portals of the west facade as well as over the portal on the north side of the cathedral. Together, these narrative friezes tell the story of the imprisonment and martyrdom of Saint Denis as contained in a book written around 1260 by the Italian chronicler and Archbishop of Genoa, James of Voragine (d. 1298). *The Golden Legend* recounts the lives of major saints and was one of the most popular books of the Middle Ages. There we learn that the Roman emperor Domitian was so enraged at the advances of Christianity in France that he sent his provost, a judicial officer named Fescennius, to Paris to stop the spread of the new religion. In Paris, Fescennius found Denis preaching, and, along with Rusticus, a priest, and Eleutherius, a deacon, he had him "bound, buffeted and spat upon, mocked, tied up with the toughest thongs." Denis was denounced by a woman by the name of Laertia, who claimed he had misled her husband into converting to the new religion. According to *The Golden Legend*, "The prefect straightway sent for the husband, and when he constantly professed his faith, he was unjustly put to death, and the saints were scourged by twelve soldiers, . . . loaded with a great weight of chains, and thrown into gaol." Fescennius tried to kill Denis by beating, fire, and exposure to hungry wild beasts, which became "perfectly tame" when Denis made the sign of the cross in front of them.

In the semi-circular area over the south portal door, known as the tympanum, Denis, wearing the bishop's miter, celebrates mass with his fellow prisoners. As James of Voragine states, "While he was offering the Mass in prison, and giving Communion to the people, the Lord Jesus appeared to him in the midst of a dazzling light, and taking the Bread in His hands, said to Dionysius: 'Take this, My beloved one, for thy reward is very great with Me!'" Christ Himself, surrounded by six angels, extends the communion wafer through the clouds, indicated by the wavy lines above Denis's head, to place it directly into the bishop's mouth. The prisoner on the left holds the cup and the one on the right, an open book. At the far left of the scene stands Laertia, her hands and body transmitting feelings of regret for having denounced Denis, for which she later

South Portal Tympanum, West Facade

repented. On the right, Fescennius, holding a scepter, issues orders, possibly to the two men between Laertia and the prisoners, one of whom holds a club and the other the executioner's blade. Two pairs of men with swords and an axe stand on either side of the main scene in the left and right archivolts, the molding along the curve of the outer rim of the tympanum that runs between the posts on either side of the door.

In the tympanum of the north portal of the west facade, the three prisoners—Denis, Rusticus, and Elutherius, "with a great weight of chains" around their necks—are led away by Roman soldiers, identifiable by their round shields and broad swords. Fescennius, again seated to the right of the prison, his arm outstretched, issues the order for their execution. Above the prisoners, Christ, separated from the earthly realm by clouds, watches as angels hold the crowns of saints to place on the martyrs' heads. In the first archivolt on either side, people are lamenting. The man on the left holds his hand to his brow in a gesture of sorrow, and the couple on the right kneels in prayer. At the top of the inner archivolt, an angel prays over what appears to be a reliquary which will house the bones, the sacred relics, of the martyrs. Above the angel, God surveys the layered scenes.

Finally, walking around the front of the cathedral to the portal on

North Portal Tympanum, West Facade

North Entrance Tympanum

the north side of the building, you will see in the tympanum over the north entrance a depiction of the actual beheadings of Denis, Rusticus, and Elutherius, their deaths accompanied by two miracles. At the top, doves descend to earth bearing the crown of martyred saints. On the left, however, we witness what may be the most celebrated miracle of the Middle Ages: the future Saint Denis picked up his decapitated head and walked, in the phrase of James of Voragine, "from the hill of the martyrs (present day Montmartre)" several miles to the town of Catulliacus, before the name was changed to Saint-Denis, while preaching a sermon on repentance. The very witty nineteenth-century French literary critic Charles Augustin Sainte-Beuve observed, with regard to the story of Denis, the cephalophore or "head-carrier," that "the first step is the hardest."

THE BIBLE OF THE POOR

I F THE FIRST Gothic cathedral looks to Rome, to the pagan past, and to the local history of the saint from which it takes its name, it is focused even more deeply upon the Bible, the Old and New Testaments as well as the apocrypha, for inspiration both outside and inside the building itself. In an age in which few could read or write and literacy was the sign of a clerical education, the cathedral was, in the popular phrase, "a poor man's Bible" and a teaching tool. The priest preaching a sermon might illustrate his lesson by pointing to the astonishing array of sculpture and stained glass illustrations of biblical figures and stories by which he was surrounded. The imagination of students in the schools attached to cathedrals was stimulated by looking at the visual version of what they read in written works during the course of their studies.

Biblical motifs all around the doors of Saint-Denis were meant to shape the spiritual state of those who entered the sacred space of the cathedral. Originally, columns flanking the three portals of the west facade were filled with life-size jamb statues of kings, queens, and prophets, which were removed by enthusiastic revolutionaries at the time of the French Revolution. We know them only from drawings made before their disappearance and from pieces that have cropped up in Harvard's Fogg Museum, the Walters Art Gallery in Baltimore, and the Museum of the Middle Ages in Paris. To judge by the drawings and by similar jamb statues that have survived at Chartres, Amiens, Reims, and Notre-Dame Paris, the height, position, and the attributes of such figures are enough to induce in the viewers, situated below and dwarfed by their size, feelings of vulnerability and awe.

There is no more crucial threshold between the exterior material world of things and the interior world of the cathedral, which is sup-

Central Portal, West Facade

posed to offer a glimpse of paradise, than the central portal, a strong point of entry not only into the church but into theological and eschatological truth, eschatology being that part of theology concerned with death, judgment, and the destiny of the soul. As we read in John 10:1, 2, 6, and 7, "He that entereth not by the door into the sheepfold but climbeth up another way, the same is a thief and a robber. But he that entereth in by the door is the shepherd of the sheep. . . . This proverb Jesus spoke to them. But they understood not what he spoke. Jesus therefore said to them again: Amen, amen, I say to you, I am the door of the sheep."

The jambs around the central portal of Saint-Denis feature a biblical lesson about being prepared as you enter the door—the Parable of the Wise and Foolish Virgins. In Matthew 25:1–13, the kingdom of heaven is compared to ten virgins who, "taking their lamps, went out to meet the bridegroom and the bride." Five of the virgins take oil with them, and five did not. And, as the bridegroom, symbol of Christ, tarries, the virgins "all slumbered and slept." When the cry came at midnight, the virgins "arose and trimmed their lamps." The foolish ones, however, realizing there was not time to fetch oil for their vessels, plead to the wise: "Give us of your oil, for our lamps are gone out," but they refused for fear of running out. While the foolish virgins are buying oil, the bridegroom comes and lets their wise sisters in the door with him to the marriage of bridegroom and Church. When their foolish sisters arrive at the door, "saying: Lord, Lord, open to us," he answered them, saying: "Amen I say to you, I know you not." The parable concludes with a warning to the hearer, "Watch ye therefore, because you know not the day nor the hour."

Four virgins in modest full dress with head coverings line the left jamb between two ornamental columns. The bottom three stand under architectural canopies, while the fourth lacks a canopy and the fifth is squeezed at the outer edge of the tympanum. The same is true of the virgins along the right jamb, but with two crucial distinctions. The virgins on the left jamb, which is the right side of Christ, are holding upturned vessels to indicate that their contents remain intact, while the virgins on the right jamb, to the left of Christ, hold downturned jars that are empty. Other visual signs mark the difference between the wise and the foolish virgins. The long pigtails which grace the faces of those for whom the door has been opened are met on the other side by virgins whose pigtails are twisted and by body language that is capped by the wise virgin standing erect over the left jamb, while the foolish one on the right bows on bended knees in a gesture of sadness and dejection. As a teaching tool, the Parable of the Wise and Foolish Virgins thus proffers a great lesson about open and closed doors, a great warning to be prepared for final things, as no one knows the hour of his or her death.

You may wonder how this central lesson of Christianity made it from the pages of the Bible to the carved visual images around the central entrance to the first Gothic cathedral. We were not there, of course, but it is not hard to imagine a conversation between Abbot Suger, the canons of the church or monks involved in the building project, and the master mason and his team of sculptors, who may have seen images of the wise and foolish virgins elsewhere. The actual artists probably did not have direct access to manuscript illustrations of the parable, but the clerics of Saint-Denis who could read might have shared the story with the carvers who embellished it with gestural and physical details drawn from their own imaginations. The bronze door itself displays eight scenes of Christ's Passion, Resurrection, and Ascension between floral rondels with spiraliform designs between them. In the second rondel on the top right, a depiction of the supper at Emmaus from Luke

24:30–31, the image of Suger floats in space at the feet of Christ and His two companions.

LAST JUDGMENT

A SCENE OF THE CRUCIFIXION fills the half-circle at the top of the tympanum, as two angels hold the cross on which Christ is stretched, with holes visible still in His hands and feet. Perched slightly above the cross are two more angels which hold the instruments of the Passion. The one on the left clasps nails in its left hand, the one on the right, the crown of thorns. Below Christ's outstretched arms, the Virgin clutches a veil to His immediate right, six disciples on either side. The upper lintel or horizontal frieze below the curved part of the tympanum is framed by two angels on the outer edges, the one on the left with a trumpet, the one on the right with a flaming sword, indicated by rippling lines from pommel to point. These are the signs, as in Matthew 24:31, of the Second Coming of Christ: "And he shall send his angels with a trumpet and a great voice; and they shall gather together his elect from the four winds, from the farthest parts of the heavens to the utmost bounds of them." As with the Parable of the Wise and Foolish Virgins, the message is one

Central Portal Tympanum, West Facade

of preparedness: "Watch ye therefore, because you know not what hour your Lord will come" (Matthew 24:42).

At the feet of Christ naked figures of the dead rising from tombs fill the lower lintel. Some face left, others right, in seeming random order meant to emphasize the great sorting that will occur once they are judged. Suger, the only clothed figure in the lower lintel, again floats in space just below Christ's right foot at the edge of the mandorla, the almond-shaped motif that covers His lower body. The abbot is clearly still alive and, while alive, makes every effort to be on the right side and as close to the Lord as possible.

Saint-Denis served historically as the burial place of royalty, and its central portal provokes a great meditation on final things. The scenes on the lower lintel, tympanum, and first archivolt illustrate the Last Judgment according to the Gospel of Matthew 25:32–33, which extends the sheep motif in John to encompass sheep and goats: "And all nations shall be gathered together before him: and he shall separate them one from another, as the shepherd separateth the sheep from the goats: And he shall set the sheep on his right hand, but the goats on his left." The dominating figure of Christ in Majesty at the center of the tympanum is unusual in that his arms, spread across the horizontal bar of the cross, are not nailed to it, but unfurl scrolls from each hand, attesting to the separation of the sheep from the goats. The inscriptions, which are restored but probably authentic, are again from Matthew 25:34–41. The banner in Christ's right hand reads "VENITE BENEDICTI PATRIS MEI," based on Matthew 25:34: "Then shall the king say to them that shall be on his right hand: COME, YE BLESSED OF MY FATHER, possess you the kingdom prepared for you from the foundation of the world." The banner in His left hand reads "DISCEDITE A ME MALEDICTI" from Matthew 25:41: "Then he shall say to them also that shall be on his left hand: DEPART FROM ME, YOU CURSED, into everlasting fire."

The tympanum above the central portal of Saint-Denis foretells a great orderly separation of the confused souls rising from their tombs into the saved and the damned displayed on the first archivolt. From the top, Christ disperses souls to heaven with His right hand, two fingers raised in a gesture of blessing, or, to hell with His left hand, full palm raised in a gesture of rejection. On His right at eleven o'clock an angel receives a small child; below, three souls in the bosom of Abraham, then an angel with two more souls, and, finally, angels and saved souls are shown dwelling in a building that represents the House of the Lord. To Christ's left, at one o'clock, a soul is turned away from a curtained door. Beginning at two o'clock, demons take hold of and devour the chaotic jumble of souls, some upside down and all suffering and tumbling in a chaotic mass to eternal damnation. The three souls in the bosom of Abraham, on the paradise side of the inner archivolt, along with the smaller figures on the hell side, are drawn from Matthew 8:11–12, where Jesus says that "many shall come from the east and the west, and shall sit down with Abraham, and Isaac and Jacob in the kingdom of heaven: But the children of the kingdom shall be cast out into the exterior darkness: there shall be weeping and gnashing of teeth."

In the second archivolt, two censing angels stand above Christ, and, in the third, the head, arms, hands, and feet of God the Father are visible beneath a disk in which He holds the Lamb, symbol of Christ, and the Cross. On the outer archivolt, the dove of the Holy Spirit hovers above both Father and Son. The scene of the Last Judgment is surrounded by the Twenty-four Elders of the Apocalypse of Saint John 5:8, seated on thrones and holding books, rebecs, "harps and golden vials." From the end of the life of Christ on earth on the doors, to the ultimate state of grace or damnation on the first archivolt, to the end of human time on the outer archivolts, we have moved from this world to the next. Let's now enter the door of the cathedral.

CLERICS OR MONKS responsible for the liturgy, everyday worship along with special prayers, entered by the south transept door at Saint-Denis, for that was where they lived. The mass of worshipers entered by one of the portals on the west side. That entrance is prepared by a bronze plaque between the actual central door and the tympanum: *Nobile claret opus, sed opus quod nobile claret / Clarificet mentes, ut eant per lumina vera.* "Bright is the noble work; but, being nobly bright, the work / Should brighten the minds, so that they may travel, through the true lights." This inscription, under which all who enter must pass, captures the essence of the doctrine of light contained in a book that came from the East to the Abbey of Saint-Denis in 827, which was translated from the Greek to Latin by Abbot Hilduin (d. 855) shortly after its arrival, and again by John Scotus Eriugena (d. 877) later in the century. *The Celestial Hierarchies* attributed to Pseudo-Dionysius, one of the three candidates for the Saint

Denis in Saint-Denis, defines Jesus as "the Light of the Father" and God, "the Primal Ray," as "the Origin of Light" and Light itself.

Gothic architecture has been said to be the translation of the doctrine of light into architectural form, and such was Suger's explicit intent, expressed in his account of cathedral building, that "the whole [church] would shine with the wonderful and uninterrupted light of most luminous windows, pervading the interior beauty."

ENTERING THE CATHEDRAL

To ENTER A GOTHIC CATHEDRAL is to experience both light and lightness. Saint-Denis is built according to a three-tier plan in which the lower arch or arcade level, the middle three-columned or triforium level, and the upper or clerestory level appear as great sheets of glass between a wall so thin as in places to be almost invisible. Entering by the narthex, the recess below the towers on the other side of Suger's west facade, and looking down the central aisle, we see a great burst of light from the transept crossing, or intersection of the long and short arms of the cross, and the rounded upper choir, beyond the short arm of the cross, at the eastern end. Unlike the old Roman basilicas, which lacked

Nave

transept arms across the central aisle, the Gothic cathedral is built in the shape of a cross, and the long part of the cross or nave, from the Latin *navis* ("ship"), is punctuated by tall piers. Some of the piers are situated along the outer wall of the cathedral, while others rise from below the broken arches or arcades and the edge of the wide central volume of the cathedral. The space between them, known as the ambulatory, from the Latin *ambulatio* ("walk"), stretches the entire length of the cathedral, even around the apse, or projection from the choir at the east end of the church. As its name implies, the ambulatory or side aisle allows pilgrims, and now tourists, to circulate around the church even as worship is in progress. The piers or vertical supports of Saint-Denis are of the composite type; that is to say, the core supporting shaft is surrounded by sheaves of smaller columns which add strength while making the whole appear more graceful and lighter than if they were a thick solid mass. Some of the lighter columns are capped by capital friezes or flowered extensions which support the broken arches running along the partial wall below the triforium, while others rise clear up to the base of the high ogival or pointed vaults that give the cathedral its stunning sense of breadth and height—"a mysticism of soaring lines," in the phrase of Jean Bony. That is where the flowered capital extensions meet the radiating curved ribs that extend across the ceiling of the nave, some of which are directly connected to the bundle on the other side and others of which crisscross at the round decorated shield bosses that, like the keystone of a simple arch, punctuate the ceiling of the nave at regular intervals.

To get to the heart of the cathedral, you have to leave by a door on the south side of the nave and reenter via the south door of the transept, one of the arms of the architectural cross. Upon reentering, I am always struck by the burst of light through the great rose window in the north transept. This great lacy wheel of delicately honed stone spindles and glass measures almost forty feet in diameter and is a nineteenth-century restoration of the mid-thirteenth-century original, destroyed in the French Revolution for the lead content between the finely cut pieces of colored and painted glass. The north rose is a version of the Tree of Jesse motif (more later) that also appears in the stained glass of the apse and that is found in almost every Gothic cathedral in France. The Saint-Denis Tree of Jesse is unusual, however, because of its round rendering of a motif that in glass at least is almost always represented as a straight line illustrating the royal genealogy of Christ from the Old Testament

Jesse to Jesus. Here you will see a sleeping Jesse at the center of the wheel and the flowering of his progeny in the radiating lozenges and circles of purple, red, and blue glass all about. The rose above us as we enter the abbey church through the south portal features God in the central medallion blessing angels surrounded by the twelve signs of the zodiac and the Works of the Months that you will recognize for their renderings in stone around the north and south door jambs of the west facade.

Gisants, prone memorial monuments, fill the interior space all around the southern entrance of the cathedral, extending to the right into the apse and to the left into the nave. The kings of France had historically been crowned at Reims, though the regalia they wore for coronation was stored at Saint-Denis and brought there, a distance of some ninety-seven miles, for ceremonies of succession. You may, in fact, still see a few late pieces, like the crown and ermine robe that restored King Louis XVIII wore for his elevation in 1815, in a side chapel on the northwest side of the building. Saint-Denis was distinguished above all other French cathedrals as the burial place of royalty, beginning with the first Merovingian king Clovis (d. 511 CE) and his wife Clotilde (d. 545), whose remains were transferred there only in 1816, and ending with the last entrail of Louis XVI and Marie Antoinette's son, Louis XVII, the Dauphin, who was buried there at the beginning of the twenty-first century.

When it comes to French royalty, there is no more speculative issue than the fate of the Dauphin, which drew the attention of Mark Twain, whose swindling Duke and Dauphin present themselves as the exiled French king and a noble in *Adventures of Huckleberry Finn*. DNA analysis, however, has narrowed the narratives connected to the disappearance of the Dauphin by discounting the claims of various pretenders—a German clockmaker, a Protestant missionary from Wisconsin—and by rendering credible the story according to which Louis XVII died in 1795 at the age of ten of natural causes, scrofula, or tuberculosis adenitis of the neck, the very disease which the kings of France were purported to cure with the "royal touch" (more later). As was the custom among royals and nobles, the young prince's innards were not interred with his body; and, in the heady aftermath of the Revolution, the physician who performed an autopsy surreptitiously removed his heart. The organ ended up in the possession of the Archbishop of Paris. When the episcopal palace was sacked in the Revolution of 1830, the heart, encased in a crystal urn, was saved and subsequently passed through the hands of several members of lateral branches of the Bourbon family with whom it travelled to Spain and Austria. At the beginning of the twentieth century, the itinerant organ was presented to the Duc de Bauffremont, president of the Memorial of the Basilica of Saint-Denis in Paris. And in 1999 a piece was forensically removed and certified, via mitochondrial DNA analysis and comparison with a strand of Marie Antoinette's hair, to indeed have a high probability of being that of the Dauphin of France. This, at least, is the tale of provenance validated by French Royalists who gathered on June 8, 2004, to bury Louis's heart in an alcove of the crypt, the protected underground area for precious relics and tombs, near his parents and where you can still see it on macabre display. In all, 150 kings, queens, princes and princesses, and high officials lie in the royal necropolis, of which some seventy of the funerary statues still remain.

CITY OF THE DEAD

SAINT-DENIS HAD BEEN a sacred burial ground since the Romans. So let's begin there to explore this enormous city of the dead. The stairs adjacent to the entrance of the south transept lead to the crypt, the site of the earliest Christian shrines predating both Suger's cathedral and another church built on the spot by Abbot Fulrad (d. 784) and consecrated in 775 in the presence of the emperor Charlemagne (d. 814). To the left of the bottom of the stairs lies a primitive cemetery that once

Gallo-Roman Graves

contained the remains of some one hundred noble Gallo-Romans and Merovingians (fourth-to-seventh centuries) in what is now a haunting array of stone sarcophagi lying in the dirt. This is the area under the altar of the cathedral and is thought also to be the place where the bones of Saints Denis, Rusticus, and Eleutherius were once interred. The archeological site beneath Saint-Denis was only discovered in the middle of the nineteenth century when Eugène Emmanuel Viollet-le-Duc began to dig beneath the tomb that had been constructed for Napoleon Bonaparte. The tomb was dismantled when the emperor's remains went in 1861 from the Chapel of Saint-Jérôme to their final resting place under dome of the Invalides in Paris's seventh arrondissement.

Opposite the archeological site of the Merovingian necropolis lie the stunning restored ruins of the Romanesque crypt constructed by Abbot Hilduin in the ninth century and rebuilt some 250 years later, about fifty years before Suger's Gothic expansion over the layers of architectural history. This great barrel-shaped vault of rough-hewn stones, cut before the regular courses of ashlar, squared masonry that will characterize the walls of Gothic buildings, is limned by a series of Romanesque or rounded arches held aloft by columns capped by carved capitals. On what would have been the floor of the ancient church lie six great black slabs with the remains of the Bourbon kings of France, including those of Louis XVI and Marie Antoinette along with Louis XVIII who died in 1824. On the other side of the old Romanesque wall and circled by it is Suger's crypt with its massive round columns and capitals decorated with a variety of floral patterns and themselves surrounded by a series of radiating chapels with windows set almost at ground level. By the stairs to the right of the Gallo-Roman necropolis, two large black plaques with gold lettering display the names of the Merovingians, Caroligians, Capetians, and Valois kings and queens whose remains are crammed into a cubbyhole in the small space between the two markers as testimony to the little that is left of the French monarchy.

The royal bones in the ossuary of the crypt endured a sad saga beginning on August 1, 1793, with the declaration of the National Convention Assembly that governed France from September 1792 until October 1795 that "the tombs and mausoleums of the aforementioned kings erected in the church of Saint-Denis . . . will be destroyed beginning on next August 10." With great zeal, crowds gathered at Saint-Denis to open the tombs and pillage the precious objects—crown, scepters, crosses, rings—that had been buried with the royal dead, right down to the lead in coffins, melted down to make bullets. The good citizens mutilated with ghoulish glee the bodies of the hated rulers of the Ancien Régime. At the exhumation of Henri IV (1553–1610), whose face apparently was still "perfectly recognizable," according to Henri-Martin Manteau, the man in charge of the military transport, a soldier cut off a piece of his beard and held it up to his face with the promise "never to wear another moustache." The mob grabbed great tufts of Catherine de Medici's (1515–1589) hair, amid accusations of having killed her husband Henri II (1519–1559). Relieved of the grave goods, the bodies once buried at Saint-Denis were dumped into two common pits. Even in the pits the theft of royal relics continued. Henri-Martin Manteau climbed down a ladder and, by his own account, "indifferent to the crowd," stealthily removed one of the thumbnails of Louis XIV. Manteau, who in 1816 edited a record of the events which he had witnessed, reports that one of the cart-drivers "made a large opening with a knife in his [Louis's] stomach," and the stuffing which had been inserted to replace the entrails of the Sun King came pouring out. Once the pits were filled, the bodies were covered with quicklime and buried until, with the restoration of the monarchy in 1815, Louis XVIII had what remained of the royal remains exhumed and interred in ten common coffins still in the cathedral crypt.

THE GISANTS OF SAINT-DENIS

THE TOP OF THE STAIRS by the ossuary opens to a field of kingly gisants, recumbent funerary figures, from the Middle Ages and Renaissance, which underwent their own journey in the period between the French Revolution of 1789 and the Restoration of 1814. Many were taken to Paris where they were displayed in the Museum of French Monuments, a former convent, which is now the École des Beaux-Arts. In this period of destruction and neglect, the Abbey of Saint-Denis was stripped of its roof for the lead which was, like the lead in the royal coffins, melted down for ammunition. This exposed to the elements the wooden roof frame and the top of the vaults below. The cathedral was at one point used as a field hospital for soldiers wounded in the Napoleonic Wars, and as a warehouse for the storage of grain. It was not until 1806, when Napoleon, true to his megalomaniacal character, took an interest in being buried at Saint-Denis that the phase of rapid deterioration came to an end; and it wasn't until 1817, with the closing of the Museum of French Monuments, that the royal mausoleums were transferred back to the abbey where they were installed in the crypt. In the middle of the nineteenth century, Viollet-le-Duc moved them into the main body of the cathedral where they are displayed, if not in strict chronological order, at least grouped by dynasty on either side of the transept and nave—Merovingian, Carolingian, Capetian, and Valois.

To stand among the reclining sepulchres of Saint-Denis is to float eerily among the dead and to experience the most profound cathedral effect. First among these is the collapse of time. The dead are resurrected collectively in white stone or marble, their earthly garb, physical appearance, and facial expression rendered so realistically that they appear simply to be sleeping in peaceful assembly. Through the close proximity of those who have lived over a period of ten centuries, space has abolished time. If heaven is a place that holds the promise of meeting one's forebears, then Saint-Denis offers the kings and queens of France a foretaste

Gisants

of that blessed state. Indeed, one of the original motivations to be buried there was to rest for all eternity close to one's ancestors, and to the saints.

Louis IX, the future Saint Louis (d. 1270), rearranged the gisants in the middle of the thirteenth century to reflect the continuity of royal successions, despite the genealogical breaks between dynasties. Dagobert (d. 639), who provided the initial endowment for the abbey church, had his special place and recess tomb to the south of the main altar with his son Clovis II and seven Carolingians nearby. Eight Capetians were on the north side, with Philip Augustus (d. 1223), Louis's grandfather, and his father Louis VIII (d. 1226) in the center of the transept crossing along with Louis IX's own future final resting place at the center of a heavenly royal court.

DOGS, LIONS, AND PILLOWS

IF YOU ARE NOT STEEPED in French dynastic succession, you will have a hard time amid the sea of prone stone and marble figures in the choir and transepts of Saint-Denis, so let me suggest that you wander among them observing remarkable features and stopping before some of the especially striking funerary monuments, all of which are labelled and dated. You cannot help but notice, for example, the numerous dogs at the feet of their owners, Blanche of Navarre (d. 1398) and Jeanne (d. 1350), daughter of Blanche of Navarre and Philip IV of Valois, or Marguerite d'Artois (d. 1311). Some dogs are pictured with a bone, others with bells around their neck. All, I suspect, accompany their masters and mistresses even into death because of the dog's almost universal reputation for loyalty. And then there are the lions. The feet of Charles, Count of Valois, look as if they were covered in chain mail socks curled around a compliant lion. Complacent and even smiling lions lie at the feet of Louis Hutin, John II the Good, and Philip VI of Valois. Lions are, of course, associated with kingship, but the remarkable tameness of the lions of Saint-Denis suggests a waning of the worldly fierceness of man and beast in the world beyond the grave.

Angels plump the pillows of Louis and Philip of Alençon (d. 1273) at whose feet lies a dog with a rabbit in its mouth. Between the two are what appear to be two students reading, a sculptural doodle equivalent to the droleries in the margins of medieval manuscripts. Many of the funerary monuments show the dead in prayer. The joined hands of

Louis of France (d. 1260), oldest son of Saint Louis, are lifted far off his chest. A loyal dog at his feet, his body reclines over a series of broken arches filled with secular and religious mourners, the procession led by two bishops. The side under Louis's feet shows the image of a beloved son carried on a bier by four kings, including his father.

Charles of Anjou, king of Sicily (d. 1285) and brother of Saint Louis, was buried in Naples, but his heart was taken to Saint-Denis, where he is portrayed in sculpture holding it on his chest over the spot it used to occupy. Saint Louis's entrails were taken to his brother Charles in Sicily in what amounts to a fraternal exchange of innards. In that same vein, Jeanne of Bourbon (d. 1378) clasps to her breast a sack containing her entrails. The attributes of status are represented alongside the dead, knights still wearing their armor, sword, and shield bearing coats of arms. The princesses of France, Blanche of Brittany (d. 1393), Marguerite of Flanders (d. 1382), Marguerite of Artois (d. 1311) all wear the veils and

Tomb of Louis XII and Anne of Brittany

mentonières or chin coverings that are the attributes of noble married women.

The extravagant renaissance mausoleums of Saint-Denis stand out among the lower-lying prone gisants and are combined works of sculpture and architecture in the Italian style, harking back to classical as well as to medieval sources. Sculpted at Tours out of marble from the mines of Carrera and carted to Saint-Denis in sixty-three crates in 1531, the funerary monument for Louis XII (d. 1515), king of France and Naples and leader of the French campaign into Italy in the early sixteenth century, and his wife Anne of Brittany (d. 1514) occupies the northwest corner of the transept crossing. The base is carved all around with images of the military deeds of Louis, whose soldiers are dressed in classical garb. Louis's crossing of the Alps, a battle, his triumphal entry to Milan, and the surrender of the Venetian General Alviano are all represented there. The classical building, with pilasters, decorated in a delicate biomorphic style, reminiscent of the designs uncovered at Pompei late in the sixteenth century, and rounded arcades, supports a terrace on top of which Louis and Anne, kneeling on pillows, are shown in prayer before two prie-dieux covered with flowing drapes.

Inside this chapel within a chapel lie the outstretched emaciated naked bodies of the deceased king whose eyes and chest are sunken, the scar from embalming and the removal of his heart and entrails still visible. He appears, along with Anne, to be taking his final breath. Particularly striking are the bare upturned feet of the royal couple, Louis's symmetrically positioned and dominated by the gigantic big toe of a conqueror, and Anne's more naturally placed against legs that seem to writhe in pain, perhaps referring to her painful death as a result of a kidney-stone attack. The contrast between the richly dressed living royal couple and the denuded cadavers below speaks to the theme of equality before death and, finally, to the vanity of earthly pursuits and the misery of the human condition. Twelve apostles sit in the arches, each with his attribute, Peter with keys, Thomas with the architect's square, James with a shell clasp on his draped robe and on his pilgrim's sack, Paul with a book. Allegorical figures of four ladies representing the cardinal virtues—Justice with a sword and globe, Prudence with a mirror and a snake creeping up its arm, Temperance with reins and a clock, and Force who grasps a column—sit perched at the four corners of the mausoleum.

KING DAGOBERT

STANDING AT THE TOP of the stairs to the left of the door leading from the crypt, you can see on the other side of the altar the extraordinary tomb of King Dagobert (d. 634), a Gothic extravaganza begun in the thirteenth century at the behest of Saint Louis and only completed in the nineteenth by Viollet-le-Duc. Dagobert was the last of the Merovingian rulers to wield significant power. Through his intelligence

Dagobert's Tomb

and ruthlessness, he managed to unite, more or less, warring Frankish tribes from Bavaria to Alsace and Aquitaine. In the spiritual line of Clovis (d. 511), the first Christian king, Dagobert supported the Church. Having endowed the Abbey of Saint-Denis, he was the first king to request burial there. According to legend and the writings of Archbishop Hincmar of Reims (d. 882), Dagobert was hunting when a stag, pursued by a pack of dogs, ran into a chapel at Catulliacus, the Roman name for Saint-Denis. The chapel, founded by Saint Geneviève (d. 512) in the previous century, now lay in ruins. By a miracle, the dogs refused to cross the threshold. Later, when Dagobert rebelled against his father Clothar II over the question of royal succession, he sought refuge from soldiers sent by his father to fetch him in the very same chapel. There he fell asleep and in a dream saw three men in white. The eldest spoke: "Know, young man, that we are Denis, Rusticus, and Eleutherius and our bodies rest here. As the humbleness of our grave has obscured our renown, if you promise to decorate our tomb, we will liberate you from your dilemma and lend you our help." Whereupon the soldiers, like the dreamer's hunting dogs, found themselves unable to enter the chapel, and his father relented. Dagobert "did not forget the vow and the promise he had made to the martyr saint Denis and to his companions." He had the saintly bodies disinterred and reburied "where they still lie, in the year of the Incarnation 630," that is, on the site of the abbey church of Saint-Denis.

Dagobert's tomb is a cathedral within a cathedral, showing as it does the characteristics of the tympanum over a portal, limned by an archivolt and capped by a gable with towers and spires on either side. Dagobert lies as an unusual gisant, on his side, his hands folded in prayer, his wife Nanthilde standing at his feet, and his son Clovis II by his head. In the lower lintel Saint Denis awakens a dreaming hermit, who is sleeping under a trefoil or three-ring arch in a miniature chapel, and tells him to pray for the soul of Dagobert, which is being dragged to hell by devils, a scene represented to the right. The reason for which Dagobert might have been destined for the underworld is not clear. In one account, he was guilty of alienating church property; in another, he was made to pay for lax morals by Christian standards. In Hincmar's account, maintaining "three queens almost simultaneously as well as several concubines" justified his condemnation. In the upper lintel the king calls upon Saints Denis and Martin, who rescue him from the devil's grasp and, in the tympanum, they carry Dagobert, dressed as a naked homunculus with a crown, to heaven. The archivolt around this trompe-l'oeil of a tympanum shows six angels waving censers to issue the king upward. The gable at the very top depicts the saints interceding with Christ on Dagobert's behalf.

Dagobert's tomb was begun just around the time of the invention of the concept of purgatory as the antechamber to a more permanent afterlife—a third space where the soul might be cleansed of earthly sin for a specified period of time before ascending to Heaven. Under such an arrangement, the time in purgatory might be lessened by pious prayers and donations before death, at the time of death, or even after death as the result of the generosity of surviving relatives. The meaning of such an arrangement for Dagobert and all who followed is clear: no matter how personally sinful the king may have been while alive, his endowment of Saint-Denis via gifts of land and precious objects guarantees that the saints who are also buried there will shield him from eternal damnation.

As you leave the stairs facing Dagobert's tomb, do not miss the floor that leads across the apse and which consists of blue and red alternating eagle- and floral-patterned tiles, the creation of Viollet-le-Duc in the nineteenth century and restored in 2015. In the curved ambulatory on the north wall of the apse, the Saint-Firmin chapel shows vestiges of a floor once covered by mosaics depicting the Works of the Months, of which only October remains. Here, a man pours wine into a barrel, the word "OCTO" visible between his face and the pitcher in his hand. The image is consistent with that among the Works of the Months around the door jambs on the south portal of the west facade. Two steps lead up to the altar in the Saint-Firmin chapel. The first bears the figure of a monk named Alberic, once part of a series of such medallions, with the inscription: "To whom I pray fervently / Whom I serve completely / Saintly martyr of God / Please remember me." The decoration on the upper step displays two crisscrossed quadrants with fantastic animals—a lion, a dragon, an eagle, and a sphinx-like figure, all in the rampant or rearing position, along with other exotic beasts. The mosaic medium, which Suger claims was also once part of the design of the north portal, points to an Eastern origin.

COLORED GLASS

WALKING CLOCKWISE around the apse, you come closer than at any point to what Suger, using an old word for a new phenomenon, calls "painting," by which he refers to the painted figures on colored glass and not on the solid walls of a traditional Romanesque church. "We caused to be painted, by the exquisite hands of many masters from different regions," the proud abbot claims like the impresario of a dramatic architectural production, "a splendid variety of new windows both below and above." The great sheets of glass at Saint-Denis are part of what makes Gothic style modern. They may have had an Eastern source in the cloisonné technique of metalwork, melted colored glass or enamel in gold or silver cells found in jewelry and other precious objects from ancient Egypt and the Byzantine world. So, too, the actual medieval glass may have been imported. Much of the stained glass in medieval cathedrals was made at the building site, and small differences in chemical composition allow for precise identification of origin, even when the glass was recast. To wit: analysis of the deep blue pieces of which Suger speaks—the *materiem saphirorum*—indicates that they came from the eastern or southeastern Mediterranean, were shipped north in lingots, melted down into sheets which were then cut, painted, and leaded along with the glass of other colors into the "paintings" on the walls of Saint-Denis.

Suger was pleased with his innovation, claiming as he does that the Lord provided the makers of the "marvelous windows a rich supply of sapphire glass and ready funds of about seven hundred pounds or more." Very little of the original glazing from the abbey church of Saint-Denis has survived, many of the pieces removed at the time of the Revolution having found their way to museums in France, England, and the United States. The provenance of authentic twelfth-century glass, like that of medieval manuscripts, is often shrouded in mystery. After 1789, some glass pieces were taken to the Museum of French Monuments, which was established by the archeologist Alexandre Lenoir to preserve the material culture of churches after the Revolution, and from there ended up in the hands of French, Belgian, and British dealers, whence their removal to the English-speaking world.

Several of the stained glass windows at Saint-Denis capture the spirit behind the construction of the first Gothic cathedral—a turning to the light as both a sensory experience and as a process of understanding, enlightenment, that God, according to *The Celestial Hierarchies* of Pseudo-Dionysius, is light.

First, the Tree of Jesse window which, in the phrase of Suger, "begins the series . . . in the apse of the church" and is placed just to the right of the axis or midpoint of the apse, this in addition to the Jesse at the center of the north rose. At the bottom right, Suger clutches a miniature version of the entire window, as if he were offering it to his church like one of the donor windows found elsewhere to acknowledge the gift of a particular urban guild, an individual, or those whose labor went into the building itself. The Tree of Jesse window illustrates the passage from

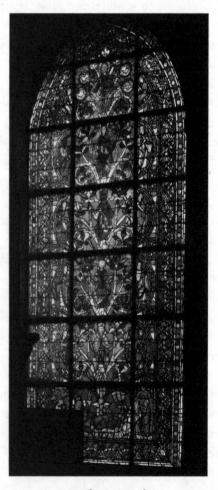

Tree of Jesse Window

the prophecy of Isaiah in which the sleeping Jesse dreams of a rod issuing from his stomach and, winding its way across the generations, terminates in the birth of Jesus. The large bottom central image is a visual representation of the prophecy of Isaiah 11:1: "And there shall come forth a rod out of the root of Jesse, and a flower shall rise up out of his root." On the left of Jesse stands the image of Matthew, one of the two evangelists (with Luke) who traces the genealogy of Christ from Abraham to King David, the son of Jesse and the father of Solomon, in forty-two generations, as noted in Matthew 1:17: "So all the generations from Abraham to David, are fourteen generations. And from David to the transmigration of Babylon, are fourteen generations; and from the transmigration of Babylon to Christ are fourteen generations."

The tracing of Christ's royal lineage could not have escaped the attention of the kings of France for whom legitimacy resided, despite dynastic breaks, in continuous dynastic succession. The first connection is genealogical. Though the line of Jesse in the Saint-Denis Jesse window passes symbolically through only three generations before arriving at the Virgin who sits directly beneath the Son, this is enough to make the continuous connection between Jesse and Jesus. On either side of the main panels whose background design confirms the flowering of one generation into the next sit the prophets who are identified by written banners in their framing lozenges: Isaiah, Moses, Jeremiah, and Samuel on the left side, and Daniel, Haggai, Amos, and Joel on the right. The second connection is semantic, as the seismic cleavage between the Old and New Testaments is smoothed by an unfolding through time of the meaning of Isaiah's prophecy. In retrospect, the Old Testament prophet's words are taken to refer to the coming of the Messiah in Isaiah 11:6: "The wolf shall dwell with the lamb: and the leopard shall lie down with the kid: the calf and the lion, and the sheep shall abide together, and a little child shall lead them." This is Paul's understanding in Acts 13:23: "Of this man's [David's] seed, God, according to his promise, hath raised up to Israel a Saviour Jesus." "And again," in Romans 15:12, "Isaiah saith: There shall be a root of Jesse; and he that shall rise up to rule the Gentiles, in him the Gentiles shall hope." From Jesse to Jesus, the partial homophony of the names makes a connection that Suger, the master of state formation at a time when claims of longevity support those of legitimacy, is anxious to affirm. If the authenticity of Jesus as Messiah reaches back across twenty-nine generations to Jesse as prophet, then the authority of King Louis VI and Louis VII might also, by analogy, reach back to Clovis, the first Christian king of France. And, so, as Suger writes, the Tree of Jesse window, sustained by the image in the lower left corner of the vain and generous abbot's gift, "begins the series . . . in the chevet of the church."

By renovating the old Romanesque church in the new Gothic style, Suger sought somehow to reconcile the two: "In carrying out such plans my first thought was for the concordance and harmony of the ancient and the new work." Similarly, he seeks the "concordance and harmony" of the Hebrew and Christian Bibles. One of the ways that they might be accommodated to each other is via the strategy of reading backward—of explaining the Old Testament preemptively in terms of the New and the New Testament retroactively in terms of the Old. Another lies in the technique of reading more deeply, what Suger terms "anagogic" understanding, which is the ability to recognize the truth of the New Law beneath the Old. Such a way of thinking is, of course, inseparable from the question of the relationship between Jews and Christians, more precisely, the Jews' reluctance to recognize Jesus as the Messiah.

Reading anagogically is nowhere more evident than in the three stained glass windows to the north of the axis of the apse—the so-called Moses, Infancy of Christ, and Anagogical windows to which Suger, more clearly than any tour group leader, serves, in his account of the building of Saint-Denis, as a trustworthy guide.

THE MOSES WINDOW

Y̲OU WILL FIND no better illustration of the cathedral as the Bible of the poor than the Moses window, which is worth examining in some detail. In third position to the north or left of the axis of the apse, it is of the narrative type, organized biographically to follow the life of the leader of the Israelites from birth to death, as contained in the Books of Exodus, Numbers, and Deuteronomy. Again, it is not clear that the glass painters of Saint-Denis could actually read the Bible, but far more likely, as in the case of the sculptors of the west facade (see p. 18), that they received instructions from clerics who participated in the esthetic design of the cathedral or from Suger himself.

The Moses window consists of five round central panels with two quarter-rounds and four half-rounds on either side. In the right quarter-

Moses Window

circle at the very bottom, Pharaoh orders the Hebrew children to be cast into the river, while, to the left, two women flee with a young child, possibly even Moses's mother and his sister Miriam, who wears a green dress as in the full circle between them. The remarkable central rondel captures in body language, especially hand gestures, the astonishment of the Pharaoh's daughter, her handmaiden, and Miriam at finding a child in the water, indicated by blue, white, green, red, and yellow wavy lines at the bottom glazing under their feet. The child, painted on a single piece of oval glass, is depicted in some detail. If you look closely, you can see what appears to be a little embryo with a large head, two hands, and no lower body.

In the left half-lozenge between the lowest and the second rondel, Moses, wearing the hat associated with the Jews and carrying a stick in his right hand, is depicted as a shepherd guarding a herd of sheep with a goat between the branches of a tree in the half-round on the right. The shepherd motif is continued in the full round just above in which the animals, shown at the bottom of the frame, surround the burning tree or bush in which God appears to Moses. The fire is rendered by a large red band all around God's head and by Moses's body language. Having removed one shoe, he grasps his foot, which must have felt the heat, with his left hand while raising his right hand in the air, in a gesture of astonishment. The inscription which floats over the heads of God and Moses reads: "JUST AS THIS BUSH IS SEEN TO BURN YET IS NOT BURNED, SO HE WHO IS FULL OF THIS FIRE DIVINE BURNS WITH IT YET IS NOT BURNED."

The left half-lozenge which accompanies God's appearance to Moses in the burning bush shows at the top God who identifies himself to Moses (Exodus 4:3) by turning his staff into a snake. On the right we see the plagues visited upon the Egyptians—the sea changed to blood, the invasion of frogs, locusts, wild flies, and the hand of God which launches a thunderstorm of hail and fire—before Pharaoh releases the Israelites from captivity. In the central full-round above, Moses, staff in hand, leads the Israelites, represented by two couples walking hand in hand, across the Red Sea, figured as wavy lines a third of the way up the panel and an undulating red line at the bottom on top of a chariot wheel and the fragmented and twisted bodies of the Egyptian army. God, surrounded by a red nimbus, observes the scene from on high.

At the center of the fourth full rondel, a barefoot Moses, suspended in midair, receives the tablets of the Law on Mount Sinai, while, below, the Israelites are seated at a table at one end of which the golden calf stands in obvious reference to the betrayal of the covenant with Yahweh. The scene of idolatry is depicted in the right half-lozenge, while, on the left, Moses smashes the tablets before an architectural structure featuring the rear part of the calf under an arch. In the final half-circle on the right, the destruction of the rebellious opponents of Moses, as recounted in Numbers 16:31: "the earth broke asunder under their feet: [32] And opening her mouth devoured them with their tents and all their substance." On the left, with his finger outstretched, God orders Moses to Mount Nebo, as written across the middle of the glass, "and see the land of Chanaan, which I will deliver to the children of Israel to possess, and die thou in the mountain" (Deuteronomy 32:49).

The top central panel of the Moses window, which we know from Suger's description should have been placed below the reception of the Law, shows Moses pointing to a griffin-like figure on top of what looks like a Romanesque column and capital, while the Israelites who surround it raise their hands in wonder. The scene captures the last of the stories of the discontent of the Israelites, who began to murmur against God and Moses in Numbers 21:5: "Why didst thou bring us out of Egypt, to die in the wilderness? There is no bread, nor have we any waters: our soul now loatheth this very light food." Which brings punishment in 21:6: "Wherefore the Lord sent among the people fiery serpents, which bit them and killed many of them." The rondel features serpents at the base of the column and at the feet of those gathered around it. Asked by the Israelites to intercede on their behalf, Moses prays to God, who instructs him in 21:9 to "[m]ake a brazen serpent, and set it up for a sign: whosoever being struck shall look on it, shall live." The Israelites looking up at the brazen serpent also take in the cross at the top of the pole on which we can make out in green grisaille the image of the Crucifixion. An inscription arrayed horizontally across the panel between the bronze serpent and the arms of the cross reads, "JUST AS THE BRAZEN SERPENT SLAYS ALL SERPENTS." It is completed at the bottom, under the feet of the Israelites, "SO CHRIST, RAISED ON THE CROSS, SLAYS HIS ENEMIES."

Moses, who sacrifices himself to save the Israelites, prefigures Christ, and the scenes of his life from the window that bears his name, correctly understood, foreshadow the life of the Christian Savior. Thus, Suger, reading anagogically, notes that the scene of discovery of the child in the water in fact signifies Christ and the Church: "Moses in the ark is that Man-Child Whom the maiden Royal, the Church, fosters with pious mind." The submergence of Pharaoh's army in the sea is a foreshadowing of the sacrament of baptism. The Law that Moses receives on the mount is, according to the Pauline formula adapted by Suger, a dead letter that awaits the grace of Christ who "invigorates it": "Grace *giveth life, the letter killeth.*"

THE BIRTH AND INFANCY
OF JESUS WINDOW

THE INFANCY WINDOW, which, as currently constituted, is also a Life of the Virgin window, sits in first position to the north or left of the axis of the apse, closest to the east and to the sunrise associated with rebirth. It contains the essential elements of the Infancy program found in almost every cathedral in northern France. The bottom central panel depicts the Annunciation by which the angel Gabriel informs Mary that she would conceive and give birth to Jesus. At the top, we see the dove of the Holy Spirit and, at the bottom, an image of Abbot Suger lying prostrate at Mary's feet. As if there could be any question, the title just above his tonsured head reads "SUGERIUS ABAS," while that between the heads of Gabriel and Mary reads "AVE MARIA." The enterprising abbot is everywhere underfoot: at the feet of Christ of the Last Judgment on the tympanum of the central portal, at His feet at the Supper at Emmaus on the door below, at the bottom of the Jesse Tree window, and at the feet of the Virgin at the Annunciation—all part of Suger's "colossal but profoundly humble vanity," in the phrase of the great art historian Erwin Panofsky. To the right and left, two modern rectangular panels depict an angel informing Joseph of the virgin birth in a dream and the scene of the Visitation of Mary with her cousin Elizabeth who is pregnant with John the Baptist.

The birth of Jesus fills the second medallion. Mary lies on a bed with a lamp over her head. The child, whom Isaiah foretold and Moses preceded, lies on an altar-like pedestal to her left, a yellow star, an ass and an ox over His head. Joseph sits to the far left of the image, all three under a triple arcade which separates them from a host of angels. In the left and adjoining rectangle, shepherds are informed of the birth by an angel descending from heaven with a scroll; and, to the right, the Presentation of Jesus in the temple. Simeon, who identifies Jesus as the Messiah, is shown taking the child in his arms: "Behold this child is set for the fall and for the resurrection of many in Israel and for a sign which shall be contradicted" (Luke 2:34). This last image had special meaning for Saint-Denis, as Suger maintained that the abbey possessed among its relics "the arm of the aged Saint Simeon," here shown in direct contact with the infant Jesus.

The Infancy window is filled with scenes that a cleric, standing before it, might have emphasized in preaching. Even the most illiterate visitor to Saint-Denis might have heard the story of Jesus's birth, and, in hearing, forms pictures in the mind. Yet, seeing such vivid color images feeds the imagination more potently than any oral account. We can no longer hear the story, or read it, without thinking that the Infancy window renders the way it really was. So, moving to the third rung, you might see the story of the Magi who, in the central panel, follow a star to the place of Jesus's birth. On the right, they gaze upon Mother and Child in the scene of the Adoration; and, on the left, they are warned in a dream by an angel not to return to Herod. The panels above depict the slaughter of the innocents on left and right while, in the middle, Joseph, having been warned in a dream by the angel which peeps through the clouds, flees with Mary and Jesus on the back of a long-eared donkey. I, for one, can never look at a scene of the Massacre of the Innocents and the Flight into Egypt without thinking of the pogroms that sent my ancestors into flight from Russia or the slaughter of innocent Jews in the Holocaust of the last century. This, as we shall see (see p. 300), is how Marc Chagall, commissioned to create stained glass windows to replace those lost at Reims in World War II, imagined the profound connection between the events of the New Testament, medieval "paintings," to borrow Suger's phrase, and the world in which we live.

In the fifth position of the Saint-Denis Infancy window, Jesus, who at the age of twelve has become separated from his parents in Jerusalem, is found "in the temple, sitting in the midst of the doctors, hearing them and asking them questions" (Luke 2:46). Mary and Joseph look on from the adjoining rectangles. At the very top, in a panel of painted glass that was originally not part of the Infancy window, we witness the death of Mary, surrounded by the apostles and angels in the triangular side panels.

If the Moses window, in third position from the axis of the apse, anticipates the Infancy window, in first position, they are joined by the so-called "Anagogical" window, which is situated between the two and makes a connection between them. The first three round panels of the anagogic window form an interpretive whole. In the bottom frame we see Christ standing between two women and in front of a wheel with a central disk and six disks on spokes. If you look closely, you will

Anagogic Window

observe that each disk contains a bird which represents as a group the seven doves of the Gifts of the Holy Spirit as elaborated by the Early Church Fathers—the gifts of wisdom, understanding, counsel, fortitude, knowledge, piety, and fear of the Lord. Christ bestows a crown on the woman to his right, who is holding an open book in her hands and who is identified by the title next to her as "ECCLESIA," the Church. With His left hand Christ takes a covering off the head of a woman who holds tablets in front of a title which reads "SYNAGOGA." The message of this bottom medallion could not be clearer in its emphasis upon Christ as the bridge between the Synagogue and the Church, between the crowning of the New Law, contained in a book, and the unveiling of the Old Law, the Law of Moses, inscribed on tablets.

The unveiling of Moses occupies the whole of the next rondel where he stands holding the tablets of the Old Law, surrounded by three men wearing the hats associated with Jews, while a fourth, without a hat and possibly the figure of Jesus, removes a piece of cloth from his head. In what Suger calls the medieval "concordance and harmony" of Old and New Testaments, Moses is a prefiguration of Christ who reveals or unveils the truth of the Hebrew Bible. Though this panel of the Anagogical window is not original and may, indeed, have been inspired by Suger's description of what he observed in the twelfth century, inscribed in the banner around the human figures, it visually embodies his words: "Also in the same window, where the veil is taken off the face of Moses: 'What Moses veils the doctrine of Christ unveils. They who despoil Moses bare the Law.'"

Above Moses we observe two men carrying sacks over their shoulders and a third turning a long shaft attached to a millstone in what is one of the great metaphors of reconciliation of the Hebrew and Christian Bibles, a grinding of the grain of the Old Testament into the New, a removal of the flour, which is edible, from the chaff, which is not. Again, this recreation of the original window according to Suger's description written in the encircling banner shows the "Apostle Paul turning a mill and the Prophets carrying sacks to the mill. The verses of this subject are these: 'By working the mill, thou, Paul, takest the flour out of the bran. Thou makest known the inmost meaning of the Law of Moses. From so many grains is made the true bread without bran, Our and the angels' perpetual food.'" At the top of the Anagogical window, a majestic God holds a cross on which the Crucifixion is painted in front of a box on wheels which may be the ark of the covenant, from the Book of Exodus, which contained the Ten Commandments. The scene, which, again, visually reconciles the Old Law with the New, is situated above a rondel illustrating a motif known as the Tetramorph, images of the four figures of the evangelists under the guise of winged animals, also found in the four corners around the clock on the west facade. On the upper left and moving clockwise, Matthew, the Man, extending a book toward God; John, the eagle; Luke, the ox; and, on the lower left, Mark, the lion. The paradigm of the Tetramorph originated in the Old Testament Book of the prophet Ezekiel, who, while in exile in Babylonia circa 550 BCE, used the symbolism of Babylonian astrology to describe a vision in which the likeness of four living creatures came out of the midst of the fire (Ezekiel 1:10). The motif was reappropriated in the Apocalypse of Saint John, who alludes to Ezekiel's vision: "And the first living creature was like a lion; and the second living creature like a calf; and the third living creature, having the face, as it were, of a man; and the fourth living creature was like an eagle flying" (Apocalypse 4:7).

A GLIMPSE OF HEAVEN ON EARTH

ABOVE AND BEYOND the stories told in the stained glass windows of Saint-Denis is the wondrous experience of looking up at the luminous glass and at the colored light that passes through at certain times of day, tinting whatever it hits, mostly stone, like a fuzzy kaleidoscope. As a foretaste of heaven, the Gothic cathedral was made to appeal to the imagination, to reproduce the effects of what it would feel like, while still on earth, to be in the New Jerusalem described in the Apocalypse of Saint John: "Having the glory of God, and the light thereof was like to a precious stone, as to the jasper stone even as crystal" (21:11). If you have ever visited a Romanesque church with thick walls, interior surfaces tinted with conventional pigments and not "painted" with glass, and with small windows that block more light than they admit, you will appreciate Suger's determining transformation of the cathedral effect.

The Gothic cathedral aims to excite and please the senses to an extent that would have been unthinkable in the churches built just fifty years earlier. Though they may have been suited to instruct and to inspire the faithful, and some are exquisitely beautiful, Romanesque buildings were not meant to dazzle or delight. On the contrary, pleasure taken in the medium through which sacred truths were expressed detracted from the message. The Early Fathers of the Church, in the line of Plato's distrust of the senses and especially of images, warned against esthetic tampering with the natural things made by God. "Whatever is born is the work of God," Tertullian (d. ca. 220), the first Christian author, maintains. "Whatever, then, is plastered on (that) is the devils work." At the turn of the fifth century CE, Saint Augustine observed that one might write the name of God in gold or in ink. The former would be worth more to men, but the meaning of the word would be the same.

The earlier medieval rejection of the senses in favor of the intellect or mind versus Suger's appeal to visual pleasure, two ways of knowing God, captures the essence of one of the great debates of the High Middle Ages. It marks, in fact, the difference between theology and philosophy at the root of a personal conflict between Suger and his contemporary Saint Bernard of Clairvaux. The most influential monk of the twelfth century and the founder of the austere Cistercian order, Bernard condemned in no uncertain terms the building of large religious buildings with rich decorations. He may even have had Saint-Denis in mind when he spoke of "major abuses" in churches, their "vertiginous height," "extravagant length," "inordinate width and costly finishings," their "elaborate images that catch the eye and check the devotion of those at prayer within." "O vanity of vanities, but above all insanity! The walls of the church are ablaze with light and colour, while the poor of the Church go hungry." Bernard censures fancy decorations in churches as a "form of idol-worship," a confusion of outward glitter with inner worth. "When eyes open wide at gold-cased relics, purses do the same. A beautiful image of a saint is on show: the brighter the colours the holier he or she will be considered. Those who hasten to kiss the image are invited to leave a gift, and wonder more at the beauty than at the holiness they should be venerating."

Suger, on the other hand, gives free rein to the senses and allows himself to become fixated upon the beautiful things that are part of the structure he has built, stained glass and sculpture, as well as the appointments—wall hangings, rugs, furniture—and liturgical objects—altarpieces, crosses, vases, and chalices—with which the interior of the church was adorned. In a stunning account of the acquisition of precious stones for a golden cross to adorn an altar in the upper choir of the new church, the shrewd abbot is giddy with delight at outsmarting monks from the abbeys controlled by his abstemious rival Bernard:

When I was in difficulty for want of gems and could not sufficiently provide myself with more (for their scarcity makes them very expensive): then, lo and behold, [monks] from three abbeys of two Orders—that is, from Cîteaux and another abbey of the same Order, and from Fontevrault—entered our little chamber adjacent to the church and offered us for sale an abundance of gems such as we had not seen in ten years, hyacinths, sapphires, rubies, emeralds, topazes.

Suger is doubly elated. He no longer has to search for precious stones for the altar he has designed, and he has struck a good deal on behalf of the abbey he directs. We "thanked God," he exudes, "and gave four hundred pounds for the lot thought they were worth much more."

You may catch a glimpse of what such a display of riches might have looked like from this painting (ca. 1500), now in the National Gallery,

Mass of Saint Giles (Presented by the Art Fund / National Gallery, London)

London, the Mass of Saint Giles, by the Master of Saint Giles. Here, the Frankish king Charles Martel or even Charlemagne himself, kneels upon an oriental carpet before a cloth-covered prie-dieu. Surrounded by interior sculpture, the wooden top of a prayer screen, which separates that part of the cathedral where the public prays from that reserved for clerics, and Dagobert's tomb, which can be seen in the upper right, the priest officiates at the altar of Saint-Denis on which sits a triptych retable topped by the cross of Saint Eloy in which the gems amassed by Suger are set.

In his extraordinary account of the building of the new abbey church of Saint-Denis, Suger does not shy away from—indeed, savors—the inner glee we all feel at getting a bargain. His revelatory mental gesture is a symptom of the birth of the bourgeois who with cleverness triumphs economically over his or her rivals in the way that warriors and the knights of medieval epics or romance once conquered their opponents by physical force. The growth of Gothic cathedrals coincided, after all, with a revival of the circulation of money and rise of cities in the twelfth and thirteenth centuries. Nor does Suger hesitate to invoke the kind of rationalization familiar to all of us when we have done something, or gotten away with something, we know is wrong by some standard we have transgressed. Thus, the deal which Suger strikes with the monks of Cîteaux may seem venal by the strict moral gauge of Bernard. It is, however, in the eyes of the avaricious abbot, part of a sacred duty "to cover" the ashes of the saints "with the most precious material we possibly can: with refined gold and a profusion of hyacinths, emeralds and other precious stones." Here is where Suger, as human as any of us, begins to exaggerate. He interprets the miraculous appearance of such an abundance of wealth as a sign from God. "The Holy Martyrs themselves were telling us with their own lips" to seize a bargain when they saw one. Had they not been martyred, it is what they would have wanted: "so many [gems and pearls] were brought to us for sale from nearly all the parts of the world . . . that we should have been unable to let them go without great shame and offense to the Saints." In reading this passage, I have always been struck that Abbot Suger, a great Gothic entrepreneur and supreme rationalizer, shows himself to be one step away from a Protestant for whom riches are a sign of election by God for salvation in the world to come.

At one time the treasury of Saint-Denis contained an immense collection of precious objects alongside the relics that gave the cathedral its aura. The royals and nobles who were buried there brought with them the attributes of office—crowns, scepters, jewels, and rich robes. A few of the gifts which belonged to the abbey in the twelfth century survived the pillaging of the Revolution and are on view in museums in France and the United States. Dagobert's throne, a bronze folding chair on the Roman model, with four legs in the shape of leopard's bodies, fierce heads at the level of the seat and paws on the ground, fascinated Napoleon Bonaparte, who insisted on sitting upon it for his coronation ceremony in 1804. It can still be seen in the Cabinet des Médailles of the Bibliothèque de France. A rock crystal vase, which Suger describes as "looking like a pint bottle of beryl" and which had been a gift from Eleanor of Aquitaine (d. 1204) to her husband Louis VII, a porphyry vase which Suger had retrofitted with double wings and the head of an eagle, a copy of *The Celestial Hierarchies* of Pseudo-Dionysius with a velvet, ivory, and jewel cover from the fifteenth century—all belonged once to Saint-Denis and are currently on exhibit in the Louvre's medieval collection.

Sardonyx Chalice

One object, however, stands out above all the others—described by Suger as a "precious chalice out of one solid sardonyx," with gold and silver-gilt handles, rim, and stem full of (replacement) rubies and sapphires, and a base with the images of Christ in the Byzantine style. The sardonyx chalice was actually used to celebrate a mass on June 11, 1144, in the presence of King Louis VII and Queen Eleanor, who had come to Saint-Denis for the consecration of the chapels off the ambulatory behind the main altar of the cathedral. It was, in other words, present at the birth of the Gothic style. And not only present, but, having touched the lips of the king and queen of France along, presumably, with those of Suger himself, it still resonates with an aura of historic authenticity, of symbolic cultural capital, that only a few objects—the Rosetta stone, the Dead Sea Scrolls, the Sutton Hoo helmet, the Liberty Bell in Philadelphia—can claim. In the aftermath of the Revolution, Suger's chalice was taken to the Cabinet des Médailles from which it was stolen in 1804, smuggled in a plaster cast of the classical Laocoön first to Holland, then to England, where it passed through the hands of several dealers and eventually was purchased in 1922 by Joseph Widener, a wealthy breeder of racehorses. Today it resides in the National Gallery in Washington.

In our journey from the west facade of Saint-Denis to the treasure amassed by the man responsible for the first Gothic cathedral, we have come full circle—from sculptures dominated by final things, martyrdom, and Last Judgment, to the worship of precious, shiny, material things.

How can the two be reconciled?

The answer lies in Suger's concentration upon the cross of Saint Eloy which leads him to think that the two realms, physical and spiritual, may be closer than we think. The cross was a gift to Saint-Denis from Dagobert, and, though it has disappeared, we know it from the Master of Saint Giles's painting of the interior of the abbey church (see p. 48). Looking at the "loveliness of the many-colored gems" in "that incomparable ornament," the abbot's "delight in the beauty of the house of God" distracts him from worldly cares. He takes an inward turn that, far from the early medieval fear of fixation upon earthly goods, detaches him from them. He begins to dwell, "as it were, in some strange region of the universe which neither exists entirely in the slime of the earth nor entirely in the purity of Heaven." Beautiful things lift Suger outside of time, which may account for the time travel of the meditative abbot who appears throughout the cathedral he built in different zones of historical and theological time—at the feet of the Virgin at the time of the Annunciation, at the feet of Christ at the supper at Emmaus, at the bottom of the Jesse window in the real time of the construction of Saint-Denis, and at Christ's right foot at the Last Judgment and the end of human time.

Suger's experience of simultaneity affirms the most basic cathedral effect: the abolition of time by space. And I wonder how different it is, really, from what I feel when I visit museums in which the vestiges of Saint-Denis or other works with a hallowed provenance are housed. The experience is not the same, of course, for a Jewish male of a certain age as it was for the medieval churchman. A museum space is not as authentically enveloping as the high vaulted, expansively long and wide, at once dark and brightly colored, interior of a Gothic cathedral with its moist smells alongside the smoky residue of candles, and, on occasion, the deep vibrations of organ music and the sound, like angels, of a solo singer or chorus. Standing in front of the sardonyx chalice in Washington's National Gallery, the eagle, or the Eleanor vase in the Louvre, or the heads from the west facade of Saint-Denis in the Cluny Museum of the Middle Ages in Paris, the Walters Museum in Baltimore, or Harvard's Fogg, I savor some of the same delight in beautiful things as Suger before the cross of Saint Eloy, and some of the same abstraction from material things that hovers between the slime of the earth and the purity of heaven. At best, such moments of spirituality, whether in a cathedral or a museum, take me out of myself, out of my body, outside of chronological time.

The sensuous narcotic loss of self which Suger associates with the beauty of the cathedral and its contents was part of a new philosophical order according to which it is no longer necessary to turn one's back on the material world; rather, one might seek, as the twelfth-century abbot does, to "transcend it by absorbing it," in the phrase of Erwin Panofsky. Such "anagogical" uplift signals a momentous cultural shift that will manifest in almost every area of human endeavor, but nowhere more fully than in the construction, after Saint-Denis, of some 180 Gothic cathedrals which, beginning with Notre-Dame Paris, are sumptuous sites of worship, esthetic wonderlands, and among the most astonishing architectural achievements the world has ever known.

NOTRE-DAME
The Cathedral of Paris

NOTRE-DAME PARIS. EASTERN END OF
ÎLE DE LA CITÉ, PARIS 4E.

Access by subway (Cité) or foot. Begun 1163 CE, cathedral of Paris, and, eventually, all of France, site of learning next to University of Paris (Sorbonne), gathering place for dramatic national events, heavily restored in the nineteenth century, damaged in the catastrophic fire of April 2019. Do not miss the chance to climb the north tower and walk among the "chimères" on the balustrade and visit the beloved bells in the south tower.

U NDER THE GUIDANCE OF THE BISHOP OF PARIS, MAURICE DE Sully, and in the presence of Pope Alexander III, the cornerstone of the choir of Notre-Dame was laid in 1163 among the complex of religious buildings on Paris's Île de la Cité. The high altar was consecrated on May 19, 1182, by a papal legate. In May 1185, Heraclius, archbishop of Caesara and patriarch of Jerusalem, declared the Third Crusade on the steps of Notre-Dame, which for the last 850 years has been a functioning church and the geographic center—*kilomètre zéro*—from which all distances in France are measured. Napoleon crowned himself emperor there in 1804. On November 11, 1918, soldiers from allied nations converged at Notre-Dame to the clanging of its big bell Emmanuel to celebrate the end of the Great War. The liberation of Paris on August 25, 1944, culminated the next day in a victory parade down the Champs

Élysées and a *Te Deum* service in Notre-Dame. Kings may have been crowned in Reims and buried in Saint-Denis, which remain as vestiges of the Old Régime, but Paris is the place, even after the Revolution, in which the nation marks great national and international events. Notre-Dame was and still is the beating heart of France.

ROMAN AND MEDIEVAL PARIS

Paris of the twelfth century was one of the great stopping places of history. The city had been settled by a Celtic tribe, the Parisii, in the third century BCE. The Parisii were conquered by the Romans, who in 52 CE established a Gallo-Roman settlement in and around the Île de la Cité, known as the "Lutetia Parisiorum," or "the place near a swamp" of the tribe of the Parisii. France was Christianized in the third century CE, and occupied by the Germanic King Clovis, who, at the urging of his wife Clotilde, converted to Christianity around 496. Clovis made Paris his capital in 508. In the second half of the eighth century, Charles the Great or Charlemagne had managed to unite all of Europe under his rule and maintained relative peace throughout the empire. When he died in 814, however, Europe found itself vulnerable to invasions—Muslims from the Mediterranean, Magyars from the East, and Vikings or Norsemen from Scandinavia who raided England, Ireland, and France. In 845 Paris was attached by Viking invaders who sailed their fierce long ships up the Seine. Axe-bearing warriors from the North scaled the city walls and looted and burned what they could. Charlemagne's grandson Charles the Bald paid 7,000 pounds tribute to keep the raiders at bay. But the same thing happened in 876, and again in 885. Finally, the French King Charles the Simple, so-called for his forthrightness and not his lack of wit, concluded a peace treaty with the Viking leader Rollo in 911; and decades of peace, which grew into centuries, meant that Paris prospered as it never could have in the chaos following Charlemagne's death. The population of the city grew from an estimated 20,000 at the low point of the Viking raids, to an estimated 110,000 in 1200, to some 250,000 at the time of the Black Death of 1348, which may have killed as many as 800 people a day.

Peace brought tremendous economic growth, with the opening of long-range trade routes between the Middle East and the North, between England, the Low Countries, Italy, and France, all of which accompanied a growth in population. This was a period in which the rural economy of what Marc Bloch calls "the first feudal age" gave way to a rise of cities, with all that cities imply by way of money, commerce, markets, and judicial institutions, new urban social arrangements like the municipal government of the commune, artisan guilds and corporations, universities, and, in the Parisian basin, the Gothic cathedrals that were both engines of economic development and the place where change was registered in the written documents, the visual works of art, and the very shape of the buildings themselves.

Paris had long been a religious center, going back to pagan sites of worship during the Roman settlement of Lutetia. With the legalization of Christianity under Emperor Constantine in 313 CE, the city assumed a certain religious authority centered around a Roman-style basilica, reinforced in the sixth century by a Merovingian church, dedicated to the first Christian martyr, Saint Stephen. This structure may have been renovated in the ninth century, and either rebuilt in the Romanesque style or replaced by a Romanesque church some two hundred years later. The complex of sacred buildings on the Île de la Cité, which included the earlier churches, a monastery, and the bishop's house with its dependencies, coalesced in the mid 1100s into the cathedral of Notre-Dame, which has dominated the religious landscape of Paris ever since.

FROM ALL DIRECTIONS

THE ENORMOUS SIZE OF the cathedral of Paris is impressive from whatever direction you approach it. From the north, its towers are visible in the distance. Then, crossing the plaza in front of City Hall and the bridge over the Seine, they disappear, only to loom gigantically at the end of the rue d'Arcole. From the west, all along the Quai des Grands Augustins on the Left Bank, the massive frontality of Notre-Dame stands in high relief against buildings that in today's Paris are not much higher than their medieval counterparts, which were, in fact, a lot closer to the cathedral than at present. This is the angle that impressed Victor Hugo in his monumental 1831 *Notre-Dame de Paris* (*The Hunchback of Notre-Dame*) where the protagonist Claude Frollo, archdeacon of the cathedral, observes from his window, "the immense church of Notre-Dame, whose black silhouette, with its twin towers, its ribs of stone and its monstrous cruppers, stood out against the starlit sky like an enormous two-headed sphinx sitting in the midst of town." From the south, as from the north, Notre-Dame appears suddenly as you walk down the busy rue Saint-Jacques or take the oblique rue Dante to the Square René Viviani just across the Seine from the south tower of the church. Ideally, try to approach Notre-Dame from the east, upriver along the Quai de Tournelle on the left bank, or across the bridge from the Île Saint-Louis. This is the gateway of photographers, the classically romantic view of Notre-Dame, which exposes dramatically the flying buttresses synonymous with the cathedrals built in the High Middle Ages.

Architectural historians, structural engineers, anyone who has looked closely at the outer perimeter of Notre-Dame has wondered how such a thin tall wall might stand. Even at the time of its construction, those who saw it were astonished. The Norman monk and chronicler Robert de Torigni (d. 1186) exclaimed that "if it is ever completed, nothing on this side of the mountains [Alps] will be able to compare with it." Others were terrified and saw in a building so high a violation of the law of God. "It is a sin to build the kind of churches which are being built nowadays," the Parisian theologian Peter the Chanter wrote in 1180. "It is a sickness of epidemic proportions." The race to build tall churches took a quantum leap in Notre-Dame, whose crossing vault reaches a height of 108 feet and whose towers are more than twice as high.

The wonder of Gothic design, which produced buildings higher than anything in the ancient world, involves a piece of visual magic. There is theoretically no limit to how high the stones used to build a cathedral might be piled, and specialists in masonry stress calculate that such a pile might reach a height of two miles before the rocks at the bottom begin to crumble. Yet, anyone who has tried to stack stones on top of each other knows that the stack quickly reaches a point at which it starts to topple. So the answer to the question of how the masons of Notre-Dame built as high as they did lies less in a tall piling of cut rock than in an equilibrium struck high in the air between stones working with each other against gravity's downward tow. The soaring walls of Notre-Dame do not stand alone but are part of a balanced system of support. The wide ogival or pointed vaults, which make for such dizzying effects when inside the church, exert an outward thrust against which no vertical wall could resist were it not for the counterthrust of the flying buttresses which meets it with equal and opposite force at the point at which vault, wall, and buttress coincide.

The flying buttresses of Notre-Dame stand up and out in the diversity of their parts, each of which plays a distinct role in offsetting the lateral thrust of the cathedral's high vaults. The outer base, the intermediate terminal, and the church wall are all linked by diagonal flyers and a great whirligig of struts, the highest of which arcs to the roof line where it comes to rest between the windows of the upper elevation like the long limb of a dancer whose extended hand compels the upper parts of the structure to stay in place. The syncopated, coordinated flying buttresses of Notre-Dame are intricate, dynamic, rhythmic. They are movement in stone.

As Viollet-le-Duc observed in the nineteenth century, builders in the Gothic style transformed the Romanesque principle of weight and mass into one of vectors and forces acting counter to each other, held in balance to produce a third force, in counterpoise, which is neither, all part of an architectural system that functions both inside and outside of the main structure. Like the exposed posts, beams, and even pipes, wires, and ducts of the postmodern Beaubourg cultural center, Notre-Dame unveils all around the choir and on both sides of the nave just how the outward push of a wide vaulted ceiling is offset by the diagonal inward push of flying buttresses, how, in other words, the cathedral's high walls have managed to stand plumb through the ages. The system was tested in the Notre-Dame fire of 2019. When the wooden roof framing over the vaults, which acts as a brace upon both vaults and buttresses, went up in flames, it was feared that inward pressure from the external flyers would cause the walls of the cathedral to collapse. When that did not happen, braces were quickly constructed to offset the newly released tension from the buttresses.

Offsetting the lateral thrust of the high vaults of Notre-Dame by the counterpressure of an external buttressing system required, of course, calculations above and beyond anything resembling trial and error. Preparation prior to actual construction involved the assembling of wooden forms on which the stones of the ribs and vaults as well as those of the arched buttresses were positioned and joined by mortar. Once the mortar dried, the forms were removed. In a reversal of this process, those responsible for saving Notre-Dame after the fire of April 2019 and loss of the bracing effects of the roof framework quickly restored curved wooden braces on the underside of the buttress flyers in order to prevent their collapse. Structural engineers who have studied Gothic construction refer to the moment when the supporting forms are removed as the "five-minute rule": if a wall, held in balance by the counterpressures of buttress and vault, like that of Notre-Dame, stands for five minutes, it will last for five centuries.

To judge by the results, the computations of the medieval master masons were overwhelmingly true, the most notable exception being the famous collapse of Beauvais Cathedral (about forty miles northwest of Paris), which was never completed beyond the transept crossing. According to a now lost recording of the minutes of the chapter, the union of the canons of Beauvais, "on Friday November 29, 1284, at eight o'clock in the evening, the great vaults of the choir fell and several exterior pillars were broken; the great windows smashed; the holy châsses of Saint Just, Saint Germer and Saint Evrost were spared; and the divine service ceased for forty years." The eminent art historian Stephen Murray, who has measured Beauvais scrupulously, estimates that the collapse at Beauvais was the result of "a critical lack of lateral buttressing."

It was not by chance that Arabic knowledge of Classical and Indian mathematics and science, filtered through the universities of Spain, arrived in France in the decades preceding construction of the first Gothic cathedrals. Adelard of Bath (d. 1142), the natural philosopher, translated Euclid's *Elements* from Arabic to Latin at a time when only a few theorems were known in the West. In 1145 Robert of Chester translated Al-Khawarizmi's (d. ca. 850) *Compendious Book on Calculation by Completion and Balancing*, which marked the advent of algebra in Europe. Though no design drawings or documents showing computations survive from this initial period of cathedral construction, it is hard to believe that architectural feats of such magnitude and requiring such delicate calculations of vectors and forces were possible without the new mathematical sciences from the Muslim East. In the case of Notre-Dame, calculation was ongoing. New construction and renovation went hand in hand for some time. In their initial construction, the flying buttresses were of a double type, allowing for two windows in the upper part of the cathedral, a small lancet or pointed window below a round spoked opening of the oculus type. Beginning in 1225–30, however, the flyers were altered to allow an increase in the size of the upper windows. The original double flyers were replaced with single extensions, some of which were restored to their earlier shape as part of Viollet-le-Duc's restoration in the 1840s.

To reach the front of the cathedral from upriver, you cross the Pont de l'Archevêché at the eastern tip of the Île de la Cité. Then you can either traverse the Square Jean XXIII to the rue du Cloître, where the monastic quarters attached to Notre-Dame, a city within a city, had been situated throughout the Middle Ages. Or, you can walk on the southern side between the cathedral and the Seine. The first itinerary takes you along the end of the curve of the choir and past the so-called "red door" through which the canons entered the cathedral and directly accessed the choir stalls reserved for them in that sequestered part of the choir where they celebrated the divine office. Just two bays beyond the red door, the entrance under the north transept offers in the lintels and tympanum above its double portal a visual rendering of the Infancy of Christ and of one of the most popular legends of the Middle Ages, "The Miracle of Theophilus."

The lower lintel of the portal of the Cloister displays an astonishingly compact rendering of the life of Jesus up until the family's flight into Egypt. On the far left, Mary has just given birth to Jesus, who lies in the crib under her bed. An ox and an ass poke their protective heads at either end of the swaddling, with Joseph at the foot of the bed and the dove of the Holy Spirit hanging from a curtain draped in the background. The scene just to the right shows Joseph bearing a basket of birds as an offering alongside Mary's mother Anna. Mary hands the infant to Simeon

North Entrance Tympanum

over the altar in the familiar Presentation in the Temple. Just beyond the middle of the lintel, King Herod, a little devil whispering in his left ear, gives the order to kill all children under the age of two near the city of Bethlehem. The slaughter depicted to the right of the order is particularly gruesome. A mother begs a Roman soldier, whose sword is poised upon the chest of her child, for mercy. In the final scene, Joseph with Mary and Jesus on a donkey escape the carnage.

THEOPHILUS

THERE ARE FEW MEDIEVAL LEGENDS more sustained over time or more widespread than that of Theophilus, a lowly cleric, who lived in Sicily in the sixth century, and who served the bishop as his steward. So effective was Theophilus as an administrator that when the bishop died, the populace acclaimed him their new bishop. Theophilus was a humble man, however, and insisted that someone else be named bishop in his place. The new bishop, perhaps recognizing with envy the superior administrative skills of the man he displaced, deprived Theophilus of his original office. This caused Theophilus to fall into such despair that he sought the advice of a Jewish sorcerer. The sorcerer summoned the devil, who agreed to help Theophilus so long as he would renounce Christ and His Mother along with the Catholic faith, and that he sign in his own blood a written contract to that effect. Theophilus's clerical stipend is thus restored, and he becomes a generous distributor of riches and goods to the poor. In time, however, Theophilus comes to his senses, is filled with regret, and seeks the help of the Virgin Mother, who scolds Theophilus, but takes him back, as he renounces the devil and professes his faith in her and her son. The Virgin then retrieves by force Theophilus's contract, and the redeemed sinner went straight to the bishop to recount what had happened. He died peacefully three days later.

Theophilus's story was the subject of numerous sermons and vernacular literary works contemporaneous with the building of Notre-Dame. It was reproduced in many illuminated manuscripts and programs of stained glass and sculpture. Some of the fullest and most interesting stone renderings of this tale of error and repentance lie on the northern side of Notre-Dame, dedicated to the miraculous powers of the Virgin to intercede on behalf of those who come to church to seek forgiveness. To the east of the red door, the entire story is depicted in a single quatrefoil, a frame in the shape of a four-leaf clover, heavily damaged by the hammers of destructive revolutionaries. On the right, Theophilus appears as the devil's man, the charter held between them and a Jew, identifiable by the length of his beard and the skullcap associated with figures from the Old Testament in the background. In the middle he prays on his knees to a statue of the Virgin floating in the air at the level of Satan's right hand, folded around Theophilus's shoulder. On the left, the Virgin, whose face is disfigured, reclaims the charter from the devil's hand.

The Theophilus story is further elaborated in the lintel over the northern entrance to Notre-Dame. On the left of the upper frieze, the cleric compacts with the devil, who, as lord, places his hands over those of his vassal. In the middle left, Theophilus as bishop distributes alms, a little devil at his side. On the right, the penitent Theophilus prays to a statue of the Virgin, which is, like the reliquaries in the shape of a church, itself enclosed within a miniature cathedral, the two towers and a trefoil tracery topped by a gabled roof, a church within a church. In her answer to the repentant cleric's prayers, the Virgin is depicted as a muscular Christian who conquers Satan using the cross as a weapon. According to Rutebeuf, the mid-thirteenth-century Parisian poet whose writings were contemporaneous with the building of the north transept of Notre-Dame, "Our Lady raises her cross, the Devil falls and she treads him underfoot." In the top triangle of the tympanum, the bishop, with Theophilus in attendance, tells his story while holding up a book from which hangs a seal as a guarantee of the authenticity of his testimony and of the tale itself. The monks entering the cathedral under the sculpted images of Theophilus thus encountered a great lesson in the consequences of giving in to temptation, of conniving with the devil, who, as in our contemporary imagining of unconscious thoughts, was always ready to pounce. "Now hear my words," Rutebeuf's Virgin instructs. "Go to the Bishop, do not wait; / Give him the charter that you made, / To read aloud / Inside the church, before a crowd, / So that good men are not seduced / By such deceit."

SAINT STEPHEN ON THE SOUTH SIDE

THE SOUTH SIDE OF Notre-Dame, built around Saint Stephen's portal, attests to Notre-Dame's original dedication to the first Christian martyr, who, renowned for his rhetorical gifts, was murdered around 35

Saint Stephen Portal Tympanum

CE. Though access to the south entrance is limited by the fence around the sacristy and treasury building and the guardian's house, one can still peek between them to the sculptures on the exterior of the south transept. The trumeau or post at the center of the south portal shows Stephen dressed in deacon's robes and carrying a book. The protomartyr Stephen, having elicited ire in various synagogues because of his teachings, was accused of blasphemy. He is seen in the lower lintel disputing with his fellow Jews. In the left two tableaux, a seated Stephen holds forth by gesturing with his hand as if he were engaged in heated debate. The others, who are both standing and sitting, seem confused. Two seated men look at their opponent, while those standing gaze either into the distance or at each other. The bearded man, second from the left in the back row, is holding both his beard and his head, as if he were genuinely confounded.

On the right hand side of the lintel, Stephen stands with three of his opponents seated below him, seemingly on the ground. The man on the far right in the background is taking notes. Having vanquished his opponents in the synagogue, Stephen is taken by force to the Jewish court of the Sanhedrin where he is tried for blasphemy against Moses and God for saying that "Jesus of Nazareth shall destroy the temple, and shall change the traditions which Moses delivered unto us" (Acts 6:12–14). He is seen in the right third of the narrative tableaux being led before the judge by a black Roman soldier who grasps Stephen by the hair on the top of his head.

At the end of the argument with his enemies, "Stephen, full of the Holy Spirit, looked up to heaven," and said, "Behold, I see heavens opened and the Son of man standing on the right hand of God" (Acts 7:54–55); at which point a mob "crying out with a loud voice, . . . ran violently upon him" (Acts 7:56). Stephen was stoned to death by a crowd led by no other than Saul of Tarsus, the future Saint Paul. If ever there were a change in life stories, it is the conversion of Stephen to the Christian cause and of Saul to Paul. In the right portion of the upper lintel, Stephen's body is placed in a sarcophagus by Saints Gamaliel and Nicodemus, while overhead, Christ, flanked by two angels and separated from the earthly realm by clouds, watches on.

The entrance devoted to Saint Stephen, which depicts and shows the consequences of his powers of debate, both faces the nascent University of Paris and is flanked by a series of thirteenth-century plaques known as "dados" devoted to everyday life in the medieval Latin Quarter. The meaning and purpose of these have been contested. It is thought that the image on the lower left on the west side of the door, which shows horses in the left lobe of a quatrefoil, depicts the arrival of a student in Paris where he is greeted by a master in a long robe, his arm around the new recruit. Alternately, it has been suggested that this is a scene of adieu for students preparing to leave Paris.

STUDENT LIFE IN AND OUT OF THE CLASSROOM

SEVERAL OF THE DADOS depict classroom activities. In the image on the upper right of the left set, three figures on the left are discussing a particular page in a book, their fingers all pointing to the same passage, with a fourth head looking on from behind them. The three figures on the right examine what looks like a scroll. The upper left dado on the right side shows students engaged in heated dispute, as the figure dressed in what seems like a monk's cowl on the right points an accusatory fin-

Student Dados, Exterior Wall, South Side

ger at his interlocutor. In the quatrefoil just to its right, the magister may
be lecturing to students assembled, sitting and standing, at his feet; or, as
suggested by the symmetry, animated gestures, and cocked heads of the
two figures to the right and left of the magister at the level of his elbows,
they may be engaged in debate, at the end of which the teacher, his own

hand raised as if to decide between the two disputants, pronounces a judgment or *sententia*. Not all of the bas reliefs depict classroom activity. The lower left image to the right of the door shows students at leisure, while the upper left image to the left of the door displays what appears to be a student residence from which two figures, framed by the roof and arcade of the building on the right edge above the quatrefoil, lift glasses in a possible reference to student drinking. Their fellows on the left look down at the scene below.

THE WEST FACADE

WALKING DOWNRIVER along the sandy path between the flying buttresses that support the nave and the river, you reach the fortress-like southwest corner of Notre-Dame, from which you can appreciate the size of the parvis or open space in front of the cathedral of Paris—almost 400 feet in depth with a breadth of a little over 130 feet. If you cross the parvis, which is often where the (surprisingly quick moving) line of visitors queuing to enter the cathedral ends, you will notice on the Seine side of the plaza a nineteenth-century bigger-than-life statue of Charlemagne (d. 814 CE) and his guards. Together with Roland and Oliver, heroes out of the first Old French epic poem, composed right around the time of the First Crusade or sixty-five years before the beginning of the building of the cathedral, the emperor stands as a reminder of the roots of medieval France in the glory of Rome. For what remains of Rome lies just below your feet in the excavated streets and buildings of Gallo-Roman Lutetia, discovered in the 1960s in the course of building an underground parking lot and accessible via the archeological crypt of the Île de la Cité at the western end of the parvis.

The great open space in front of the cathedral summons the layers of history that culminated in Notre-Dame Paris, built in stages from east to west over the course of a century. The first "campaign," which lasted from the laying of the cornerstone in 1163 to 1182, was supervised by the Bishop of Paris. Maurice de Sully raised the necessary funds—from pious donations from the diocese of Paris, revenues from surrounding estates, his own fortune, and a donation of 200 pounds from King Louis VII—to begin construction. Odo of Châteauroux (d. 1273), a theologian, papal legate, and cardinal, observed, in what is surely an exaggeration, that "it was in great part with the 'oboles' (halfpennies) donated

West Facade

by women that the cathedral of Paris was built." The bishop also organized the chapter or the canons of the church into the equivalent of a
building committee, a "fabric," which, like Suger at Saint-Denis, hired
the masons, carpenters, and artists in metal and glass, located and transferred the materials, some of which was reclaimed from previous buildings on the site, and managed the transformation of the center of Paris
in what was the largest urban renewal project of the High Middle Ages.

In this first phase, the choir was built up to the transept which was
closed off temporarily so that services could be conducted at the main
altar while work progressed to the west. When Maurice de Sully died
in 1196, he left one hundred pounds for the completion of the roof.
Maurice's successor, Eudes de Sully (d. 1208), apparently not a close
relation, initiated a second building campaign, involving both arms
of the transept along with parts of the nave and the buttresses up to
the level of the doors along the west facade. By 1220 the nave was in
place, and the west facade had risen to include everything up to the
top of the great rose window flanked by two double lancets, each
capped by an oculus. The last medieval campaign ended around 1245
with the raising of the southern and northern towers and the high
gallery between them. There is some question as to whether planning
for the towers of Notre-Dame included pointed spires to be added to
their square tops, as was the case at Saint-Denis and, as we shall see,
at Chartres. Viollet-le-Duc concluded, after an evaluation of their
structural strength, that the towers could have supported the extra
weight of frontal spires, though we will never know with certainty
whether or not they were originally intended. Gargoyles were added
to the top of the outer edges of the buttresses after 1230. And, in the
course of the thirteenth century, private chapels, which are accessed
from the ambulatory on either side of the nave, enclosed the open-
ings between the bases of the buttresses, so that, looking at the cathedral from the outside, we have the impression of a continuous wall
out of which the flyers rise. Such private spaces of worship, erected
by wealthy families, urban corporations, or important court officials,
were continued as radiating chapels around the choir. The original
spire rose from the roof of the transept crossing and was completed
around the middle of the thirteenth century, by which time the south
rose window was also in place. In its medieval form, Notre-Dame was
built in just under 150 years, though the building, a "living organism"

in the phrase of Viollet-le-Duc, has evolved through repair, renovation, and restoration ever since.

Looking at a great Gothic cathedral for the first time produces feelings of familiarity and of the strangeness of relatively small differences, all part of the cathedral effect. Some things are the same everywhere, and others vary from place to place. Medieval churches were destinations for pilgrims and other travelers who circulated among them, and they work psychologically deep in that zone where the visual perception of space and place shapes emotions and belief to create the impression that the same eternal truths are to be found wherever one goes. This did not, however, in the quest to build higher, and bigger, and more beautiful in the mode of Suger's "anagogical uplift" from material to spiritual things, prevent innovation and intense competition for architectural distinction.

ARCHITECTURE AND
SCULPTURE COMBINED

Notre-Dame is a Janus-faced building. It looks back to Saint-Denis and forward to the cathedrals built in its wake—Chartres, Bourges, Amiens, Reims, Laon, and Beauvais. It is a watershed in the development of the Gothic style which hit its stride in the cathedral of Paris. The west facade shows the same three-portal structure, two towers with a bridge between them, that we encountered at Saint-Denis. Yet, by the end of the twelfth century, the semi-circular transverse arch over the doors of the earlier church had evolved into the broken equilateral arch, graduated toward a point at the top. The change may have been the result of observation of sagging at the keystone and haunches of rounded arches. It must also have involved some awareness of the structural advantages of the broken arch, which, by current calculation, is twenty to twenty-five percent stronger than its rounded predecessor. Broken arches thus support the added weight imposed by the height to which the builders of new high churches in the Gothic style aspired.

Notre-Dame is covered all around by striking sculptural programs. The west facade, in particular, presents as a multi-layered visual field with distinct zones and types, from the free-standing statues along the bottom of the western rose window, to the lacy stone tracery in the rose and oculi windows, the horizontal arcades between the tops of the columns of the high gallery of kings, the trumeaus in the portals, the jamb statues between them, the dados or bas reliefs at the base of the buttresses, and the lintels and tympana with their surrounding archivolts above the doors.

Beginning at the top, the Virgin and Child flanked by candle-bearing angels dominates the high balcony, her head, from the ground perspective, directly in the center of the western rose window. In front of the double lancets to her right Adam stands woefully, one arm draped to his side and the other held to his cheek, signaling, in the gestural language of Gothic sculpture, feelings of sorrow or regret. Eve is situated symmetrically on the other side. All three figures are raised on pedestals above the edge of the balcony such that, standing below, one wonders how they manage not to fall.

THE LONG SAD JOURNEY
OF THE KINGS OF ISRAEL

THE TWENTY-EIGHT STATUES between columns stretching across the entire breadth of the cathedral just under the balcony separate the bottom third of the building from the mid-section containing the rose and high-columned open bridge and the top defined by the two towers, which are not exactly alike. The north tower is one meter wider than its southern twin. In keeping with the genealogical bent of the west facade, these figures, which measure almost twelve feet in height, represent the kings of Israel and Judah, the descendants of Jesse and the human ancestors of Mary and Jesus whom we encountered in the Tree of Jesse at Saint-Denis (see p. 36). Placed there originally in the middle of the thirteenth century, the Old Testament kings of Notre-Dame's gallery of kings were, however, almost from the start associated with the kings of France. And not only by the common people, but by scholars who in the eighteenth century began to inventory and to make detailed drawings of religious monuments.

The confusion between the kings of Israel and Judah and the kings of France accounts for the unhappy fate of these larger-than-life statues during and just after the French Revolution. When the National Convention, which governed France between 1792 and 1795, declared that all signs of the Ancien Régime were to be removed, vandals armed with hammers climbed to the gallery of kings and began to knock off their

Heads from Gallery of Kings

crowns. The statues themselves were passed between the columns and
lowered to the ground beginning in December 1793, losing their heads
in the process of what must have felt like a symbolic reenactment of the
mass guillotining of royals and nobles during the Reign of Terror (1793–
1794). The rubble from the original gallery of kings and other statuary
from the west facade of Notre-Dame laid in a pile at the foot of the north
tower where it was used as a public urinal for a period of three years. In
1796, the rubble was removed, its destination a complete mystery until
in 1839 some of the kings' bodies turned up as a boundary marker for a
charcoal depot in Paris's thirteenth arrondissement. In 1977, twenty-one
of the heads were discovered at 20 rue de la Chaussée-d'Antin in the
course of excavation for the Banque Française du Commerce Extérieur
in the former Hotel Moreau. They are now displayed in beautiful array
in the Museum of the Middle Ages (Cluny) not far from their original
home on the Île de la Cité. Gazing at these regal faces, traces of paint still
visible on their faces and in the pupils of their eyes, I am always moved
by their remarkable journey and by the sad solidarity dignity they have
recovered in a museum which today has taken on some of the esthetic
aura of the cathedral.

Between 1793 and the 1840s, the niches between the columns of the west facade remained empty in what was delicately referred to as the "toothless" Notre-Dame. Eugène Emmanuel Viollet-le-Duc and Jean-Baptiste-Antoine Lassus, the restorers of Notre-Dame between the mid-1840s and mid-1860s, reproduced the original figures of the gallery of kings on the basis of drawings made prior to the Revolution and similar statues elsewhere. Interestingly, and this is a detail hardly visible even to specialists, the head of the eighth king from the left is the sculptural portrait of Viollet-le-Duc, the twenty-third head, that of Lassus. If such sculptural signatures seem inappropriate in this day and age, they would have not been so in the Age of Cathedrals, as we recall the multiple images—in glass and in stone—of Suger in his cathedral at Saint-Denis.

The far right or south portal as we face the cathedral is devoted to Mary's mother, Saint Anna. Its central post or trumeau depicts Saint Marcel (d. 436), ninth bishop of Paris, who is described by his biographer as having slain a man-eating dragon terrorizing the countryside around Paris. Thus, you see here Marcel blessing the faithful with his raised right hand and, with the bishop's curved staff in his left hand, he subdues an only mildly menacing dragon at his feet. Marcel's relics were kept behind the altar of Notre-Dame in a rich reliquary in the shape of a miniature church encrusted with precious jewels. Along with so many rich sacred objects, it disappeared at the time of the Revolution, as did the original of the trumeau statue, the remains of which are also on exhibit in the Cluny Museum.

THE BIRTH OF JESUS IN STONE

IN ONE OF THE RICHEST and most detailed narrative friezes to be found anywhere, the lintels and tympanum above the Saint Anna portal dramatize visually the events proximate to Jesus's birth. Scenes on the lower lintel were taken from the apocryphal Pseudo-Gospel or Protevangelium of James (second century) and the Gospel of the Nativity of the Blessed Mary or the Pseudo-Matthew (ca. 800 CE). These works are little known today. Yet, they were widely copied in Greek and Latin manuscripts, and their elaborations of the more canonical story of Jesus's birth contained in the synoptic Gospels of Matthew and Luke circulated widely in the Middle Ages, as attested by the prevalence of stories drawn from them in Gothic sculpture and stained glass.

South Portal Tympanum, West Facade

The actual sculptors and glass painters might not have had any direct contact with the apocrypha of the early centuries of Christianity, but they did copy readily from each other and even rendered motifs from one medium into another. You may wonder, then, what happened at the outset? Art historian or not, we are obsessed by sources. The aura of authenticity belonging to an original is undeniable, as if the first example of a work of art partakes of the wonder of creation itself. So, assuming that a sculptor or glass painter did not copy from what they had seen, it is easy to imagine from the start a canon or cleric who belonged to the "fabric" or building committee of Notre-Dame stimulating the artist's imagination with scenes from the lives of the parents, the Nativity, or the Infancy of Jesus as contained in the apocrypha. This is, after all, the way both verbal and visual narrative works: the writer, painter, or sculptor may be aware of an event or an idea, but they must fill in the particulars of setting—what the angel speaking to Mary looked like at the time of the Annunciation, what Mary was wearing, and what she was doing—reading or spinning. The same is true for the details of Mary's parents' initial appearance in the synagogue, Joachim's exile in the desert, their reunion at the Golden Gate, or Joseph's activity— sleeping or looking on—while Jesus lies in bed with His Mother.

The right third of the lower lintel of the Anna portal features Anna and Joachim, Mary's parents, who have lived for many years without bearing children, as they enter an arcaded temple with offerings. If you look closely, you will observe details of Jewish liturgical objects and ritual in the ancient synagogue. Anna, holding doves in her hands, and Joachim, a small lamb, stand in front of the bima or Jewish altar on which the Scroll of the Law or Torah is unfurled beneath the eternal lamp. With one hand, the high priest rejects the couple's offering and, with the other, points to the text of the Law, which states: "It is not lawful for thee to offer thy gifts first, forasmuch as thou hast gotten no seed in Israel" (James 1:2). Disconsolate and ashamed to return home, Joachim, a sack over his shoulder, departs for the wilderness in a scene which begins on the far right of the lower lintel and continues into the first archivolt where he is depicted among a flock of sheep. In the second archivolt an angel informs Joachim that his prayers have been answered and orders him to meet Anna at the Golden Gate on the eastern wall of Jerusalem. Their reunion is depicted in the third and fourth archivolts where Joachim, holding a staff, turns toward Anna, who appears beneath an archway like the entrance to a church with a column, flowered capital frieze, and broken arch under an architectural canopy, marking the gates of the city.

The events depicted on the left half of the frieze take place twelve years later and involve Mary's betrothal and marriage. An angel of the Lord appears and orders the high priest to "go forth and assemble them that are widowers of the people, and let them bring every man a rod, and to whomsoever the Lord shall show a sign, his wife shall she be" (James 8:3). Joseph arrives on horseback from what appears to be the first archivolt on the left. On the far right of the scene, the rods are stacked in the temple on the bima under the eternal light. Looking back to the left, you can see that Joseph holds his rod, which has flowered. Mary touches him tenderly on the forehead while the rejected suitors look on. The marriage takes place between the scene of betrothal and the bima, as the high priest takes Mary's right hand and joins it to that of Joseph while Joachim holds his daughter's other hand. After the marriage Joseph doubts Mary, but an angel reassures him and announces, in the middle of the lower lintel, the divine maternity: "And behold an angel of the Lord appeared unto him in a dream, saying: Fear not this child, for that which is in her is of the Holy Ghost, and she shall bear a son and thou shalt call his name Jesus . . ." (James 14:2). To the right of the scene of doubting

Joseph, the repentant husband kneels, signaling his wish for forgiveness while an angel looks on from above.

The upper lintel, drawn from the Gospels of Luke and Matthew, shows on the far left Mary climbing the steps of the temple in a gesture of gratitude. To the right, two scenes we encountered in the Infancy of Christ window at Saint-Denis recount events preceding Jesus's birth. With Isaiah, holding his right hand over his heart and the scroll of his prophecies of the coming of a son who will be named Emmanuel in the left, the angel Gabriel announces to Mary the birth of a son to be called Jesus. Here, you can see the Visitation of Mary with Elizabeth, who is pregnant with John the Baptist, between the Annunciation and the scene, covering the middle of the upper lintel, of the divine birth. While Mary lies in bed under two lamps, Joseph, draped in a long robe, falls asleep, his head on one hand. Meanwhile, the child lies swaddled above Mary, the ox and the ass breathing on Him, as three angels look on through the wavy lines that represent the heavens. Two angels inform the shepherds, one old and bearded, the other young and beardless, with animals, in a moment of sculptural frivolity, lapping at their feet. In the right portion of the lintel, King Herod listens to the counselors on his right and dispatches the three eastern kings who, on his left, are waiting to mount the horses on the extreme edge of the Nativity frieze.

The tympanum above the lintels depicts Mother and Child in the *sedes sapientiae* "seat of wisdom" pose, an Eastern motif attested in Byzantine sculpture as early as the eleventh century. Mary, "Container of the Uncontainable," is here shown under a canopy, signaling the earthly Jerusalem, on miniature columns with flowered capital friezes right out of a cathedral. Crowned Mary holds what looks like a scepter or a flowering rod in her left hand, her right hand around the middle of Jesus, who holds a book in His left hand and blesses all who see Him with His right. They are surrounded by two acolyte angels swinging censers, themselves flanked by a kneeling king on Mary's left and a standing bishop on her right. These figures, who both hold between their hands long scrolls from which the writing has disappeared, have been thought to represent the subordination of the secular to the spiritual realm. The kneeling monk taking notes behind the bishop remains a complete mystery. He could, of course, be in the process of recording the submission of the state to the church; or, as has also been suggested, he could be the representative of the canons involved in the construction and maintenance of the church. In the archivolts that rim the Saint Anna portal, a celestial court comprised of fourteen angels, fourteen kings, sixteen prophets, and sixteen old men of the Apocalypse, capped at the top of the broken arch by the Lamb of God and the Son of Man, all celebrate Jesus's grandparents, His parents, and the frontally seated Mother and Child.

Below the deeply recessed archivolts, life-sized jamb figures on either side of the door depict, moving outward on the left, Saint Peter, the first leader of the early Church, who is identifiable by the keys in his left hand; King Solomon, the wealthy and wise king of Israel, who is holding a scepter and a book; the Queen of Sheba, who brings gifts to Solomon while seeking his wisdom; and an unidentified king. To the right of the door stand Saint Paul, known for his establishment of Christian communities in Europe and Asia Minor in the first century; King David, Solomon's father, who is holding a harp, emblem of his musical skill and of the psalms attributed to him; David's wife and Solomon's mother Bathsheba; and, in symmetry with the facing jamb figures on the left, another unidentified king.

The north portal of the west facade, known as the portal of the Virgin, bestows on the viewer an abundance of sculptural motifs. Some repeat those of Saint-Denis, some elaborate upon what is found there, and some are new to the repertoire of Gothic imagery to be passed on to those who cut and carved stone in the wake of Notre-Dame Paris. The trumeau shows Mary with Child, a flowering rod in her right hand and angels on either side of her crowned head. Below her feet, in a three-part panorama of scenes from the Book of Genesis, we see on the left the Creation of Eve, who emerges from sleeping Adam's flank, as God, hand raised in a gesture of command, completes this final act in the creation of the world. In the middle, naked Eve eats the forbidden fruit with one hand and hands it to Adam with the other. Between them the serpent, whose head emerges as the head of a woman, is entwined in the branches of the Tree of Knowledge in this imaginative rendering of the Fall. On the right, Adam and Eve, hands covering their genitals, are issued by the archangel Gabriel "out of the paradise of pleasure, to till the earth from which they were taken" (Genesis 3:23).

The sides of the trumeau and the door jambs develop the theme of labor. Behind the standing Mary a series of rectangular plaques depict in disorderly array the Classical motif of the Ages of Man. The series begins on the upper left with a youth as naked as Adam and Eve as they leave the garden and proceeds to the plaque below it, showing an older and partially dressed version of the young man who, fully clothed in the third image, holds a mask up to his face. This association of aging and acting anticipates Jaques's speech in Shakespeare's (d. 1616) *As You Like It*: "And one man in his time plays many parts, / His acts being seven ages" (2.7.142). Below the "many parts," the man becomes a standing woman, a laborer carrying a bundle of heavy logs on his back, and, at the bottom left, a woman sitting under bundles of logs in racks on the wall, warming her hands in front of an open fire. On the right bottom, an indistinct carving lies below the scene of a young man surrounded by nature, perhaps signaling love, hunting with a bird and dog, then, beginning at the level of Mary's long dress, increasingly bearded and sinking into old age. On the door jambs themselves, as at Saint-Denis, the signs of the zodiac are paired with the Works of the Months, both analogous to the Ages of Man in their cyclical waxing and waning.

THE DORMITION OR
THE DEATH OF MARY

IN THE LOWER LINTEL OF the Virgin portal, Old Testament kings and prophets, scrolls unfurled across their laps, sit on either side of the ark of the covenant, containing the tablets of the Law which Moses carried down from Sinai and King David brought into Jerusalem. The tabernacle structure in the middle may, in fact, represent Solomon's Temple where it resided in the Holy City. The ark of the covenant is significant in the context of the Virgin portal since Mary was thought to have redeemed Eve by bringing into the world a new covenant, a New Law to replace the Old.

The upper lintel depicts the scene of the dormition of the Virgin. According to James of Voragine's (d. 1298) *Golden Legend*, a popular thirteenth-century collection of saints' lives, Christ's Mother asked before she died to be reunited with the apostles who "were plucked up by clouds from the places wherein they were preaching, and put down before Mary's door." Christ stands in the middle of the scene, with Peter and his keys second from the left, and Paul, his hand expressing fatigue, on the far left under an olive tree. On the right, James and John, the beardless young apostle who is nonetheless weary, sit under a fig tree while two angels place Mary's body in a sarcophagus decorated with circular moldings which, as one of the numerous examples of the representation of architectural detail within architecture, might have framed the windows of a Gothic church. Jesus asks the apostles what "'grace and honour, think ye, shall I now confer on My mother?' They answered, . . . 'Thou, Jesus shouldst raise up the body of Thy mother, and place her at Thy right hand for all eternity!'" Whereupon, "instantly Michael the Archangel appeared, and presented Mary's soul before the Lord." At the top of the tympanum, Mary, hands joined in prayer as she is crowned by an angel, sits at the right hand of the Son.

In contrast with the history of the imprisonment and martyrdom of the local and national Saint Denis above the south and north doors of the cathedral which bears his name, the images on the west facade of Notre-Dame portray the transcendent events of universal Christian history. Whoever designed the sculptural program of the western portals represented such events in their particulars, while bearing in mind the centrality of the cathedral of Paris, which functioned increasingly as the capital of France in the centuries following its construction. Pilgrims to Notre-Dame, regardless of origin, were part of the history represented on its frontal face in addition to the mix of local and universal saints depicted on the surrounding jamb statues and on the outer face of the intervening buttresses.

The jamb statues show on the left of the door of the Virgin portal Saint Denis surrounded by two angels, and, on the right, John the Baptist, Saint Stephen, Saint Geneviève, the patron saint of Paris, and the fourth-century Pope Sylvester. Each stands above a square bas relief under a broken arch with a representation of their manner of death: Denis, over a scene of beheading; Saint John above the scene of the executioner offering his head on a plate to Salomé. Stephen stands on the image of a man lifting one of the stones with which he was stoned to death. There is some speculation that the otherwise unidentified king on the far left of the Virgin portal is Philip Augustus, who donated to the cathedral before his death in 1223 hairs of the Virgin, three teeth of Saint John the Baptist, several of the stones with which Stephen was attacked, and the head of Saint Denis. These were first deposited in the church of Saint-Étienne, then translated to Notre-Dame in 1218. Thus, the relics of the saints in the jamb statues of the Virgin portal resided within the cathedral, their provenance attested by the bas relief under Philip Augustus which depicts the unfurling of a long scroll recording the royal gift.

The presence of saints directly connected to Notre-Dame is reinforced by the full-length figures on the four protruding buttresses on the outer edges and between the three portals at the level of the archivolts above the doors. On the north, Saint Stephen, the first martyr of Christianity, and, on the south, Saint Denis, the first Parisian martyr. In the niche between the Virgin portal and the central portal, an allegorical figure of the Church as a woman wearing a crown, holding a chalice in one hand and an unbroken standard in the other. Between the central and the Saint Anna portal, the figure of the Synagogue presents as a woman wearing the hat associated in the Middle Ages with Jews, a snake around her head. In one hand she holds the tablets of the Law and, in the other, a broken standard, several of the sanctioned attributes of anti-Semitism in the High Middle Ages.

THE CENTRAL ENTRANCE
TO FINAL THINGS

THOUGH THE GREAT ROSE WINDOW attracts our attention as the focal point of the western facade when viewed from a distance, our eyes are drawn increasingly to the main door as we approach. This central entrance to the cathedral articulates more clearly than anywhere else the drama and the stakes of passing from the world of time and of things into the monumental sacred space of Notre-Dame. The trumeau depicts Christ alive and on earth. His feet crush a viper asp, symbol of death. Beneath this visual triumph over death, figures of seven prophets clasp the scrolls that foretold Christ's Coming, and, beneath them, the allegorical representations of five of the seven liberal arts: Astronomy as a woman raising her head toward the sky, Grammar as a woman in a long coat holding in her hand switches with which to discipline a child, Music as a woman playing bells, Dialectic as a woman holding a serpent, the sign of sophistry, Geometry as a woman holding a compass. Rhetoric and Arithmetic are absent. Medicine is represented as a woman holding a vial, and, in the center, Philosophy sits with a scepter in one hand and an open book in the other, a ladder with nine rungs between her knees, indicating the nine levels of knowledge.

Central Portal Tympanum, West Facade

The lintels and tympanum of the portal of the Last Judgment portray Christ of the Second Coming at the end of human time. Around the door, as at Saint-Denis, the wise and foolish virgins with their upturned and downturned vessels limn the jambs, which are balanced on either side by life-sized statues of the apostles: on the left, moving outward, Saints Peter with his key, John, the beardless younger apostle, Peter's brother Andrew, James the Lesser, whom Saint Jerome identifies as the half-brother of Jesus, Simeon, who presented Jesus in the temple, and Bartholomew; on the right, Saints Paul, who is often depicted as bald, James the Great, identifiable by the shell on his pilgrim's bag, Thomas, patron saint of architects, shown here with a measuring rod, Jude, Philip, holding what looks like a loaf of bread because of his witnessing of the miracle of the loaves at the wedding at Cana, and Matthew, with an open book or gospel.

Dead souls rise from their tombs in the lower lintel as angels on either end sound the trumpets to signal Christ's return to earth. Again, as at Saint-Denis, this is a mixed crowd, which includes a bishop still wearing his miter, a king and queen, their crowns, a knight, his suit of chain mail, men with beards and women in wimples, young and old, and in-between, all struggling to lift the tombstones under which they have lain since the time of their death. Significantly, one of the figures is that of a young black man next to the angel on the left. The multi-racial quality of the frieze is neither unique nor the product of nineteenth-century restoration, as Blacks, known via explorers who had traveled as far as India, pilgrims and crusaders in the Middle East, and the Reconquest of Muslim Spain, figure in a number of Gothic sculptural programs, and, as we shall see, even take center stage in the person of the Black Virgin of Chartres (see p. 101). The lower lintel, partially destroyed along with the trumeau in the late eighteenth century to make way for large processions to enter the cathedral, was rebuilt by Viollet-le-Duc. The fragments of the original on view in the Cluny Museum of the Middle Ages show the young Black man who attests to a consciousness on the part of the thirteenth-century sculptor of the equality of souls before death and the eternal Judge of the Last Judgment.

At the center of the upper lintel, the archangel Michael holds a set of scales in which the souls of the dead are weighed in a comic scene with cosmic consequences. In the balance on the left, a small naked figure in prayer outweighs the grotesque figure, aided by cheaters, holding on to the chain on the right. A demon rising from below clutches the edge of the balance with a crowbar, while his colleague, a long-tailed horned demon who opposes Michael, places one clawed hoof on the top of the scale while pressing the other on the balance. To Christ's right, the elect, all of whom wear crowns and none of whom belong to religious orders, look to the heavens and march, smiling and serene, to paradise. An angel in the first rim of the voussoir welcomes them to the space surrounding this drama of salvation filled with crowned figures with beatific expressions on their faces. To Christ's left, the damned, in chains and shepherded by grinning and groaning hairy hoofed demons at either end of the lineup, are led away to eternal damnation. The condemned represent a fair sampling of noble society, from the bishop close to the front of the line, the monk in the middle, the king third from the end, to the knight who brings up the rear, along with the women in middle- or upper-class headdress in-between.

The place to which the damned are herded is depicted in the lowest rungs of the voussoirs which display in vivid detail the tortures of hell to the right of the chain gang of the cursed. In the first rim bodies fall upside down into an enormous boiling cauldron stoked by a demon with a pitchfork and toads crawling up the rim. The third voussoir ring shows demons poking and twisting the writhing bodies of the lost souls, one of which is a king still bearing his crown. Reptilian monsters rear their menacing heads from below. The images at the bottom of the fifth and sixth voussoirs are among the most hideous in all of the medieval sculptural arts. In what appears to be punishment for the sin of luxury, a woman with a simian face (low forehead, enormous ears and mouth, protruding tongue), a chain around her neck, and enormous breasts, sits, legs spread, on the shoulders of a monk, her heels dug into the head of a bishop, still wearing his miter, and who, in turn, sits atop a king. The last row presents such a tangle of demons, other monsters, and humans that it is impossible to say who is doing what to whom. This depiction of the tortures of hell smears all distinction between monster and mankind in a prefiguring of the surreal figures of Hieronymus Bosch almost three centuries later.

From the tympanum, Christ in majesty, the stigmata on His hands and wound in His side still visible, looks upon the scene of the Last Judgment. A cruciform halo, as distinct from the angels' simple halo, surrounds His head, and, at His feet, a sculpted relief of the Celestial Jerusalem. Angels on either side hold the instruments of the Passion, the angel on the left with three nails in one hand and Longinius's lance in the other. The angel on the right embraces a nearly life-size cross. The Virgin and Saint John, witnesses to the Passion, kneel in the outer edges of the tympanum. The central entrance to the central cathedral in the central city of the center of Europe in the thirteenth century thus embodies a great theological rendering of justice.

In case one might miss the criteria by which he or she will be judged at the end of time, the bas reliefs at eye level on either side of the central portal display a series of six virtues and six vices which are less theologically than ethically motivated. The virtues, in the mode of Classical figures, are represented as women holding shields with emblems of good behavior. They sit above the vices which are less uniformly disposed and depict particular immoral acts—a relation of abstract rules to their infraction. Thus, on the right of Christ, moving outward, Faith with a shield bearing a cross above Idolatry, with a man worshipping an idol; Hope with eyes raised to heaven and a shield with a standard versus Despair as man killing himself, a sword run through his body; Charity, whose shield is decorated with a sheep, versus Avarice showing a man plunging his hands into a chest; Chastity with a salamander in the middle of flames on the shield versus Luxury, showing a woman holding a scales, an enigmatic image redone in the eighteenth century; Prudence, with a serpent and a stick like the Classical figure of the Caduceus, versus a man below playing with fire; Humility, with a dove in the shield, versus Pride with a horseman thrown from his mount.

To the left of Christ and next to the door, the figure of Force with a woman in warrior's garb—a coat of mail and a sword—with a lion in the shield sits above Cowardice depicted as a man running from a rabbit; Patience with a steer versus Impatience, showing an enraged figure threatening a cleric; Sweetness or Mildness with a lamb versus Hardness depicting a man kicking a servant; Concord or Peace with an olive branch on the shield versus Discord figured as a dispute between two men; Obedience with a kneeling camel on the shield versus Rebellion as a man raising his hand to strike a bishop; Perseverance with a crown for he who is faithful to the end versus Inconstancy and the image of a monk leaving the convent, his frock visibly left behind.

You enter Notre-Dame by the Saint Anna portal, and, as you enter, please stop for a moment to observe the extraordinary metalwork on the door. The filigree straps which cover the surface of the wooden doors function as enormous hinges, but they are also decorative. Upon close examination, they reveal, as in a visual puzzle with hidden pictures, an abundance of flora and fauna. Flowers, fruits, slim branches, buds, birds, animals, some real and some fantastical, lurk in the unfurling scrolls, which, stamped and soldered in the thirteenth century, serve as reminders that the Gothic cathedral is made not only of stone and glass but also of metal and wood.

INSIDE NOTRE-DAME

Unlike SAINT-DENIS, with a single aisle around the nave and choir, Notre-Dame features a double ambulatory whose two channels are separated by alternating smooth round columns and columns surrounded by slimmer shafts that run up to the level of the main arcade. Both the heavier columns and the slimmer shafts are decorated at the top by an array of flowery capitals that, along with the botanical decoration around the Virgin portal of the west facade, attest to a growing interest in nature in the thirteenth century. As you move up the ambulatory aisle on the right side of the nave, you catch a glimpse of the side cha-

pels, some of which retain their altars, confessionals, and the large seven-
teenth- and eighteenth-century paintings that once hung facing inward
from the columns on both sides of the central vessel. As you reach the
transept crossing, do not miss the statue of Joan of Arc (d. 1431) by the
southern door. Fully armed, a sword at her side, and the standard of
France clasped securely in her arms, the woman warrior saint is shown
with her head lifted toward heaven, her hands clasped in prayer. Joan's
mother came to Notre-Dame after her execution to ask for a revision

North Rose Window

of the inquisitory trial which led to her conviction in Rouen. It was not until 1920, however, that Joan was canonized. The sculpture in the southern transept was installed the next year.

On the far side of the transept crossing, the great northern rose window measures a little over forty-two feet in diameter, much larger and more complex than the roses of Saint-Denis. Pitched to the north, this "beautiful flower in mourning" in the phrase of art historian Émile Mâle receives less light and is dedicated to the Old Testament. Rather, it can be said to anticipate enlightenment, light in the Gothic imagination being synonymous with God. Circles of Old Testament prophets, patriarchs, and judges radiate from the center like an orderly starburst of deep-hued jewels. In the first ring Hosea sits at the very top; to the left at eleven o'clock, the prophet Isaiah; at eight thirty, Jeremiah; at three, Daniel; at four thirty, Ezekiel. They are recognized as Old Testament prophets because of the hats associated with Jews in medieval icongraphy, and because of the emblematic scrolls that might ordinarily contain their words of prophecy, but which in the instance display their names. The middle circle contains another series of thirty two Old Testament figures: at twelve thirty, King Solomon; at five o'clock, King David with his harp; and to the left of David, at five thirty, sits Moses, holding the tablets of the Law, on one of which is written the word "Judices" ("Judge"), and, on the other, "Moses." An outer rim of another thirty two medallions enclosed in trefoils is dedicated to kings and priests, the most notable of which is Moses's brother Aaron, at four o'clock. The lancet windows below present a gallery of Old Testament kings, which mirrors in glass the sculpted gallery of kings on the west facade of the church.

At the center of the northern rose, the object of anticipation, the Virgin Mary, holding the stem of a lily as on the trumeau of the northern portal, sits with her son, surrounded by eight doves. Though to the eye the Old Testament ancestral figures around her seem to radiate outward, the meaning of the window is centripetal. The course of human history converges inward toward the coming of Christ.

The southern rose window, completed about a decade after that on the north, is a variation of its earlier model. At the center, Christ of the Apocalypse, the sword of judgment on His lap, reigns supreme over the celestial court around Him, beginning with the Tetramorph, winged symbols of the four evangelists: on top, the eagle, John, along with

Matthew, the man; to His right, Mark, the lion; and to His left, Luke, the ox. Twelve rays emanate from the center, and contain the images of apostles, saints, virgins, martyrs, and kings. Among the identifiable figures, Saint Lawrence. When asked by the Prefect of Rome in the middle of the third century CE to produce the material goods of the church, of which he was the guardian, the future saint brought forth the poor to whom alms had been distributed. Lawrence is seen holding the grill on which the prefect tortured him to death in the second ring at two o'clock; Denis holds his severed head in the second ring at four. A third ring of circular medallions features twenty-four assorted saints, virgins, and martyrs as well as the Annunciation at ten thirty. The outer row of twenty-four trefoil clovers shows angels with various accessories—crowns, incense, candles—mixed with several New Testament scenes such as the Holy Family's flight into Egypt at nine o'clock, or, in the square panel at the far right corner outside the perimeter of the rose, the Resurrection. On the whole, the southern rose is less well organized and coherent than that on the north. Many of the figures remain unlabeled and unidentifiable, others are generic. A few scenes from the Old Testament are scattered among the overwhelming iconography from the New Testament. In the first ring at nine thirty, the Judgment of Solomon comprises two women standing in front of the king with the baby in the middle and a man with raised sword ready to cut the baby in half. At the very bottom left, outside of the circle of the rose, an image of the Fall of Man can be seen in the trefoil at six thirty. Moses and Aaron appear at the center of the analogous trefoil at seven thirty.

The question of the content and arrangement of the multitude of scenes painted on the rose windows of Notre-Dame is vexed by the reworkings over the centuries of thousands of shards of glass that have been damaged and replaced, sometimes by the same motifs and sometimes by an available component scene which fits the empty space. The case of the lancet windows beneath the great south rose is, however, special. The glass filling these tall panels was lost in the eighteenth century and replaced as part of the restoration of the nineteenth on the basis of windows at Chartres, whose glazings were much better preserved than those of Notre-Dame. The central lancets show the evangelists of the New Testament sitting on the shoulders of the prophets of the Old: Matthew on the shoulders of Isaiah, Luke on Jeremiah, John on Ezekiel, and Mark on Daniel. On either side, prophets with scrolls and books in their hands.

THE WESTERN ROSE

THE OLDEST ROSE WINDOW of Notre-Dame is that of the western facade. Unlike the Old Testament in the north, and the New in the south, this opening belongs to the "encyclopedic" type. A mirror of man and of nature, the western rose displays the signs of the zodiac, the Works of the Months, and the virtues and vices like those that limn the area beneath the jamb statues of the central portal. The virtues are represented in the top half of the outer circle as women bearing allegorical shields. There, at eleven thirty, Faith with a cup and a cross; Hope at one, with a banner; and, at eleven, Charity with the Lamb of God. The vices reside in the top half of the middle ring: at eleven thirty, Idolatry as a man worshiping a horned idol; and, just to the right, Anger, as a man raising his unsheathed sword against another; at two thirty, Cowardice, as a knight who has dropped his sword when pursued by a rabbit; and at ten thirty, Luxury or Vanity as a richly dressed woman admiring herself in the mirror. Mary and the infant Jesus sit at the center of the western rose, surrounded by twelve Old Testament prophets with their scrolls. In the middle ring of the lower half, the signs of the zodiac, and, on the outer rim, the Works of the Months surround the Virgin and Child as they do in the Virgin portal of the west facade.

The astrological signs and their corresponding labors are only partially visible because of the enormous pipe organ of Notre-Dame which sits across a wide tribune or gallery above the first bay of the nave. Music has always played a great role in the development of Notre-Dame, whose construction coincided with the development of polyphony at the School of Paris. In the century between the beginning of the construction of the cathedral in 1163 and the completion of the great rose windows in the 1260s, the unencumbered line of Gregorian chant, which moves in its unified harmonies in a single direction, gave way to a multiplicity of musical voices, sometimes simultaneous with each other and sometimes in dialogue, the first step in the direction of the great contrapunctual composers—Vivaldi, Bach, and Mozart—of the Western tradition. There have always been organs at Notre-Dame, beginning with the medieval instruments in the choir and culminating with the great symphonic organ, created in the eighteenth century, renovated by Viollet-le-Duc in the nineteenth, and electrified in the twentieth, with its five keyboards, 109 stops and nearly 8,000 pipes—the biggest in France.

Filled as it is with biblical figures, the cathedral functioned, in an age in which only a small portion of the population could read, as a Bible for the poor and as a teaching tool. Those who prayed might look to sculpture and stained glass as a way of visualizing the people and events contained in the Bible. Those who preached might use such images to remember, illustrate, or emphasize the subjects of their sermons. How is it, then, that so many of the forms belonging to the great rose windows of Notre-Dame and elsewhere are not visible from the ground to the naked eye? Could it be that it did not matter? Light came through the window as a kind of grace that rendered sacred whatever it touched, making biblical history part of the present. Or, could it be that, like certain figures on the tops of cathedrals visible only to God, the illegible figures of stained glass nonetheless drew His blessing upon the community of the faithful? In this way, the myriad illegible images in Notre-Dame can be compared to the frieze which ran around the inside of the lintels of the Parthenon in Athens and which worshipers inside the building could see only with great difficulty.

The indecipherability of much of the Notre-Dame glass is offset by what it feels like to be in the cathedral—the cathedral effect. Without knowing who or what is painted on the walls, it may be enough to know that so many of the figures of the Old and New Testaments as well as symbols from the pagan world of astrology or the Classical world of ethical abstractions are to be found there. The flood of colored light is more important than the identity of particular prophets, priests, or kings. All the more so, since the whole is enhanced by non-figural elements of pure design: shards of glass with no painting or bounded circles, semi-circles, and trilobes with vegetable, crosshatching, or other geometric patterns, some ringed in pearl-like strings, which create the impression of an enormous wall of glowing glass like that which John describes in his vision of the Apocalypse as belonging to the Celestial Jerusalem: "And the foundations of the wall of the city were adorned with all manner of precious stones. The first foundation was jasper: the second sapphire: the third, a chalcedony: the fourth, an emerald. [20] The fifth, sardonyx: the sixth, sardius: the seventh chrysolite: the eighth, beryl: the ninth, a topaz: the tenth, a chrysoprasus: the eleventh, a jacinth: the twelfth, an amethyst. [21] And the twelve gates are twelve pearls, one to each: and every several gate was of one several pearl. And the street of the city was pure gold, as it were, transparent glass" (Apocalypse 21:19–21).

The shimmering colored light coming through the rose windows of Notre-Dame has a double effect. Where it falls on columns, walls, or the floor, it dematerializes the stone. Looking directly at the kaleidoscope of colors also helps to imagine what paradise will look like when and if the time comes. The history of the stained glass at Notre-Dame did not, however, always take these two effects into consideration. Throughout the eighteenth century, medieval stained glass was removed in favor of transparent glass through which daylight penetrates without the filtering stain of color. The return to the spirit of the Middle Ages as part of Viollet-le-Duc's nineteenth-century restoration involved the repair of damaged panes along with the recreation of medieval stained glass motifs in some of the windows that had been removed by the light-seeking enemies of Gothic style at the time of the Enlightenment. Convinced that plain clear glass lacked the mystery of its medieval antecedent, Viollet-le-Duc installed patterned grisaille glass, executed in schemes of grey or another neutral color, in some windows of the side chapels. He supervised the installation of a Tree of Jesse in the Saint Anna chapel, the second from the transept on the north side of the nave. He commissioned set scenes of the Glorification of the Virgin at the right side of her Son between an Annunciation and a Visitation in the upper windows of the axial chapel at the easternmost point of the church. The great restorer also provided for an eclectic range of familiar subjects in the Gothic style on either side of the axis. There, portraits of the patriarch Abraham, the prophets Ezekiel, Isaiah, Daniel, and Jeremiah, the priests Aaron and Melchizedek mingle with the evangelists Luke and John, the martyrs Stephen and Lawrence, Saints Denis and Marcel (see p. 71), Popes Gregory VII and Leon III, the bishop builders of the original cathedral, Maurice and Eudes de Sully, the emperor Charlemagne, and Louis IX of France.

A project for new glass in the modernist mode began, but was abandoned, just before World War II. After the war, Minister of Culture and renowned author André Malraux revived the effort to install modern glass at Notre-Dame, and, beginning in the early 1960s, the artist Jacques Le Chevallier designed twelve windows for the upper part and eighteen for the tribune level of the nave. Pure abstractions without recognizable subjects, or with familiar subject types suggested by splashes of color against a clearer background, these may shock the viewer by their resonance with the abstract expressionism that was part of the rebellious artistic spirit of the 1960s. And, yet, in their respect for the basic colors of medieval stained glass and in the way in which the layers of patterned color play off against each other, there is a case to be made for the latest additions to the windows of Notre-Dame which not only preserve the mystery of the originals but also recreate the effects of pure light and color as a visual foretaste of heaven.

Turning in the transept crossing between the two rose windows, you catch a glimpse of that part of Notre-Dame that still survives from the renovations of the neoclassicism of the seventeenth century and the Enlightenment of the eighteenth. Beyond the modernist altar where daily mass is conducted, and beyond the wooden prayer stalls where the canons of Notre-Dame sit, stands the altar where services were conducted for the clergy before the Revolution. Behind that, the sculpted Pietà looms larger than any piece of sculpture inside the church and can also be seen from the sides and rear through the grillwork around the choir.

In 1638 King Louis XIII, in an official act registered in the Parliament of Paris, the supreme court of France, published a solemn document, offering his kingdom to the Virgin Mary. The "Vow of Louis XIII," an alliance of church and state unimaginable in the secular democracies of the West, was accompanied by a project to redesign the choir of Notre-Dame, which did not come to fruition until the end of the century under Louis XIV. Beginning in the first half of the eighteenth century, the columns around the choir were covered in marble, a feature still visible in the painter Jacques-Louis David's *Coronation of Napoleon* (1807), but subsequently removed by Viollet-le-Duc. The prayer screen separating the choir from the transept and the nave was removed, and the sculptural installation that fills the round point of the choir was put into place. This array of marble and bronze figures turns around the Pietà of sculptor Nicolas Coustou (d. 1733) which casts back to the Pietà of Michelangelo (1499) in Saint Peter's Basilica, Vatican City. While the Italian rendering has a pyramidal composition, which gives it a great sense of stability, the more dynamic French version is built around intersecting diagonal lines which fill it with motion. Christ looks like He is falling, and His Mother is there to catch him. While Michelangelo's Mary, sorrow on her face, looks down at the finality of the scene before her, Coustou's Mary looks toward the viewer, as if imploring us to see the tragedy before us, as well as upward, in keeping with the skyward visual magnetism of the Gothic church. The angel to Mary's left follows the finger of Christ's left hand, his other arm hanging limply, in quotation of Michelangelo's model. The baby angel or putto at Mary's right side looks on the scene with wonder and reinforces the Virgin's stature as Mother. To Mary's left, the kneeling figure of Louis XIII offers his crown and scepter to her, while, on her right, a kneeling Louis XIV places his hand over his heart as a pledge of faith. In front of each column between the choir and the ambulatory stands a bronze angel bearing the instruments of the Passion: the lance, the scourges of the flagellation, the inscription "INRI" (*Iēsus Nazarēnus, Rēx Iūdaeōrum*, "Jesus of Nazareth, King of the Jews"), the vinegar-soaked sponge, the nails of the cross, and the crown of thorns.

The outside of the choir is now open at the western side, but between the columns at the rounded end, both the south and the north sides of the once impenetrable enclosure retain a high wall with relief sculpture at eye level. These tableaux, which date from the end of the thirteenth century, were repainted as part of Viollet-le-Duc's restoration, and resemble nothing so much as a kind of dynamic visual narrative one finds in the Bayeux Tapestry account of the Norman Conquest of 1066 or in a contemporary graphic novel or cartoon strip. The north side of the enclosure displays fourteen scenes from the life of Jesus: the Visitation, Annunciation to the Shepherds, Nativity, Adoration of the Magi, Massacre of the Innocents, Flight into Egypt, Presentation in the Temple, Jesus among the Doctors, the Baptism of Jesus, the Wedding at Cana, the Entry to Jerusalem, the Washing of Feet, the Last Supper, and the Agony in the Olive Garden at Gethsemane the night before the Crucifixion. The wall of the south enclosure displays scenes of the resurrected Jesus: successive apparitions to Mary Magdalene, to the Holy Women, to Peter and John, to the pilgrims of Emmaus, to Thomas, who is shown sticking his finger in Christ's wound, and to the apostles by the Sea of Galilee. In Galilee, Christ is shown sending the apostles into the world to preach, and, in a final scene, He is on the Mount of Olives after the final dinner with the apostles the night before His ascension.

THE TREASURY

I F YOU FOLLOW THE SEQUENCE of reliefs around the ambulatory, peering through the grill at the elaborate installation around the altar and Pietà, you might miss the entrance to the treasury of Notre-Dame. The original sacristy or vestry, which was built alongside of the medieval cathedral, had fallen into such disrepair that it was replaced in the middle of the eighteenth century by a building that was, in turn, destroyed in the violence that attended the urban uprisings of 1830 and 1831 in Paris. In a wave of anti-royalist rage that continued after the replacement of the Bourbon king Charles X by the Orleanist Louis-Philippe, a mob ransacked the church of Saint Germain l'Auxerrois before moving on to the nearby archbishop's palace where the rioters threw its elegant furnishings into the river. Eugène Emmanuel Viollet-le-Duc, who had no formal architectural training but claimed to have learned how to build and restore by drawing, was a witness to the event, about which we know in part because of a rapid sketch he did, at the age of seventeen, of the joyous destruction of the massive symbol of episcopal excess on the southeast corner of the cathedral.

The sketch, which shows the looting from the other side of the Seine, upholds Viollet-le-Duc's contentious claim about architectural educa-

Viollet-le-Duc Sketch of Sacking of Bishop's Palace, Notre-Dame Treasury

tion in so far as the drawing of destruction was a first step in restoration. He and his partner Jean-Baptiste-Antoine Lassus rebuilt the sacristy of Notre-Dame in the neo-Gothic style as a house for the chapter of canons to meet as well as for the few relics and precious liturgical objects that had survived the Revolution of 1789. The original relics of Notre-Dame, kept behind the altar in the choir, included, *inter alia*, objects or body parts associated with Saints Denis, Geneviève, Marcel, Stephen, and the Virgin. As powerful catalysts of faith wrapped in an aura of sympathetic magic, the relics were scattered to prevent the resuscitation of religion allied with the crown as part of the Ancien Régime. With the appropriation of church property during the Reign of Terror, the rich reliquaries in which the relics were housed were picked clean of their

Viollet-le-Duc Reliquary for Crown of Thorns,
Notre-Dame Treasury

precious stones. Their metal contents were taken to the Paris mint where they were melted down for cannons or coins.

Among the objects currently in the treasury of Notre-Dame are several relics of the Passion, which, as we shall see, were, in the middle of the thirteenth century, purchased by Saint Louis for the Sainte-Chapelle, notably, a piece of the True Cross and the crown of thorns (see p. 162–63). An elaborate reliquary for the crown was commissioned by Napoleon I in 1806. It shows three angels holding a golden globe on top of which sits the Lion of Judah and a cross, the ensemble part of imperial iconography harking back to the cruciform orbs of the Carolingian and Ottonian emperors of Europe. It sits empty, as the crown of thorns is currently housed in an elaborate reliquary designed by Viollet-le-Duc, whose remake of Notre-Dame extended beyond the structure to the painted decoration of the inner walls of the choir in the French medieval revivalist style alongside the English medievalism of William Morris, and, beyond that, to furniture and to liturgical objects like the crown of thorn's current housing, which was a gift of Napoleon III to the cathedral. Set on a trilobe base with gold filigree between the jewels around its edge, Viollet-le-Duc's reliquary exhibits a seated Saint Louis who holds the crown of thorns in his hands while wearing the crown of France on his head. The whole is shaped like an hourglass, and the ornate canopy behind Louis's head narrows to a bejeweled neck on top of which sits a case in the shape of a crown. Statuettes of the twelve apostles, recognizable by the attributes associated with them, stand under tiny gables all around a circular glass ring as if they were jamb statues on the facade of the cathedral or the tall bronze apostle figures on the cathedral's roof. They are separated from each other by miniature Gothic window frames through which one can see the round crystal housing of what is left of the crown of thorns itself. The glass portion of Viollet-le-Duc's reliquary is topped by another gold filigree and jeweled band capped by fleurs-de-lys identical to the ones on Saint Louis's crown. On the first Friday of each month the crown of thorns is removed from its reliquary and processed around the inside of the cathedral in a rite that attracts tourists and faithful alike.

Several of the treasury objects of less importance are also associated with Saint Louis. A jewel-studded reliquary from the middle of the nineteenth century in the shape of the bust of the king, replete with his distinctive hair and crown, reproduces the one in which Louis's head was originally housed, first at Saint-Denis, and later in the Sainte-Chapelle. The king's hair shirt along with the ivory-handled scourge with which he had himself flagellated in rituals of mortification of the royal body that some have taken for Louis's staging of his own saint-hood are also on display there. Other sacred objects have arrived at the cathedral from private collections or from other churches. A point of one of the Holy Nails of the cross, left by Anne Gonzaga (d. 1684), an Italian French noblewoman, to the Abbey of Saint-Germain-des-Prés, ended up in a refashioned reliquary in the treasury of the cathedral of Paris. A reliquary containing a part of Saint Paul was given in 1825 by Pope Leon XII to Archbishop Hyacinthe-Louis de Quélen, who left it to the mother church. In addition to the few relics that survived the Revolution, a wealth of liturgical objects—a monstrance, an Easter candle holder, and clerical robes, all designed by Viollet-le-Duc, numerous chalices, ciboria, pattens, croziers, crucifixes, and medals—make the treasury of Notre-Dame more of a museum than a working vestry.

GARGOYLES AND CHIMERA

Rounding the choir and descending the nave on the north side, one exits Notre-Dame by the Virgin portal and is practically in front of the entrance to the north tower. Looking up, hundreds of gargoyles hover at three levels along the nave and all around the choir. These monstrous protrusions were not part of the initial building but were installed in the thirteenth century. There has been much discussion of the original purpose of gargoyles. Were they the signs of evil expelled from the church? In their horizontal sleekness, which contrasts with the overall verticality of the Gothic church, they indeed appear to be screaming, leaping from its sides. Were they meant to keep demons away? Were they there, like the wise and foolish virgins or the rapacious devils in the voussoirs around the portal of the Last Judgment, to warn worshipers about the stakes of entering the sacred space on the other side of the walls? The answer may involve any or all of the above, but may, in fact, be much simpler.

Gargoyles function to drain water from the roof. Water is the enemy of cathedrals, and, in the period after the Revolution, when roofs were stripped for their lead content and were otherwise left to decay, the infusion of water in the eaves and below threatened them with ruin. The gargoyles whose facial gestures seem to shriek from on high had by that time fallen into disrepair, and many had been replaced by simple lead pipes. The restoration and repair of Notre-Dame in the nineteenth century recognized the importance of drawing water off the roof, the flat space between the bottom of the roof's slope, and the balcony that runs all around the church. The myriad of monstrous creatures projected horizontally up and down the flying buttresses were replaced by a system not unlike the mechanism that returns balls in an American bowling alley. Water that accumulates on the roof or terass runs down a drain to the top of the flying buttress, then down the grooved top of the flyer to the gargoyle whose open mouth disgorges it onto the street below. And though the gargoyles of Notre-Dame no longer serve to handle water from above, they nonetheless contribute to the spectacular visual aura of the church.

Those hearty enough to climb the hundreds of stairs to the balustrade level of Notre-Dame are rewarded by spending time there among the cathedral's fifty-four chimera, fantastical sculpted beasts that comprise a "mystical zoology" overlooking the skyline of Paris. Some resemble the creatures found in medieval bestiaries, catalogues of the nature of real and imaginary animals. Others have taken on such an iconic status via photographs, postcards, movies, and books that it is hard to believe that they were not there from the start. Unlike the gargoyles, however, they are wholly the creations of Viollet-le-Duc and Lassus in the 1840s and '50s and serve no function other than to provoke the kind of strong reactions they have elicited ever since. Only a few of the beasts on the balcony sit tranquilly on their perch, a docile elephant on the southeastern edge of the north tower, and a stork and pelican in the same area overlooking the roof of the nave.

It would be hard to make a case for the esthetic beauty of the chimera, which appear aggressive and menacing. Their bodies are perched on the rim of the balcony which many grasp with rapacious claws. The birds found there are not the cute little creatures that Saint Francis addresses as "My sweet little sisters, birds of the sky," but swooping vultures of the Apocalypse of Saint John. Remarkably, all but a couple are depicted with their mouths open, and a few with tongues hanging out, less like the gargoyles who are screaming and more like beasts of prey observing the scene below and ready to pounce. A few have already seized their quarry, like the demon on the north side of the north tower who is squashing a toad, or the horned creature with the body of a man and the head of a demon who consumes a bone on the northwestern corner of the balcony around the south tower, or the half-dog and half-cat that, crouched over the southwest edge of the same tower, devours a cluster of grapes, or the eagle with a rat in its claws on the inner balcony of the southwest side of the north tower.

Though a number of the chimera, no matter how aggressive, belong to the natural world, the majority embody the very kind of bestial combinations that Saint Bernard censures in medieval manuscript illuminations. "But what can justify that array of grotesques in the cloister where the brothers do their reading," he asks, "a fantastic conglomeration of beauty misbegotten and ugliness transmogrified? What place have obscene monkeys, savage lions, unnatural centaurs, manticores? . . . Here is a quadruped with a dragon's tail, there an animal's head stuck on a fish. That beast combines the forehand of a horse with the rear half of a goat, this one has the horns in front and the horse's quarters aft." The unnatural animals on the balustrade of Notre-Dame project the most frightening elements of the demonic. They are the stuff of nightmares. For the chimera play powerfully on the permeable boundary between man and beast, and no matter how ferocious they may appear, they all to some extent bear human faces with humanlike expressions, and many clutch the balustrade with human arms and hands. An ape-satyr resembling an orangutan peers from the south tower. A man with the face of a lion on the prowl haunts the southwest side of the north tower. A horned demon looks out over the parvis in front of the cathedral from the edge juxtaposing the northwest corner of the south tower. His emaciated body and human hands grasping the knobby top of a decorative floral scroll combine with a devilish beard, sharp chin, large open mouth, deep-set eyes, satyr's ears, and sharp protrusion on the top of his skull to strike terror in all.

Two of the chimera have drawn particular attention, the "stryge," "strix," or vampire and the figure of Ahasver, or the Wandering Jew. The stryge of Notre-Dame is an enigmatic monstrous figure. Propped on its elbows on the northwest side of the north tower, it rests both human hands on its cheeks between an oversized ear, which seems to originate in its neck, and a large mouth. Between the wide eyes of the stryge's low simian-like forehead sits a nose of the type used to caricature Jews in the anti-Semitic propaganda of the period as well as during

The Stryge

Ahasver (© Étienne Revault / CMN
Dist. Art Resource, NY)

the Dreyfus Affair of the 1890s, and, of course, the occupation of Paris and deportation of Jews in World War II. The double horns on its head, shaped like that of a neanderthal, resemble those on the head of Moses in medieval representations based upon the widespread mistranslation as "horns" of the word *keren* for the "rays of light" emanating from Moses's head when he descended from Sinai. For all his devilish appearance, the stryge wears a pair of angel wings on his back, in a mixture not only of the animal and the human but also of the demonic and the divine. Unlike many of his fellow chimera who threaten the beholder, the look on the face of the stryge is benign, the gestural language of the hands on his cheeks one of pensiveness rather than anger. But what about the tongue protruding from between his lips? It is impossible to tell on the basis of his ambiguous bodily features and facial expression whether the stryge sticks his tongue out at the city of Paris out of disdain, disgust, derision, resignation, or contempt.

On the northeast balcony behind the south tower, the figure of Ahasver presents as an old man wearing the pointed hat associated with Jews in the manuscripts, stained glass, and sculpture of the period. This is the only wholly human face among the chimera, yet to place such an unmistakably identifiable figure of the Wandering Jew among the beasts on the balustrade is dehumanizing enough to speak for itself. The forward incline of Ahasver's body along with the pitch of his head render the wandering part of the Wandering Jew who often also carries a walking stick. Ahasver's eyes are fixed not below, as in the case of the animals on the lookout for prey, but in the distance. He looks prophetically to the future.

THE BELLS

THE BALUSTRADE OFFERS access to the forest, the wooden beams under the roof and above the vaults, and the bells of the south tower. The bells of Notre-Dame have through the ages been an object of fascination, all the more so since Victor Hugo's *Notre-Dame de Paris*, whose protagonist Quasimodo is the bell-ringer of the church. They represent one of the vestiges of the past that gives the impression that one might experience the sound of the Middle Ages exactly as Parisians did eight centuries ago. Which is true only to a degree: like the sculpture, stained glass, and even some of the structural elements that have been replaced over the years, the bells have endured the ravages of time and a succession almost as hallowed as the kings of France.

Each bell has the status of one of the great living personalities of Paris, the member of a sonorous court with a history all its own. Some are bigger and more important than others, the hierarchy running from the big "bourdons," to the medium sized "cloches," to the small "moineaux" or "little monks." Each has a name. The big bells in the north tower were originally Jacqueline and Marie, Gilbert, Guillaume, Nicholas, Pasquier, and two "moineaux," joined in 1453 by Thibault. Gilbert was replaced in 1472 by Gabriel. A new bell, Henriette-Jérôme, was added in 1765. In the course of the Revolution, however, one hundred thousand church bells in France, including those of Notre-Dame, were melted down for money, cannons, or cannonballs. The melting of bells accompanied the scattering of relics. Four bells, having been blessed by the bishop on the parvis in front of the cathedral, were restored to the north tower in 1856, one of which, Sebastopol, was brought back by Napoleon from the Crimean War. It was returned in 1913 to the now destroyed convent of Chersonesus where, repurposed, it still serves as a fog bell off the Ukrainian coast.

The mechanism for ringing the bells has evolved over the centuries, from the heavy arm work of pulling medieval ropes, to the use of feet and pedals, to an electric system installed in the 1920s and '30s. The north tower currently boasts eight bells, whose names reflect the ethos and the history of the cathedral: Gabriel, the messenger of God, 4,162 kg, $A\#_2$; Anne-Geneviève, which honors Saint Anna, mother of the Virgin, and Saint Geneviève, patron saint of Paris, 3,447 kg, B_2; Denis, for Saint Denis, 2502 kg, $C\#_3$; Marcel, for Saint Marcel, 1925 kg, $D\#_3$; Étienne, for Saint Stephen, 1494 kg, $E\#_3$; Benoît-Joseph, named in 2013 for Pope Benoît XVI, Joseph Ratzinger, 1309 kg, $F\#_3$; Maurice, for Maurice de Sully, 1,011 kg, $G\#_3$; Jean-Marie, in honor of Mgr Jean-Marie Lustiger, Archbishop of Paris (1981–1205), 782 kg, $A\#_3$.

Leaving Notre-Dame by the circular staircase of the south tower, you emerge in front of the archdeacon's or guardian's house. I have always been struck in this quiet corner fenced off from the crowds on the parvis by how close one comes to the courses of stone along the base of the church. A careful look reveals little fossils and shells that were once encrusted in the tertiary rock quarried to build the cathedral. The foraminifers, miliolidae, and mesalia or sea snails visible and even touchable indicate that this rock was formed some forty-five million years ago, probably in the Val-de-Grace area, mined since antiquity, of Paris's fifth arrondissement. From there it was floated in small boats down the Bièvre River, now covered, which empties into the Seine just across from the Île de la Cité. The little creatures whose traces linger in the stone of Notre-Dame provide some temporal perspective upon the layers of time beneath the materials—stone, metal, glass, and wood—worked over a mere matter of centuries, into the living organism of the cathedral of Paris.

CHARTRES
The Queen of Cathedrals

NOTRE-DAME CHARTRES. 16 CLOÎTRE
NOTRE-DAME, CHARTRES, FIFTY-SIX
MILES SOUTHWEST OF PARIS.

Access via train from Paris's Gare Montparnasse. Be sure to sit on the left side of the compartment and look for the spires of the cathedral as you approach town. Begun 1194 CE, site of renewal of classical learning in the High Middle Ages, less damaged than other cathedrals in the Revolution of 1789, splendid intact jamb figures on the west facade and deep blue windows throughout, interior restored 2009–19.

T HE APPROACH TO NOTRE-DAME CHARTRES IS AS IT WAS IN THE Middle Ages. From the rich wheat fields of La Beauce, its spires can be seen in the distance as a reminder of the ways in which the cathedral dominated the countryside which nourished it not only via the taxes which contributed to construction, but via the grain and wine which flowed from countryside to town as part of the economic renewal of the twelfth and thirteenth centuries. Chartres is situated some fifty-six miles southwest of Paris, and, if you take the train from the Gare Montparnasse, the towers of the cathedral appear off to the left. From the station, they guide you to the parvis which is intimate and provincial—peaceful even—compared to the busy broad city space in front of Notre-Dame Paris.

A HISTORY

As in the case of Saint-Denis and Notre-Dame Paris, Chartres was the site of a pagan shrine long before the arrival of the Christian community. In his account of the Gallic Wars, Caesar (d. 44 BCE) mentions Chartres as one of the places where Druids, Celts who were displaced by the Roman occupation of Gaul, gathered both to worship and to render justice: "These Druids, at a certain time of the year, meet within the borders of the Carnutes, whose territory is reckoned as the center of all Gaul, and sit in conclave in a consecrated spot. Thither assemble from every side all that have disputes, and they obey the decisions and judgments of the Druids." The seventeenth-century historian Victor Sablon specifies that the Druids were idol worshipers who lived in forests because of the mistletoe that was the main object of their cult, and that they were especially populous in the area of Chartres because of the numerous "caves, caverns, grottos, and places hollowed in the rocks" to be found there. In one such underground shrine, the Druids consecrated an altar to a virgin who was to give birth, *Virgo paritura*, which links Chartres to a cult of virginity even before the arrival of Christianity. When "the Druids left the shadows to follow the Truth, their caves and caverns were converted into oratories, and the Christians assembled in this subterranean spot dedicated to the Virgin and celebrated a divine service there daily." Sablon describes the Virgin as "black or Moorish in color, as are nearly all the images of the Virgin in Chartres, and the Druids are thought to have given her this color because she came from a country more exposed to the sun than ours." This is the famous Black Virgin of Chartres, a statue in wood small enough to fit on an altar, which was destroyed publicly in front of the cathedral on December 20, 1793, when the cathedral, in the aftermath of the French Revolution, was rededicated as a "temple of reason." We know it visually only from engravings made prior to its disappearance.

The parvis in front of Notre-Dame Chartres is so peaceful that you might never guess that the medieval cathedral was built in fire and tumult, in the chaos both before and after the reign of the emperor Charlemagne, who is commemorated in a stained glass window of the choir. An entry in an annal account from the city of Metz recounts that in the year 743 CE "Hunald, Duke of Aquitaine, crossed the Loire with a large force, and, having ravaged the countryside, he reached Chartres

West Facade

which he burned along with the episcopal church dedicated to the honor of Mary, Mother of God." After the death of Charlemagne's son Louis the Pious in 840, his eldest son Lothaire marshaled troops in Chartres to attack his younger brother Charles the Bald. The treaty which they signed two years later near Verdun, the Strasbourg Oaths, is recognized as the first written document in the French language, or Old French. As in Paris (see p. 54), the Vikings raided Chartres, which was known as a site of resistance. In 857 or 858 CE, the invaders from the north, having burned Paris and extracted tribute from Saint-Denis, took Chartres. Frotbaldus, the forty-third bishop of the diocese, was massacred along with the faithful who took refuge in the cathedral. Their bodies were thrown into a well which was known as the Lieu-Fort, "Strong Place," still visible on the south side of the crypt.

In 911 Chartres was again besieged by the Viking leader Rollo. According to Jehan le Marchant, the author of a series of miracles of Our Lady of Chartres, written first in Latin around 1200 and translated into Old French toward the middle of the thirteenth century, "This tyrant led into France a great force, / Which he assembled / Out of pagans and Saracens. / They destroyed everything on the coast, / And laid waste France and the country. . . . He got as far as Chartres, / Which he attacked on both sides." Unable to resist the Vikings and the siege engines that reigned stones and fire upon them from all sides, the Chartrians implored the aid of their protectress, the Holy Virgin, "who has dominion over Chartres." More important, they displayed upon the walls of the city what was, before the arrival of the head of John the Baptist in Amiens in 1206, the most precious relic in Western Europe. That is, "The Holy Tunic / Of the Mother of God," which Charlemagne was reputed to have brought from Constantinople and which came to Chartres as the gift of Charlemagne's grandson Charles the Bald in 876 CE: "The Chartrians took the tunic / And placed it on the walls of the city / In the place of an insignia or banner." At first the enemy began to laugh and to hurl "rocks and arrows from Turkish bows and crossbows. / But God, who saw their defiance, / Showed divine vengeance: / He blinded them such that they lost / Their sight, and couldn't see a thing, / So that they could neither retreat / Nor could they go forward." Defeated by the power of the relic, Rollon fled, converted to Christianity, and made peace with King Charles III, the Simple. With the Treaty of Epte (911) began the Viking settlement of Normandy, which took its name from the men from the North. The relic itself was once thought to be, as Jehan le Marchant assures us, the garment that Mary wore when "carrying Jesus Christ, the son of God, in her belly." For a long time, received wisdom held that this was the saintly garment that Mary wore at the time of her delivery. The power of the Holy Relic of Chartres lay in sworn testimony that the Christ Child had touched the tunic.

As saints intervened through relics that were either part of their body or had touched their body, it would be hard to imagine a more powerful relic than Mary's tunic. A series of quatrefoil panels in the Miracles of Our Lady window (bay 38, see p. 129) depict its procession through the streets of the city. In the vertical leaves of the quatrefoil, the sick and infirm fight for contact with the relic along with the lucky ones who thank the Mother of God for having been cured. When the medieval reliquary, thought to contain Mary's tunic, was opened for inspection in 1712, it was discovered not to be a garment at all, but a piece of cloth about five meters in length. Thus, the designation was changed from "tunic" to "veil." The length of the veil was shortened in the aftermath of the Revolution of 1789. Apparently the object of some contention, it was cut into smaller pieces, one of which is still on display at the eastern end of the apse.

FIRES

CHURCH-BUILDING IN THE Middle Ages was often a question of church rebuilding—and rebuilding, the result of fire. The cathedral of Chartres burned in 962, 1020, 1119, and 1134 when it was rebuilt around the time that Suger undertook the reconstruction of Saint-Denis, though not in the new and innovative Gothic style. According to the monk and abbot of Mont-Saint-Michel Robert de Torigni, "In this same year (ca. 1145), primarily at Chartres, men began, with their own shoulders, to drag the wagons loaded with stone, wood, grain, and other materials to the workshop of the church, whose towers were then rising. . . . One might observe women as well as men dragging [wagons] through deep swamps on their knees, beating themselves with whips, numerous wonders occurring everywhere, canticles and hymns being offered to God."

The current cathedral of Chartres is an amalgam of the west facade of the church, built after the fire of 1134, and the rest of the church, begun after the great fire of 1194, which, Jehan le Marchant claims, destroyed most of the city. I remember watching the images on television of the fire that ravaged Notre-Dame Paris on April 19, 2019. As the roof and spire, consumed by flames, collapsed and fell through the vaults into the main vessel of the cathedral, I thought of Jehan le Marchant's description of medieval Chartres: "The damage was astonishing, / Neither vault nor other building were left standing, / Beams and posts collapsed." The images that later emerged of great heaps of melted lead on the floor of Notre-Dame Paris, like the drippings of sandcastles that children build on beaches, render the comparison with the medieval example even more powerful. "In the heat of the fire," Jehan continues, "the lead [of roofs] all melted; / Walls and ramparts went crashing, / Belfries and glass went flying, / All was turned to perdition, / Either by fire or collapse." When the fire of 1194 started, frightened clerics carried the Holy Relic into the crypt. Their emergence three days later, like the risen Christ, with the Sancta Camisia intact had all the drama of relief with President of the Republic Emmanuel Macron's announcement around midnight on the night of the Notre-Dame Paris fire that the cathedral had been saved.

In the medieval account, it was a miracle that the most precious relic of Chartres was saved, and almost a miracle that the papal legate, a man by the name of Melior, happened to be in Chartres at the time. In fact, the legate of Pope Celestine III was Cardinal Melior of Pisa, and he urged the assembled clergy not only to rebuild, but to build bigger and better than before, his very name *Melior* meaning "better" in Latin. Known as a great rhetorician, the cardinal persuaded the bishop, the canons, and the townspeople of Chartres to devote all their income beyond what was needed for bare subsistence for a period of three years to the rebuilding of a cathedral "[s]uch as could not be found anywhere else in the world." The nobles of Chartres came to the rescue of the devastated cathedral. On October 3, 1195, Manassès Mauvoisin, a knight, endowed a fund solemnly contracted "on the altar of the glorious Virgin," which produced an annual income of sixty sous "for the work of this church." But Chartres was also known for its rich bourgeoisie and developed urban trades. Robert Wace, a vernacular poet who wrote on historical topics around the middle of the twelfth century, noted that, "There were rich bourgeois there, and a great deal of money; / A beautiful church, very venerable; The Holy Virgin Mary, Mother of God / was there and her tunic held very dearly." Again, fundraising to rebuild Chartres after the great fire of 1194 summons the enthusiastic pledges by wealthy individuals of almost a billion euros alongside the contributions of 340,000 individuals all over the world after President Macron's announcement that Notre-Dame Paris would be rebuilt.

There is some reason to be suspicious about the origin of the Chartres fire of 1194. The presence of an emissary of the Pope who, as it turned out, was also an excellent fundraiser, along with the speed with which the cathedral was rebuilt, has provoked the curiosity of historians. The damage to the old Romanesque structure could not have been as horrendous as Jehan le Marchant's account alleges. The west facade survived along with a bay of stained glass, la Belle Verrière (ca. 1180), from behind the main altar. Exaggeration of the damage might have been motivated by a desire to encourage contributions to reconstruct. Indeed, funds to rebuild accumulated at a startling rate and were in place only eighteen months after the event. Further, rebuilding began at a pace that suggests that plans to replace the old structure may have existed even before it collapsed. The most recent fire at Chartres occurred in 1836 and destroyed the timber frame under the roof much like the Notre-Dame Paris fire of 2019. The wooden eaves, which dated to the Middle Ages, were replaced by an iron framework which, in the era before shipping by rail, engendered another campaign of carts in which the heavy iron components for girders were loaded on to wagons and hauled some 180 miles from the foundry at Fourchambault to Chartres where they were reassembled to support the new roof. Fragments of the medieval oak tie beams left in the old roof frame were analyzed by dendrochronological methods in 1990 and show the date of 1195 for the felling of the trees from which the roof support was made and between 1210 and 1215 for those of the nave and choir. This means that the initial cut took place a very short time after the fire of the previous year, and shows, overall, an extraordinary pace of building for a structure the size of the cathedral of Chartres, especially if it had been damaged to the extent alleged in Jehan le Marchant's account. Part of what makes Chartres as beautiful as it is stems from an architectural unity that is the result of the exceptionally short time frame for rebuilding—from the fire of 1194 to the transepts of the 1250s and 1260s, a period of less than seventy years.

Finally, the rebuilt church of the middle of the twelfth century was in the old Romanesque style, and by the 1190s, after the experience of Saint-Denis and Notre-Dame Paris, it must have appeared, amid the burst of cathedral building in northern France, to be outdated. The Gothic or modern style pointed toward the future. This amounts to an allegation of ecclesiastical arson, but there was always the precedent of Vézelay, which had burned in 1165 with a similar miraculous rescue of the relics of Marie Madeleine. It appears that a conflict between the noble Abbot Guillaume de Mello who, with the support of King Louis VII, wanted to reconstruct a new apse in the "French" or Gothic style, and the more conservative monks who wanted to keep the Romanesque apse, only sixty years old, was resolved by a fire of mysterious origin.

THE JAMB FIGURES OF CHARTRES

THE FRONTAL FACE OF Chartres combines familiar elements of Gothic design—three portals, broken arches, two towers, one rose window, and a gallery of kings—with elements that are unique. The gallery of kings is placed on top of the bridge between the towers, above, and not below, the rose window, as at Notre-Dame Paris. The three portals do not extend across the full breadth of the west facade but are confined to the space between the two towers, which makes Chartres look smaller than other cathedrals of the same size. The lack of buttresses between the portals makes for a continuity between them, an inviting visual flow less present in more monumental entrances. Such coherence is reinforced by two horizontal bands that cover the width of the royal portal—a series of twenty-four jamb statues, separated by columns decorated with

Royal Portal

floral designs or an interlace of humans and animals in a scroll-and-vine pattern, and the capital frieze that runs along the top of the columns to which the jamb statues are attached.

Carved at the time that the west facade was erected in the mid-twelfth century, the extraordinary array of jamb statues on both sides of the three doors of the royal portal are among the most stunning examples of Gothic sculpture anywhere. As a horizontal whole, they are striking in their verticality. Indeed, the bodies are exceedingly long, the heads disproportionately small, in some cases by a ratio of twelve to one rather than the naturalistic ratio of six or seven to one. They are imposing in their immobility, at once emotional and physical. Placed high above the viewer entering the cathedral, the elongated jamb figures look out, not down, their gaze fixed in the distance, their faces marked by expressions of serenity. Part of what draws us to them is that they are so indifferent to us. Physically, the jamb statues are stationary, almost mummy-like. Their feet rest on pedestals, each with its own geometric design. Their legs are straight, and though their arms do not exactly fall naturally to their sides, they do clasp various objects—books, scrolls, a scepter, a purse—closely to the chest. No action is suggested by the limbs of the jamb figures, which, again, may be a function of their noble indifference: they simply are, without the need to act. Suspended in space, they seem to levitate.

The constraint of the jamb figures may also be a function of the materials of which they are made. The stone used for the building of the bulk of the cathedral came from the nearby quarry of Berchères-les-Pierres, eight miles southeast of Chartres, from which it was no doubt hauled to the building site by cart. Cut in large blocks, it was adequate for the laying of foundations and the erection of walls but porous enough to make fine carving difficult. Suitable stone for the jamb statues of the royal portal was, according to petrographic analysis conducted in the 1970s and the presence of microfossils similar to those in the stones of Notre-Dame Paris (see p. 99), brought from the Parisian basin, most likely by boat down the Oise River to the Seine, or directly from the Seine, and up the Eure River to Chartres.

The *liais de Paris* or Lutetian limestone is denser than the rock of the Chartres region, which means that it can be carved with greater detail. It is more durable, as there are no places for water to collect, freeze, and eventually crack the rock. There is, however, some debate about whether the jamb statues of Chartres were carved in Paris or on site, or in some combination of the two. Recent evidence points to fabrication at the quarry site of standardized modular columns that were then shipped by boat or overland for installation as component parts at a particular building site. Alternately, stone was roughed out at the quarry and shipped to the cathedral for finish work. Or, as was likely in the case of Chartres, stone arrived at the construction site in roughed blanks that were carved according to the sculptural program developed, at the time that the order for Paris limestone was placed, by the canons of the church responsible for the planning of the building, along with the sculptors who transformed the roughed blanks into finished works of art. The arrival of the raw material in blocks of a limited diameter also explains the closeness of the limbs of the jamb figures, which might not extend beyond the bounds of the standardized modules of rock.

The jamb figures of the royal portal are carved with an extraordinary naturalism and richness of detail, rendering the local look of contemporaneous objects and dress—books and book clasps, knotted rope belts, the brooch on a blouse, the textures and even the feel of an embroidered hem, diadems, skull caps, crowns, jewels in the crown, shoes, or the bare feet of the figure hobbled by a curious claw grasping his left foot on the statue on the right side of the door of the right portal. Hair and hair style were particular objects of fascination for the sculptors of the royal portal, who distinguish adroitly different types of men's hair and beards, and who have assembled for the women a display of the longest pigtails in all of Western art. The pigtails of Chartres fall naturally to the side; or, as in the statue of the queen on the far right of the columns, one braid droops as far as her right arm, then curves around it before continuing the downward trajectory to her knees.

The cloth of the garments worn by the jamb figures was no less of an object of fascination for the sculptors of the royal portal. It is an extraordinary thing to imagine, but the twenty-four figures, male and female, all appear to be wearing clothes made from the same bolt of cloth. Whether a head covering draped like a veil around the neck, a mantel with pendulous sleeves, a long skirt, or a man's robe, the pleated material fills, like a giant curtain, the space between and on either side of the doors. The textile panorama goes further than the naturalistic damp-fold drapings of togas on seated figures of Roman sculpture or the so-called "Muldenfaltenstil," with deep looped troughs of cloth that suggest the curves of a body, to a staging of cloth itself. Which can have only one source: the Holy Relic, the "gem and the glory of the city," in Jehan le Marchant's phrase, the garment thought to be the one Mary wore when she gave birth to Jesus. Further evidence lies in the swirls of pleated and crinkly material that cover the enlarged abdomens of several of the women—on the far left, to the right of the central door, and on the far right—and that thus wrap conception in cloth.

Attempts to identify the jamb figures of Chartres rest upon circumstantial evidence. It has been suggested that the trio on the far left represent Sarah, Abraham, and Hagar, a conclusion drawn from the simple presence of a man between two women. Similarly, the queen and king to the right of the central portal have been identified as the Queen of Sheba and Solomon, who actually appear on the right portal of the north side of the church. Men wearing skull caps and not crowns are assumed to be Jewish. The man holding a scroll on the left side, nearest the door, of the central portal has been taken for Isaiah, though scrolls are the attributes of prophets more generally. With the exception of David, who holds a harp, and Moses, who clasps a fragment of the tablets of the Law, it is hard to recognize the jamb figures other than as Old Testament prophets, patriarchs, priests, judges, heroes and heroines, kings and queens. Given that a third of the statues are of women and the others are hard to identify, the jamb statues of the royal portal have only a weak claim to the royal genealogy of Christ in the tradition of the Jesse Tree found in the stained glass on the other side of the west wall.

It has been argued with some credibility that the jamb figures are to be understood in the context of the rivalry between the kings of England and of France. Unlike Saint-Denis to the north of Paris, or the cathedrals of Picardy, Amiens, and Beauvais, or churches even further east like Laon and Reims, Chartres is located only twenty miles from the frontier of Normandy, and Normandy was a possession of the king of England between the Norman Conquest of 1066 and its recapture by France in 1204.

The Plantagenets of England had come to power in 1154 with the succession of Henry II, who married Eleanor of Aquitaine when she divorced Louis VII of France in 1152 and who, as Duke of Normandy and Count of Anjou and Maine, ruled over England and most of western France. The dynasty had solidified their kingly claims by playing upon a legendary ancestry reaching back to the Classical past. Brutus, the first king of Britain, from whom the island derived its name, was the descendant of Aeneas, and Aeneas, the founder of Rome, was an exiled Trojan. Britain thus imagined itself a New Troy. The Capetian dynasty, on the other hand, had not, in the middle of the twelfth century, gained the solidity that it would after 1179 with the succession of Philip Augustus. So, in an age in which longevity was the equivalent of legitimacy, the kings of France sought deeper genealogical roots in the biblical past than the Plantagenets of England, who could only trace their ancestors back to Troy. At his coronation in 1108 Louis VI (d. 1137), the first Capetian to assert French claims against the English occupiers of Normandy, was lauded as being strengthened by the faith of Abraham, the clemency of Moses, the strength of Joshua, the humility of David, the wisdom of Solomon. Pope Gregory IX (d. 1241) acknowledged that "just as it was Judah among the Patriarch's sons whose tribe was taken up to receive special blessing, so the kingdom of France is distinguished above all the other peoples of the world by being singled out for honor and grace by the Lord." The sculptors of the jamb statues of the royal portal did their part to suggest visually the primacy of the French in the panoply of Old Testament figures limning the front.

THE CAPITAL FRIEZES OF CHARTRES

THE BEAUTY AND COHERENCE of the west facade of Chartres are enhanced by the narrative capital frieze that runs along the breadth of the royal portal. These scenes from the life of Jesus, His parents, and grandparents are so finely carved that one might mistake them for mere decoration like the scroll-and-vine work on certain of the vertical columns. And yet, they display in miniature many of the set motifs of the Incarnation and Passion found in the lintels and large sculptures all over the cathedrals of northern France. Sitting atop the large jamb figures, they hold, like the illuminations in a medieval manuscript, the fascination of miniatures. Set below a running crown of mini-arcades with gables in the shape of a tiny city, there is something of a dollhouse quality to the capital frieze of the west facade, which, in its narrative flow from one scene to the next resembles nothing so much as the Bayeux Tapestry, an embroidered account in running tableaux of the Norman Conquest of 1066. The tapestry, created some sixty years before the royal portal of Chartres and likely displayed in the cathedral of Bayeux, where it may have been embroidered and where it was discovered in the fifteenth century, might easily have been known by the carvers of Chartres.

The story of Christ's immediate genealogy and his life is not told in a straightforward manner from left to right but spreads from the center to the margins in such a way as to suggest that Christ, who dominates the central doorway, has neither beginning nor end. Incarnational history, unlike human history, radiates outward symmetrically and is folded in upon itself. The narrative cycle from right to left over the jamb statues to the left of the central door begins, as in the Saint Anna portal of Notre-Dame Paris, with the refusal of Anna and Joachim's gift in the temple and Joachim's exile in the desert, and ends with the Annunciation, Visitation, Nativity, the Magi before Herod, the flight into Egypt, and the Massacre of the Innocents—all set scenes from the Protoevangelium of James, the pseudo-Matthew, or the synoptic Gospels (see p. 71). The cycle of the Childhood of Christ unfurls from left to right on the right of the central portal, beginning with the scene of Jesus's Presentation in the Temple, Jesus's Baptism in the Jordan River, the Temptation in the Desert, the Last Supper, the Kiss of Judas, Placement in the Tomb, the Visit of the Three Marys, the Dinner at Emmaus, and the Dispatching of the Apostles. In this series, you may have noticed the absence of the Crucifixion, which I think may simply have been too grand a subject to depict in miniature.

THE ROYAL PORTALS

THE ENTRYWAYS OF THE royal portal display familiar images of the Christological drama. Ten prophets or apostles sit along the lintel of the left or north portal. Some hold books and others scrolls, which may correspond to the displacement of the scroll of the Old Testament by the codex of the New Testament with the advent of Christianity. If they are apostles, that would suggest that there has been some tailoring of the stone which might have originally contained the full complement of twelve. The eyes of the figures on the lower lintel are fixed upon the scene above where four angels, heads turned downward, are suspended below an oscillating wavy band signifying the heavens in the iconography of Gothic sculpture. In the tympanum, the ascending Christ has pierced the layers of the sky through a scalloped gauzy shell surrounded by angels who proclaim that He has risen. Alternately, it has been pro-

North Portal Tympanum, West Facade

posed that the area above the north door of the west facade illustrates Christ, hidden from the eyes of those on earth, before the Incarnation. James of Voragine (d. 1298), quoting Saint Ambrose (d. 397), combines both explanations in his description of Christ's "great leaps": " 'By one leap Christ came into the world; He was with the Father and came into the Virgin, and from the Virgin leapt into the crib, went down into the Jordan, mounted the Cross, descended into the grave, came forth from the sepulchre, and took His seat at the right hand of the Father.' " Christ's leap either into earthly time or into eternity is framed by two archivolts which display the familiar signs of the zodiac along with the Works of the Months, which we have encountered at Saint-Denis and Notre-Dame Paris (see pp. 8, 76), and that also figure prominently in a stained-glass bay on the south side of the choir inside the cathedral.

If the lower lintel of the north portal shows too few apostles, that of the central portal shows too many, their number joined, it has been suggested, by the Old Testament precursors Enoch and Elijah, who also ascended to heaven, at either end. Together, the twelve seated apostles and two standing prophets are pictured beneath rounded Romanesque arches separated by decorated columns topped by miniature capital reliefs. The tympanum shows Christ in Majesty, rimmed by an almond-shaped mandorla and surrounded by the figures of the evangelists with wings, the Tetramorph: in the upper left, Matthew, the man, who is indistinguishable from an angel; on the upper right, John, the eagle. The bodies of both figures face Christ at the level of His chest. Below John, Luke, the ox, and below Matthew, Mark, the lion. Mark's and Luke's bodies, at the level of Christ's knees, face outward as their necks strain to look back. These figures from the Apocalypse of Saint John are bordered in the first archivolt by twelve angels and, in the outer two rings, by twenty-four elders of the Apocalypse holding in their hands musical instruments—harps and rebecs, and long-neck pear-shaped vials.

The lintels and tympanum of the right or south portal show in the lower level, moving from left to right, scenes of the Annunciation and the Visitation along with the Nativity, with Joseph standing at the head of the bed and Baby Jesus atop a crib arrangement that resembles nothing so much as a children's bunk bed. At the foot of the bed stands an angel who belongs to the scene of the Annunciation to the Shepherds with their flock at their feet. The shepherd on the right holds a musical instrument up to his mouth, and the figure to his left (our right) is cut off by the edge of the archivolt, suggesting that this particular component of the Infancy of Christ panorama may originally have been placed elsewhere and moved to the west facade at the time of its construction in the

South Portal Tympanum, West Facade

mid-twelfth century, or may simply have been obscured by miscalcula-tion. The upper lintel shows the Presentation of Christ in the Temple, the headless and armless figure atop an altar surrounded by a procession of onlookers, some of whom bear gifts. In the tympanum Mary and Child are pictured in the *sedes sapientiae* "seat of wisdom" pose associated with the frontal quality of Byzantine images of Christ and generously scattered throughout the church, as are the censing angels on either side.

CHARTRES AS A CENTER
OF CLASSICAL LEARNING

THE FIGURES IN THE archivolts of the south portal of the west facade of Chartres mark a moment of turning in the history of the West. They do not concern themselves with New Testament history nor with theol-ogy, but with secular learning as early warning signs of the Renaissance of the High Middle Ages, which was every bit as powerful culturally as that of the sixteenth century. Chartres was a center of learning in the eleventh and twelfth centuries, and the images in the voussoirs of the south portal represent the seven branches of knowledge from late Antiquity that make up the liberal arts and were the basis of education throughout the Middle Ages. Each of the arts of language—Dialectic, Rhetoric, and Grammar—and the arts of things or science—Geometry, Arithmetic, Astronomy, and Music—is represented as a seated woman and associated with a preeminent authority in the field. Thus, begin-ning on the lower left, the figure of Dialectic or Logic is shown holding what looks like a flowering branch pointed upward in her left hand and a reptilian beast, possibly a basilisk, in her right, signifying the power of dialectic to point toward truth or to sting. John of Salisbury, bishop of Chartres from 1176 to 1180, defined logic as "the science of verbal expression and [argumentative] reasoning." It was in this chronologi-cal window that King Louis VII began the campaign to outlaw private warfare and judicial duels for the resolution of disagreements between well-armed nobles, substituting for combat judgment at the Parliament of Paris, the place where one speaks instead of fighting, and it can be no accident that the arts of formal debate, which will culminate in the scho-lasticism of the thirteenth century, began to occupy pride of place at the University of Paris. Peter Abelard (d. 1141), who taught in the Parisian region in the early decades of the twelfth century, notes that in the filial economy of his family of birth, his brother took on the role of a knight, while he became a scholar. Abelard equated logic with war, emphasizing its potentially dangerous effects. "I preferred the weapons of dialectic to all the other teachings of philosophy, and, armed with these, I chose the conflicts of disputation instead of the trophies of war." Below Lady Dialectic sits Aristotle, known in the Middle Ages as the dialectitian par excellence. On the inner voussoir opposite Aristotle and Lady Dialectic, two sculpted signs of the zodiac, Pisces, or two fish, and Gemini, or the twins. Both seem oddly out of place, indicating that the component stone blocks from which they were carved originally belonged around the tympanum of the north entryway with the other astronomical signs.

Above Dialectic at eleven o'clock sits Lady Rhetoric, the art of persuasion, and, between Rhetoric and Dialectic, Cicero, the author of two rhetorical treatises, the *Rhetorica ad Herrenium* and *De Inventione*, at his

Grammar and Music, South Portal Tympanum,
West Facade

desk before an open book. If you observe the second figure from the bottom of the outer right voussoir, you will see the third representative of the language arts, Lady Grammar. Grammar, the art of imposing the right words for things and of correct speaking, administers a lesson to two boys. One is semi-nude and also rude. He has put down his book in favor of pulling the hair or ear of his fellow pupil who wears a monk's cowl, an open book on his knees as a sign of studiousness. The figures offer a contrast in moral values like the virtues and vices at the base of the buttresses of the central portal of Notre-Dame or the wise and foolish virgins at both Saint-Denis and Paris. Lady Grammar holds an open book in one hand and, in the other, a switch with which to discipline the naughty boy, an element found in manuscript illustrations of the Grammar Lesson as well as in the life of the medieval classroom. In a passage that I hesitate to assign to my students, for fear that it might reappear among end-of-the-semester teaching evaluations, Guibert de Nogent (d. 1124) complains that his teacher "pelted him almost every day with a hail of blows and harsh words while he was forcing me to learn what he could not teach." Gilbert de la Porrée (d. 1154), who taught at Chartres from 1124 until he became bishop of Poitiers in 1140, had a pupil named Garnier "thoroughly beaten" for misplacing a noun with respect to its modifying adjective—*Fecitque eum optime uerberari*. The figure of Lady Grammar, in other words, might appear unduly harsh or even open to charges of child abuse by current standards, yet her pedagogical switch was thoroughly in keeping with contemporaneous teaching methods. The authority below Lady Grammar, a wax tablet on his lap and styli for writing on the wall, has been identified alternately as Donatus, a mid-fourth-century grammarian, or Priscien, the sixth-century author of the *Institutes of Grammar,* both known throughout the Middle Ages.

In the first voussoir opposite Lady Grammar sits Music, an active figure who strikes a bell with a hammer while holding a harp on her lap. A stringed instrument or viol hangs on the wall under the bell. Below Music, the figure of Pythagoras, a man of numbers and of rhythms, credited with the discovery that musical harmonies functioned according to mathematical formulae. Indeed, in the thinking of medieval philosophers, mathematics and music were allied through the ratios that produce musical sound, and that also operated in the wider universe, according to the ratios of planetary orbits, to produce the music of the spheres. The great conduit of the Pythagorian alliance of mathematics and music was the sixth-century philosopher Boethius (d. 524 CE), who wrote both the *De institutione arithmetica* and the *De institutione musica*, and who sits at one o'clock on the outer right voussoir just below the figure of Arithmetic at the left top of the broken arch. Below Boethius, the figure of Astronomy looks skyward, pointing with her right hand toward the skies, while Ptolemy, an astronomical authority, writes at his tablet, his head cocked in a gesture denoting thought. To complete the four components of the quadrivium, Geometry, situated at the top left of the arch, holds a tracing pad on her lap. She is missing her right hand, which may have held a compass. Below her, Euclid writes on a wax tablet that is the attribute of all the authorities of the ancient world seated around the lintels and tympanum of the right portal. While it may be true that only the clergy benefited directly from the learning symbolically staged around the tympanum of the south portal at Chartres, both the language arts and the sciences represented there celebrate the arts of construction—the geometrical, mathematical, and even musical calculations, as acoustics were an important part of what went into the making of a great Gothic cathedral like Chartres.

As for the language arts, the depiction of intellectual activity, as distinct from theological belief portrayed in the gestural language of prayer, is remarkable on the founding face of a twelfth- or thirteenth-century church. The wax tablets on which the authorities of the ancient world write along with the styli or writing instruments hanging on the wall point to the significance of writing for a culture which, outside of cathedral and monastic schools, had operated to a large extent without it. Along with the revival of learning at the beginning of the twelfth century, writing entered every area of human endeavor from economics and bookkeeping, to legal procedures like inquest and appeal dependent on written records, to the rise of vernacular literature—epics, love lyrics, and romances—written in Old French, to the revival of learning at intellectual centers like Paris, Laon, Reims, and Chartres. The intensity with which the scholars of the royal portal are either bent over their work or are lost in thought signals the importance of the cathedral school of Chartres which was among the most significant centers of learning in Europe.

The School of Chartres can be said to have begun when Fulbert, bishop of the cathedral, arrived in 990 CE from Reims where he had learned about music and mathematics. Fulbert was famous for rebuilding Chartres after it burned in 1020, and for his learning. His obituary from the Ides of April 1028 acknowledges that "Fulbert died, beloved of God and men, a very eloquent man, as much in divine things as in the books dealing with all the liberal arts." Indeed, the attempt to reconcile divine things with the liberal arts characterizes the School of Chartres, which was the gateway by which Platonism reached the West, in particular, *The Timaeus*, which deals with the Creation and the nature of the physical world. The Platonic account of Creation, beginning with the disorder of shapeless elements (earth, air, fire, water) on which the demiurge imposed differences and clarity was read by the Platonists of Chartres as a veiled account of the Christian understanding of how the world came into being. Such understanding only became clear, however, after the birth of Christ, who replaced Moses, as the New Law replaced the Old, a process that Suger referred to as "anagogical uplift" (see p. 52).

LEARNING AND BUILDING

THE CHARTRIANS WERE great analogical thinkers. Not only did they imagine world history before and after the birth of Christ as analogous, one prefiguring the other which fulfills it, but they imagined a great analogy between nature, the cosmos, and man, the microcosm of the wider world. All operate along the lines of arithmetic proportions or ratios which function not only for mathematics, but for Astronomy, the harmonious movement of the stars according to mathematical ratios; Music, which produces harmonies of sound along with the music of the spheres; and Geometry, by which things, like cathedrals, are constructed. All embodied things, Augustine insists, exist in proportion and number, for "numbers are the thoughts of God," which, by analogy, also inhere in human reason, the "ratio" in rationality. A magnificent illumination on the frontispiece of a thirteenth-century moralized or picture Bible depicts the Creation: God, the architect, traces with a compass a perfect circle inside of which a wavy line represents the heavens, two small round spheres the sun and the moon, and a giant globule in which the point of the compass rests, the earth, center of the universe.

We know that cathedrals were not constructed by measurement, but, in their initial layout, by means of pegs fixed in the ground and cords rotated around them to yield the ratios by which pillars were planted. Ratios, when measured, often yield odd results. Each side of the "old" or south tower of Chartres measures 16.44 m., and it is no accident that the width of the transept crossing is also 16.44 m. The length of the crossing is only 13.99 m., which has led the art historian Otto von Simson (d. 1993) to wonder just "what geometrical method yielded such a length?" The answer, it turns out, is a pentagon with a side of 16.44, circumscribed by the radius of a circle 13.984 m., a "surprising exactness of results." The master mason who laid out the dimensions of the cathedral knew, as did Pythagoras, the relationship between the pentagon and the golden section, the most perfect of proportions. When you are in a church like Chartres you are not, of course, consciously aware of the calculation that went into determining its dimensions. You do sense, however, the balance of its design as something so beautiful and wrapped in mystery as to summon the sacred—numbers as the thoughts of God, to repeat the Augustinian phrase.

ENTERING CHARTRES

ENTERING CHARTRES CATHEDRAL can be something of a surprise. Even on a sunny day, it is darker inside than other Gothic cathedrals. The abundance of original stained glass, which has not been replaced by transparent or patterned grisaille panels, as in many churches brightened in the seventeenth and eighteenth centuries, renders a hushed, deep, blue hue—more a mood than a color—in the narthex or entryway and nave. The glass at Chartres is more deeply saturated with color than elsewhere, the actual panes twice as thick as those in the light-flooded Sainte-Chapelle. In terms of interior design, Chartres differs from Notre-Dame Paris in that the tribune or open gallery level has been eliminated in favor of a triforium, a space above the nave arcade and below the large windows above, which consists of four rounded arches with columns between each of the supporting piers. The triforium cuts a horizontal band around the church at a level equidistant between the nave arcades and the clerestory or upper windows, yielding the impression of studied measure. Again, it is possible to sense the equilibrium of the elevation of Chartres without being aware of the actual dimensions

Labyrinth

of its vertical components or even why the effect of the poise of the whole affects us as it does.

The enormous labyrinth that stretches across the stones of the floor in which it is set between the fourth pillars of the nave elicits further surprise. The labyrinth of Chartres which, along with that of Amiens, is one of only two still in existence, dates to the original construction of the main body of the cathedral in the 1220s. One hundred and thirteen gear-like teeth etch the outside of a circle with a diameter of a little over forty-two feet, while, inside, a complex course of thirty hairpin turns defines the inner itinerary. If you walk the labyrinth of Chartres, you will cover 858 feet from the entrance to the center which, up until the time of the Revolution (1792), displayed a bronze plaque on which was inscribed the motif from Classical mythology of the combat between Theseus and the Minotaur. It also may have shown Ariadne with her ball of thread. By unwinding and rewinding the ball, Ariadne delivered Theseus, who had come to Crete to liberate Athens from the obligation to send its youths as tribute to Cretan King Minos, from the labyrinth where they were devoured.

As in the geometric plotting of the transept crossing and the elevation of the cathedral, there may be an architectural or structural signifi-

cance to the labyrinth whose center is exactly the same distance from the
west door as the door is from the center of the west rose window above,
making the distance between the center of the labyrinth and the center
of the rose the hypotenuse of an isosceles triangle. In the other direction,
a line traced between the center of the curve at the eastern end of the
apse, the center of the north facade, the center of the south facade, and
the center of the labyrinth forms a perfect square.

The meaning and function of the labyrinth are unclear. Some have
suggested that, in the figural thinking of the Middle Ages, Christ can
be seen as a new Theseus, who, descending to the underworld as labyrinth, vanquished the forces of evil in Satan as Minotaur, the Athenian
youths liberated by Theseus from the complicated maze being those
whom Christ redeems. If the labyrinth of Chartres is walked, or even
negotiated on one's knees, it might serve as a miniature pilgrimage route
enabling a journey to Jerusalem, placed on medieval maps at the center
of the world, without leaving home. In the legendary guide to Chartres, Malcolm Miller claims that the labyrinth "symbolizes our journey
through life, culminating not in death, but, in a Christian context, eternal life in Paradise," of which the cathedral offers a foretaste. Alterna-
tively, it has been understood as a means of working one's way out of
the errors—from the Latin *errare*, "to wander"—of the material world.
In the first case, one would begin at the outside and work one's way in,
while in the second, one would presumably start at the center and work
one's way out. There is some evidence that the labyrinth was used in the
late Middle Ages as the site of a ritual dance after baptisms on Easter
Sunday, again, a triumph of Christianity over pagan myth. Local legend
has it that the bishops of Chartres down to this day have had trouble
stopping schoolchildren from playing skipping games on the seductive
pattern of the Chartres maze.

THE STAINED GLASS OF CHARTRES

CHARTRES POSSESSES THE greatest assembly of original stained glass
of any Gothic cathedral, its windows covering twenty-eight thousand
square feet in approximately 170 bays. They are noted for their deep
blue cobalt color, the richness of scenes from both the Hebrew and the
Christian Bible, and for the representation of everyday life in the pan-

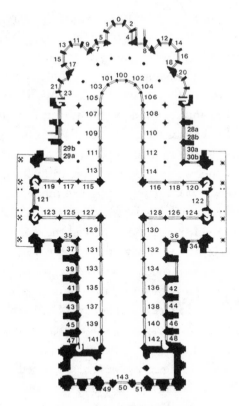

Map of Window Bays

els at the bottom of a large proportion of windows which acknowledge their donors in the same way that gifts to the university or religious and cultural institutions affix plaques with the names of benefactors.

DONOR WINDOWS

Some of the donors belong to the upper echelons of society, their gifts found for the most part in the highest windows. The north rose window was the gift King Louis IX and his mother Blanche of Castile, and the south rose, the offering of Pierre Mauclerc, Count of Dreux, and, by marriage, Duke of Brittany. Thibaut VI, Count of Blois and Chartres (d. 1218), is represented in a number of windows, including the Life of the Virgin (bay 28b), St. Martin (bay 20), and the zodiac and Works of the Months window (bay 28a). Moving down the social ladder, the odd knight appears as a benefactor, as in the Saints Margaret and Catherine window (bay 16), which depicts two knights—Geffroy de Meslay and Guerin de Fraize—identified by the coats of arms on their shields. We also find clerics, as in the Saints Simon and Jude window (bay 1), the Saint Pantaleon window (bay 11) with a cleric by the name of Nicholas Lescene, the Saint Remigius window (bay 12) with an unidentified religious donor, or the signs of the zodiac and Works of the Months window (bay 28a) with its clerical bell ringers alongside Thibaut VI.

While donor windows do appear in other cathedrals, they are by no means as numerous as at Chartres, nor, given the predominantly noble benefactors elsewhere, do they offer such a panorama of the urban trades of those who profited from the building and the daily liturgical life of the medieval church. The majority of donor windows at Chartres feature local merchants and provide a special inventory of medieval material culture. As a grouping, they give the impression of a medieval fair of the type that was held twice a year at Saint-Denis, the Fair of Lendit, as well as at Chartres. These gatherings of merchants who brought their wares to market were sponsored by the local bishop, or, as in the case of the famous fairs of Champagne, by the Count himself, who guaranteed the safety of roads and the fairness of transactions and took a percentage of the profits of exchange. The windows of Chartres are filled with the goods that pilgrims need and consume, beginning with the shoemakers at the bottom of the Good Samaritan window (bay 44) on the south side of the nave. The Parable of the Good Samaritan is a story of a traveler, a pilgrim: "a certain man (*homo quidam*) went down from Jerusalem to Jericho" (Luke 10:30). He was attacked along the road, neglected by a priest and a Levite, and saved by the Good Samaritan. An inscription identifies the pilgrim, but a less clear subtitle appears in the right quadrant of the donor's panels where a group of shoemakers offer their donation to the church, just as Suger appeared in the Tree of Jesse window extending his gift of a stained glass panel to the abbey church of Saint-Denis (see p. 36). The hand of God emerges from a cloud on the upper right, indicating His acceptance of the offering. Pilgrims depend on good shoes, and the cobblers of Chartres stood at the ready.

Alongside the shoemakers stand the suppliers of leather, the tanners of the Saint Thomas Becket window (bay 18) in the first radiating chapel on the south side of the apse and the beltmakers of the Miracles of Saint Nicholas window on the north side of the nave (bay 39). When it comes to shoes and travel, humans are not the only walkers, and we might infer that at least some pilgrims moved about, like Chaucer's Canterbury pilgrims, on horse. Thus, the blacksmiths of Chartres who donated the Typological Passion window (bay 37). On the left, two men, wearing protective body and headgear, stoke a fiery forge with coal from bags; in the middle, dressed in the leather smocks of blacksmiths, they beat redhot metal on an anvil; and, on the right, two farriers saddle a horse while a third holds the reins.

A number of windows display the commodities that pilgrims need when they get to town, beginning with money. There was no universal currency in the twelfth and thirteenth centuries, and each civil authority, beginning with the counts of Champagne, Chartres, and Blois, minted money alongside the denominations in towns which stamped their own coins. The urban origin of coins was reflected in their name such as the *denier Tournois*, the penny from Tours. Upon entering Chartres, pilgrims changed money much as we purchase euros with dollars when entering the eurozone. The street which abuts the south entrance of the cathedral is to this day called the rue des Bancs, the *banc* or bench denoting the money changer's table, and the origin of the word "bank." The Joseph Patriarch window (bay 41) to the left of Saint Nicholas features money changers weighing different currencies in a scale, behind a bench with two sacks filled with coins of different denominations as indicated by their differing colors. This is not Joseph the father of Jesus, but Joseph the Patriarch who in Genesis 41:45 was sold by his brothers into slavery in Egypt, money here being a possible link between the donor and the narrative in glass.

Once supplied with money, pilgrims needed food. The butchers of the Miracles of the Virgin window (bay 38) on the south nave show a butcher killing a pig in the lower right quadrangle and carving a suspended side of meat in the lower left. In the center stands another butcher, knife in hand, with two clients, meat hanging in the background, and, on a table in the foreground, what looks like a sheep's head and a rack of ribs.

Bakers figure in the Lives of the Apostles window (bay 0) in the axial chapel where, in the left quadrant, a man wearing a baker's apron working at a trough kneads bread in a giant mound in whose folds some claim to see the head of Jesus—a humorous play upon the bread of the sacrament. His assistant, dressed in green, brings a pitcher of water, while

Bakers Donor Panel (© Painton Cowen)

bread rises in a cauldron to the right and stretched strands of dough are draped to dry on a pole stretching across the back of the kitchen. In the right quadrant three men roll the dough into round loaves which pass between the two small figures beneath the rolling table. In the panel between the two scenes of bread making, a customer carrying a sack with at least five loaves, hands a coin to the baker behind the counter who hands him a loaf from among the abundance of bread before him as well in a basket on the floor. Bread was important not only for the sacrament, but wheat was a mainstay of the economy of the surrounding region and one of the sources of money that built the cathedral after the fire of 1194. The wealth of the clergy, canons to some extent, but especially the bishop, along with the wealth of the counts of Chartres and Blois, came from the agricultural richness of the wheat belt around Chartres.

Chartres was an important stop along the pilgrimage routes between northern Europe and southern France or Saint James of Compostela in northwest Spain. Many of the donor windows thus involve meeting the comestible needs of travelers, beginning with something to drink. The Mary Magdalene window (bay 46) on the south side of the nave was apparently sponsored by the water carriers of Chartres, and features an image from Luke 7:38 of a woman bathing Christ's feet with her tears and drying them with her hair. But Chartres was also well known for its wines, "clear, healthy, clean, and delicious," in the phrase of Jehan le Marchant who recounts in one of his miracles stories the tale of a mute and a one-eyed man who travel to the cathedral to be cured. The former, "a glutton and a guzzler," became waylaid at the tavern and leaves town just as he came, while his companion, who prayed to the Lady of Chartres in church, regained his power of speech.

WINE

SEASONAL WINE PRODUCTION is depicted in the zodiac window (bay 28a), which shows the harvesting of grapes opposite Libra for the month of September and placing wine in a cask opposite Scorpio for October. Wine, however, takes center stage in the Saint Lubin window (bay 45), the second bay on the north (left) side of the nave as one enters the church. Saint Lubin, born in the sixth century into a rural family near Poitiers, worked as a shepherd. As legend has it, he learned to write from local monks, eventually took religious orders, and worked his way up the ecclesiastical hierarchy to become bishop of Chartres. He was thus one of the most important local saints of the region. But Saint Lubin had also been a cellarer, the man within the monastic community or cathedral chapter responsible for all its provisions, including the wine cellar. You can observe at the bottom of the window dedicated to his honor an image of the so-called wine crier, who, like a circus barker, advertised the wine served in a tavern by calling out its quality and price

Saint Lubin Donor Panel

and sometimes offering free samples. *The Play of Saint Nicholas*, written around 1200 by an author from the town of Arras, features the call of a wine crier:

> *New wine, just freshly broached,*
> *Wine in gallons, wine in barrels,*
> *Smooth and tasty, pure full-bodied . . .*
> *Fresh and strong, full, rich-flavored,*
> *As limpid as a sinner's tears,*
> *It lingers on a gourmet's tongue—*
> *Other folks ought not to touch it.*

Two scenes depicting processions fill out the lower panel, one showing a pilgrim with a wine vessel, while others wait outside of a church, possibly for the arrival of the annual offering of new wine to the chapter storehouse. The round section of glass above illustrates the transportation of wine in a giant barrel mounted on a cart with horse and driver. In the rondel above, a monk, surely Lubin, taps a barrel of wine which flows into his pitcher. In the top full round, two priests perform mass, which emphasizes not only the pleasures of drink but also its liturgical significance, while in the rectangles that run the length of both sides smaller figures extend cups of wine, produced, transported, stored, and served in homage to local viticulture.

The relationship of the tradesmen of Chartres to the windows that show them so vividly at work is a vexed one. Only a few of the lives of the saints in the bays relate, like that of Saint Lubin, to the trade of the donor. The vast majority do not. Are the windows whose donors cater to the needs of pilgrims and of ordinary townspeople to be considered a form of publicity, of thirteenth-century advertising in the most venerated venue in town? What is the relationship between the clerics and individual donors who may even represent trade guilds, though the guild system was not as strong at Chartres as in other urban centers? Did the canons who planned the sculptural and stained glass programs or the bishop approach donors as today's fundraisers or development officers approach wealthy benefactors with the particular needs of universities, hospitals, cultural, and religious institutions, which would explain the lack of connection between the theme of the windows and a specific commercial activity? Jane Welch Williams, who has done the fullest study of the Chartres donor windows, maintains that they express urban tension between the canons of the church and the secular Count of Chartres and Blois. Under such an account, representation of the trades of the town is a means by which the clergy visually asserted religious authority over local merchants and craftsmen.

The donor panels at the bottom of many of the windows celebrate the building trades of Chartres and, indeed, may have been offered by those directly involved in the construction of the cathedral. If we follow these images, which do not necessarily appear in sequence, we can follow the making of the edifice, beginning with the architect or master mason. In the second full panel of the Miracles of the Virgin window (bay 38), a section of glass that was damaged and restored on the south side of the nave, a planner has laid out the blueprint of a cathedral with the recognizable design of transept and apse on his workbench, while an assistant with a rod for laying out ratios looks on. Above them three rondels show oxen pulling a cart to the building site, a man carving moldings, strong bare-chested men carrying stone up ladders, carpenters lifting big tie beams. On top, four masons put the finishing touches on a tower. Masons are shown in the donor portion of the Pope Saint Sylvester (d. 335) window (bay 8) just to the right of the door to the axial chapel. On the left, two hods carry a large block of stone; on the right, an array of moldings, builder's tools, and even the drawing of a column with base and capital shown as if in a sketchbook of architectural design. The middle panel of the donor portion shows two masons completing a building, while a man to the left pounds a large block of stone and his colleague on the right sculpts the delicate features of the statue of a king. Masons at the bottom of the window on the north side of the apse dedicated to Saint Cheron (bay 15), a Roman who was martyred at Chartres, are shown on the left cutting and dressing stone, while on the right, sculptors prepare two statues of royals of the type that can be seen on the gallery of kings above the porch of the southern transept.

The Saint Julian the Hospitaller window (bay 21) in the radiating chapel on the north side of the apse is one of several windows donated by carpenters, one of whom sharpens an adze and the other of whom works on a barrel in the middle donor quadrant. To the right two men are bent over workbenches in a workroom filled with woodworking tools on the wall, and, on the left, two woodworkers put the finishing touches on a

roof frame fixed to solid masonry—columns, capital friezes, arches—
below. Again, though images of cathedral construction appear in medieval manuscript illustrations, the *Chronicles of Saint-Denis*, in particular,
nothing matches the breadth and detail of the celebration of the building
trades at Chartres.

NOAH

To THE LEFT of the Saint Lubin window, the Noah window (bay 47)
was also donated by carpenters who have a special relationship to the
Noah story. In the lower left donor quadrant, a man sharpens an adze
for woodworking; in the right lower quadrant, a cooper, wooden mallet in hand, pounds into place the rings of a barrel; and in the middle,
two men strip the bark off a tree to make lumber. The similarity of the
first two of these images to those of the Saint Julien the Hospitaller window makes them appear as set pieces, possibly even from a pattern book.
Together, the preparation of lumber and the making of a barrel allude
to the principal themes above—the construction of the ark and Noah's
predilection for wine.

Two quatrefoils above the donor's panel of the Noah window illustrate the portion from Genesis 6:4: "Now giants were upon the earth
in those days," as do the two marginal semi-circles above them, both
of which contain giants towering over others. In the first full central
diamond panel, God warns Noah, "Make thee an ark of timber planks"
(Genesis 6:14), which occupies the second full diamond above two quatrefoils, one of which shows Noah's three sons, Shem, Ham, and Japeth,
while the other shows his wife with her three daughters-in-law. Moving up the center of the window, Noah, wielding an adze like that in
the left quadrant of the donor section, is shown building the ark, which
is a prime model not only for the ark of the covenant in the Hebrew
Bible, but for the nave—from the Latin *navus* for "boat"—of the cathedral. The lateral semi-circles portray Noah, still dressed as he was in his
encounter with God, instructing his wife to enter the ark, while animals
on the other side gather in pairs, a process which continues in the two
quatrefoils above. In the next full diamond, the ark, built as per God's
instructions, with a window, features a hull in the shape of a cathedral.
The columns, capitals, and courses of stone supporting the cabins above
acknowledge the assimilation of church and ark. The semi-circles on

Noah Window

the edge along with the quatrefoils on each side depict the flood in which men and animals float like debris on violently undulant waves of water. The diamond on top of the quatrefoils features a dove released from the window, while, above that, Noah sticks his head out, and the animals issue from the ark.

Panels concerned with Noah's life after the flood dominate the top portion of the window. Thus, he harvests grapes and makes wine, as per Genesis 9:20: "And Noah a husbandman began to till the ground, and planted a vineyard." In the opposite semicircle, Noah drinks: "and drinking of the wine was made drunk, and was uncovered in his tent." The diamond between the making of wine and his drinking from a cup in the lateral semi-circles shows Noah dismissing his son Ham for having looked upon his nakedness, while the other two sons cover him with his cloak. The top diamond depicts Noah and his wife on their knees under a rainbow. God on high renews the covenant with man: "I will set my bow in the clouds, and it shall be the sign of a covenant between me and between the earth" (Genesis 9:13). Standing in front of the Noah window, I often see tourist guides telling the Genesis story by moving up the wall with a laser pointer just as preachers and teachers in the Middle Ages might have brought Noah and his family to life by pointing with their fingers. There is no more powerful example of the Gothic cathedral as a bible for those seeking knowledge than the narrative Noah window set in the north nave wall of Chartres.

JESUS ON THE WEST WALL

THE STAINED GLASS on the west wall of Chartres dates from the twelfth century and shows a high rounded bay flanked by two smaller ones, mirroring the three portal entrances of the church on the other side, with a rose window on top. The right bay displays the Tree of Jesse, with seven square panels, including those of Jesse and Jesus, and a total of fourteen intermediaries in the genealogical chain between the two, some with their names written on the scrolls they hold in their hands. (For a description of the Jesse Tree window, see that of Saint-Denis, which was copied from Chartres, pp. 36–38). The large central window is laid out in twenty-four squares with and without pearl-like circles within them. In keeping with the capital frieze that runs the breadth of the royal portal, each represents a familiar scene from the Infancy of Jesus to be read from left to right and from bottom to top—from the Annunciation, Visitation, and Nativity in the lowest row, to the Adoration of the Magi which takes up three panes in the middle, to the Presentation in the Temple, Massacre of the Innocents, Flight into Egypt, Baptism in the Jordan, and, in the top row, the Entrance into Jerusalem. Atop it all, Mary, flanked by angels, sits, as she does on the tympanum of the south portal on the other side of the west wall, in the *sedes sapientiae* position, looking out on high over the length of the cathedral.

The left window of the west wall is filled with scenes of the Passion and Resurrection in fourteen panels of double pearl-like circles, from the Transfiguration on Mount Tabor (Matthew 17:1), to Christ's explanation of the Transfiguration to His disciples on the bottom two panes, to the Last Supper and Washing of the Disciples' Feet in the second row, to the Betrayal of Judas and the Flagellation, to the Crucifixion and the Deposition, the Entombment and the Three Marys at the Tomb, to the scene of *Noli me tangere* after the Resurrection in which Jesus says to Mary Magdalene, who has recognized Him before the empty tomb, "Do not touch me: for I am not yet ascended to my Father" (John 20:17). In the top portion of the Passion and Resurrection window, the apostles receive news of the Resurrection, Jesus meets two disciples on the road to Emmaus, and dines with them there. Thus, the stained glass of the west wall of Chartres traces the prehistory and the unfolding of the Christological drama from the genealogy of Jesus's royal ancestors to his death, Resurrection, and Ascension: "And it came to pass, whilst he was at table with them, he took bread and blessed and brake and gave to them. And their eyes were opened: and they knew him. And he vanished out of their sight" (Luke 24:30–31).

The place to which Jesus vanishes is represented in the rose window above, a starburst of great globes, limned by smaller circles and lopsided lozenges radiating from the center where Christ sits in majesty, streams of blood still flowing from the wounds in His upturned hands. If you look closely, you will see that the inner circles of the lozenges, which appear as belted circles of unequal size, house eight angels in pairs interspersed with the four evangelists represented, as in the tympanum over the central portal, as the Tetramorph: the eagle above Christ's head, John; the winged man at six o'clock, Matthew; the winged lion on His right, Mark; and the winged ox on His left, Luke. Above Christ's head, in the larger of the belted circles, Abraham, rocking souls in his bosom, is surrounded by cherubim with multiple wings. The twelve apostles sit in pairs in the circles beneath them, while the drama of the Last Judgment, which we have encountered only in stone at Saint-Denis and Notre-Dame Paris (see pp. 19, 78–81), unfurls in the bottom halves of the lozenges and outer circles. In the outer ring, between two thirty and four thirty on the right and seven thirty and nine thirty on the left, souls emerge from their tombs. At six o'clock on the larger lozenge circle, Saint Michael weighs souls that are led to paradise on Christ's right, and, on the left, are prodded off to perdition by a devil wielding a pitchfork. The tortures of hell continue in the bottom two circles of the outer row, which show a giant Hell's mouth and rack upon which two devils break the bodies of sinners. In the upper four outer circles, angels sound trumpets to signal the end of human time, while at the very top they carry the instruments of the Passion—cross, lance, nails, and crown of thorns. The west rose is an iconographic jumble which cannot be read sequentially. The story of the Passion is mixed with that of the Last Judgment such that, in order to follow either story or to connect them, your eye must jump from the center to the first circle of lozenges, from the lozenges to the outer circle, from top to bottom, and back, with an overall effect of a mixing of human time and eternity, a collapse of time upon itself, in a great visual dramatization of the unfolding and the stakes of the Last Judgment at the end of human time.

THE ROSES OF CHARTRES

THE GREAT ROSE WINDOWS of Chartres, created around the same time as those in Notre-Dame Paris, are not only their match, but certain elements of the Paris windows, heavily damaged, were copied from those of Chartres (see pp. 83–86). The Chartres north rose was the gift of Blanche of Castile, mother of Louis IX, whose heraldic sign, the yellow Castile castle, is mixed with Louis's sign, the fleur-de-lys, in the four small lancets between the giant round main window and the five large pointed lancets below. The intertwining of the emblems of mother and son attests to their closeness. An image of Saint Anna, who holds a scepter capped by a fleur-de-lys in one hand and her daughter Mary in the other, fills the center of the north rose, which is dotted with fleurs-de-lys, ample testimony to the intertwining of church and state. The trumeau in the portal below this massive window shows Mary and Anna, whose head was part of the large cache of relics to reach the West after the Conquest of Constantinople in 1204. Louis, Count of Blois, sent it to his wife Catherine of Clermont shortly before his death at the Battle of Adrianople in 1205, and Catherine presented Anna's head to the cathedral of Chartres where it remained the most important relic after Mary's tunic. The north rose lays out a thematic and figural program according to which the Hebrew Bible prefigures the Christian Bible, which is a fulfillment of the earlier text. Thus, Christ is surrounded in the first ring by four doves and eight angels, and, in the second, by His ancestors, twelve kings of Judah seated in the squares of the second ring, which is, in turn, enclosed by twelve minor prophets in semicircles. Twelve quatrefoils with fleurs-de-lys fill the space between the prophets and kings.

The lancet windows below the north rose feature Saint Anna with Mary in the center, over a shield with fleurs-de-lys. The mother-daughter pair is flanked on both sides by virtuous Old Testament figures, priests and kings who prefigure Christ, above smaller figures, or Antichrists. On the left, Melchizedek, the king-priest who offered bread and wine to Abraham and for this reason was considered a forerunner of Jesus, with a chalice representing the virtue of faith, dominates King Nebudchanezzar who embodies the vice of idolatry, as per Daniel 3:1:

"King Nebudchanezzar made a statue of gold, of sixty cubits high, and six cubits broad, and he set it up in the plain of Dura, of the province of Babylon." Between Melchizedek and Saint Anna stands King David with his harp above his father-in-law King Saul, who in the eleventh-century BCE committed suicide before a battle. To the right of Anna is David's son Solomon above mad King Jeroboam, another idolater worshiping golden calves; and, on the extreme right, the high priest Aaron, Moses's brother, looms over Pharaoh who is depicted falling into the Red Sea. As we have seen in the depiction of virtues and vices in stone around the central entrance and in glass in the west rose of Notre-Dame Paris, positive values—faith, courage, wisdom—placed visually above negative ones—idolatry, cowardice, tyranny—translates into moral superiority.

THE SOUTH ROSE

THE VISUAL PROGRAM of Chartres culminates in the south rose window. Christ in majesty sits in the middle, surrounded by eight censing angels; between them, the Tetramorph or signs of the evangelists, as on the central tympanum of the royal portal. They, in turn, are surrounded by twenty-four elders of the Apocalypse, holding in their hands a variety of musical instruments "golden vials full of odours, which are the prayers of saints" (Apocalypse 5:8). The donor of the south rose, Pierre Mauclerc, Count of Dreux and, by marriage, Duke of Brittany, was a great enemy of Louis IX and Blanche of Castile, having revolted against Louis's succession at the age of twelve. His heraldic device, a blue-and-yellow checkered shield, can be seen at the bottom of the central lancet as well as in the quatrefoils between the second ring and the outer half-circles of the rose proper. Pierre and his family are portrayed on either side of the base of the other four lancets: Pierre to the right, kneeling, while his son John stands on the far right; Pierre's wife Alix de Thouars kneels to the left, their daughter Yolande standing, in symmetry with her brother John, on the far left.

The central lancet shows Mary with Child in response to Anna with Mary as child in the north rose. She is surrounded by four major prophets of the Hebrew Bible supporting on their shoulders the four evangelists of the Christian Bible: Jeremiah carries Luke; Isaiah, Matthew; Ezekiel, John; Daniel, Mark. The iconography of the lancets summons in the very place that it originated the celebrated sentence of Bernard of Char-

South Rose

tres. "We are like dwarfs perched on the shoulders of giants," Bishop
John of Salisbury quotes his fellow teacher at Chartres as saying. "We
see more and farther than our predecessors, not because we have keener
vision or greater height, but because we are lifted up and borne aloft on
their gigantic stature." The co-presence of New Testament evangelists
and Old Testament prophets collapses the difference between the past, in
which the future is latent, and the present, which is a fulfillment, both a
realization and an understanding, of the past. The lancet windows of the

south transept of Chartres affirm the deepest cathedral effect—an abolition of time by space, the sensation, in the phrase of Augustine, that the present is "a moving image of eternity."

HEBREW AND CHRISTIAN BIBLES

THE RELATION OF THE Hebrew and Christian Bibles, the one prefiguring the other, which fulfills it, is nowhere more dramatically declared than in the sculptural program of the outside of the north transept. Of the three deeply recessed porches which make up the north portal, the central entryway displays ten jamb statues arranged symmetrically in a ring structure on either side of the door. On the outer far left of the ring, Melchizedek, the priest-king of Salem who in Genesis 14:18 "brings forth bread and wine" to bless Abraham, bears in one hand a chalice with wine and bread, and, in the other, a censer which accompanies the sacrifice. Melchizedek, who stands on a small sculpted animal that was disfigured by the destruction in the aftermath of the French Revolution, is paired on the far right with Saint Peter whose chalice, also broken, contains Christ's blood, as prefigured by the intervening figures. Peter, holding his emblematic keys, wears on his chest the Old Testament priestly breastplate and the pallium of a medieval archbishop, signs of his yoking of the two traditions. On his head, Peter, the first pope, wears the conical pope's hat. His feet are perched on a rock sculpted of stone, as in Matthew 16:18, where Christ plays on the Latin *petrus*, meaning both "Peter" and "rock": "Thou art Peter, and upon this rock I will build my church."

Next to Melchizedek in the ring structure, the figure of Abraham stands with a sword in his right hand and his left hand curled around the neck and cheek of his son Isaac, whom he has been commanded by God to sacrifice. The child's hands are crossed in front of him and his feet are bound, as on the point of death. Yet, Abraham's head is cocked to the right where, under the canopy over Melchizedek's head "an angel of the Lord from heaven called to him saying: Abraham, Abraham. . . . Lay not thy hand upon the boy. . . . Abraham lifted up his eyes, and saw behind his back a ram, amongst the briers, sticking fast by the horns, which he took for a holocaust instead of his son" (Genesis 22:11–13). In the rendering on the north portal of Chartres, Abraham stands with one foot on the back of a ram and the other on the thick bush in which the

North Entrance Jamb Statues (Left)

ram is stuck. On the other side of the door, juxtaposed symmetrically to the figure of Abraham and the aborted sacrifice of his only son, stands the figure of Saint John the Baptist, his face emaciated by fasting, and his cloak hiding the skins worn emblematically by John in the desert. John holds in his hands a plate with the Lamb of God, symbol of Christ's sacrifice, in response to Abraham's sacrificial ram.

In the middle on the left side of the door, Moses holds one of the tablets of the Old Law and points on top of a column capped by a floral frieze to the bronze serpent, which cures those bitten by snakes at the end of the golden calf episode of the Jews wandering in the desert. The Moses window of Saint-Denis contains a similar image along with Abbot Suger's explanation of the meaning of the bronze serpent—"Just as the brazen serpent slays all serpents / So Christ, raised on the Cross, slays His enemies"—along with the general principle of the relation between the Old Law and the New: "What Moses veils the doctrine of Christ unveils. They who despoil Moses bare the Law" (see p. 45). In the symmetrical position on the right, Simeon holds the baby Jesus. If Moses bears in his hands the Old Law, Simeon, who presented Jesus in

North Entrance Jamb Statues (Right)

the temple, holds the New Law. Having said that he will not die before the arrival of the Messiah, Simeon, at the moment of presentation in the temple, reveals the child as Savior and thus "despoils" Moses.

Moving still within the ring structure, to the right of Moses, Moses's brother Aaron holds a lamb which he is ready to sacrifice with the knife in his right hand. The human figure below his feet stands ready to catch the blood which will mark the door posts of the houses of the Jews at the moment of their liberation from Egypt. The figure on the right side of the door, symmetrical with Aaron, has been identified as Jeremiah, the weeping prophet, who foretells the replacement of the old covenant by the new:

> Behold the days shall come, saith the Lord, and I will make a new covenant with the house of Israel, and with the house of Juda. . . . Not according to the covenant which I made with their fathers, in the day that I took them by the hand to bring them out of the land of Egypt. . . . But this shall be the covenant: . . . I will give my law in their bowels, and I will write it in their heart" (Jeremiah 31:31–33).

At the feet of Jeremiah sits a small figure whose hand on his face, the image of grief, renders in the medieval language of gestures, the prophet's lamentations.

To the immediate left of the door, King David, without his emblematic harp, bears a lance in his right hand and, it is thought, once held the other instruments of the Passion in his left hand, which is missing. In the equivalent position to the immediate right of the door, Isaiah stands atop a sleeping Jesse, from whose root (*virga*), it will be remembered, stems the genealogical tree which passes through the Virgin (*Virgo*), and Jesus— from *virga* to *Virgo*, as from Jesse to Jesus. In the archivolts above, and all around the central portal of the north transept, an arched sculptural Tree of Jesse accompanies the stained glass Tree of Jesse on the inside.

"LA BELLE VERRIÈRE"

BACK INSIDE THE CHURCH, the first window on the south side of the apse, known as the Belle Verrière (bay 30a), is an iconic image of Chartres. The upper panels which depict the Virgin in the *sedes sapientiae* pose are from the twelfth century. The lower four rows of triple panels as well as the glass framing the Virgin survived and were reinstalled after the fire of 1194. The bottom three panels tell the story in images of the Temptation of Christ in the desert. Having fasted for forty days, He met a "tempter" who, "coming said to Him: If you be the Son of God, command that these stones be made bread" (Matthew 4:3). In the left lower quadrant, the devil points to a stone, which invites the famous response, "Not in bread alone doth man live" (4:4). The tempter then brings Christ "into the holy city, and set him upon the pinnacle of the temple" (4:5), asking Him to cast Himself down, a scene shown in the middle of the bottom row where Christ's feet are delicately poised on the roof of what could be one of the pinnacles of a Gothic cathedral. The devil's finger again points downward. In the right bottom quadrant, Christ, with raised hand, dismisses the tempter: "Begone, Satan; for it is written: The Lord thy God shalt thou adore, and him only shalt thou serve" (4:10).

The three panels in the second row depict, on the left, the arrival of Christ with two disciples at the wedding at Cana, and, on the right, the arrival of Mary. In the middle panel, the betrothed, in conversation with each other, are attended by servants. The table set before them is

"La Belle Verrière" Window

shown in exquisite detail, with fruit, bread, knives, and a pitcher for wine. When the wine has "failed," Jesus asks that the six "waterpots of stone, according to the manner of the purifying of the Jews," be filled with water and carried to the chief steward of the feast. Upon tasting the water made wine, the steward is astonished by "this beginning of miracles did Jesus in Cana of Galilee and manifested his glory. And his disciples believed in him" (John 2:6, 11). Though the Temptation of Christ and the Wedding at Cana may seem unrelated at first, they are linked through the devil's challenge to turn stone to bread and Christ's transformation of water into wine. Neither, however, relates to the Belle Verrière, and their presence below it may have more to do with the insertion of framing panels of a suitable size than with thematic intent.

The top panels of la Belle Verrière show Mary holding Jesus on her lap, the painting on glass highlighting the clothes that she wore at the time of His birth and the prime relic of Chartres. The part of the window containing Mother and Child against a garnet background was apparently placed originally in the axis of the choir but was moved after the fire of 1194 to look over that place in the apse where the tunic was kept in a great reliquary chest. Mary's crown, a band of gold with jewels topped by fleurs-de-lys, resembles that worn by Charles the Bald, donor of the tunic, in a portrait from around the middle of the ninth century. Jesus raises His right hand in the gesture of benediction, while His left hand holds an open book. Mary points with her finger to the passage in the written text from Luke 3:5, *Omnis Vallis Implebitur* ("Every valley shall be filled"), the basis of a liturgical refrain sung at Chartres during Advent. She is surrounded by active angels, some holding candles, others swinging censers, including the two large incense pots on either side of her head. Below, four angels supporting columns with floral capital friezes hold up the pedestal on which Mary rests her feet as well as the throne or seat of wisdom. French novelist and Minister of Culture André Malraux declared the Belle Verrière "the pinnacle of western painting before Giotto." Indeed, though her face has been reworked over the centuries, most recently in 1906, she is the Mona Lisa of the Middle Ages.

To the immediate right of the Belle Verrière, a window (28b), offered by a knight on horseback who is pictured in the right donor quadrant, and monks pruning vines, on the right, tells the familiar story of the Virgin's parents, Anna and Joachim, the birth and betrothal of Mary, and the Nativity and Childhood of Jesus, ending with the Massacre of the Innocents and the Flight into Egypt. The Life of the Virgin window is situated directly across from the sculptural version of the same story a little above eye level all along the eighteen-foot-high barrier separating the open space of the ambulatory from the closed space reserved for the stalls of the canons, and stretching almost one thousand feet around the choir. Begun in 1514, and only completed around 1727, the elaborate carvings, punctuated by buttress statues of God the Father, Fulbert, and other bishops of Chartres, are separated into fifteen bays which narrate in statuettes a Marian cycle divided into forty tableaux, beginning with the Annunciation of the birth of the Virgin to Joachim and Anna, to the Nativity and Passion of Christ, to a Pietà after the Crucifixion, and, finally, on the north side of the choir, the Dormition, Ascension, and Coronation of the Virgin seated in heaven.

CLOCKS AND THE
MEASUREMENT OF TIME

Over the door on the south side of the high screen, an elaborate astrolabic clock from the first quarter of the fifteenth century, partially destroyed in the Revolution and restored in 2009, tells the twenty-four hours of the day along with the phases of the moon and the astrological signs of the year. Time in the Middle Ages was measured with graduated candles, hour glasses, or sundials. The advent of the clock in the fourteenth century, however, signaled a world-historical shift—an opening to the night and a liberation from the uneven canonical hours that divided the cycles of the day into uneven portions depending on the season. So radical was clock time, "bourgeois time," in the phrase of Jacques Le Goff, that it was one of the contributing factors, along with the return of money, for the rise of cities and the economic necessity of calculating with precision the length of loans, interest, and debt, in the High Middle Ages. Even poets like Jean Froissart (d. 1405), who was also known as an historian or chronicler, recognized the importance of the clock: "An instrument very fair and very notable, / And it is also agreeable and profitable; / For night and day it teaches us the hours . . . / In the absence even of the sun." The face of the astrolabic clock of Chartres, consisting of an outer rim of gold stars upon an azure field, measures the lunar cycle, which appears through a round opening whose shifting shapes follow the phases of the moon. Inside the rim of stars and the moon, the signs of the zodiac with their Latin names follow the astrological cycles of the sun. A single hand indicates the hours of the day in Roman numerals around the clock's outer edge, the minute hand an innovation of the late Middle Ages.

Directly across from the astrolabic clock, a luscious stained glass rendering of the zodiac and Works of the Months is topped by the adult Christ, arm raised in benediction and holding a book, as in the Belle Verrière. He is flanked by the Greek letters Alpha and Omega. Christ and God are marked in the Apocalypse of Saint John by the first and last letters of the Greek alphabet: "I am Alpha and Omega, the beginning and the end, saith the Lord God" (1:8 and also 21:6 and 22:13). This looping of time upon itself refers, of course, to the great sweep of Christian history, the end of time after the Last Judgment when it will be as before the Creation, but can also be seen in the cycle of the seasons pictured in the circular and quatrefoil patterns below. The Works of the Months are a reminder of the middle or human time during which, after the Fall and before the Second Coming, man earns his bread by the sweat of his brow. Two images, however, depict a different kind of labor. The lowest circle on the right shows the image of a knight with a lance and shield in one hand and his other hand raised to the crowd of those whom it was the knight's duty to protect. This is Count Thibaut VI of Blois, who, having fought the Moors in Spain, contracted leprosy there and died childless in 1218. The northern part of his land holdings were carved into the county of Chartres. The quatrefoil for the month of May depicts a knight on campaign, alongside Gemini, the twins, whose astrological sign runs from May 21 to June 20, the period during which military campaigns were traditionally launched. Together, the two images of knights and their horses remind us that Chartres was born at the time and in the spirit of the Crusades, which are represented both in sculpture and stained glass throughout the cathedral.

CHARLEMAGNE AT CHARTRES

A WINDOW FACING EAST at the corner of the south transept and the choir (bay 116) features an image of Saint Denis, patron saint of France, handing a lance with a banner to a knight who, identified by his coat of arms, is Jean Clément who became marshal of France in 1225. And not just any banner. This is the "vexillum," the "oriflamme" or standard of France, which, according to legend, descended directly from heaven. Pope Leo III bestowed the vexillum of Rome upon the Emperor Charlemagne in 798 or 799 CE. In the first French epic, *The Song of Roland*, composed around the time and in the military mood of the First Crusade (1098 CE), the oriflamme went into battle with Charlemagne and his crusading troops: " 'Muntjoie!' they shout. Charlemagne is with them! / Gefrei d'Anjou carries the Oriflamme: / it was Saint Peter's once, and called Romaine, / but in that battle it got the name 'Muntjoie.' " Saint-Denis, as the chief sanctuary of France, was the keeper of the oriflamme, which was as powerful a symbol of the crusader spirit at the time of the seventh crusade as it was at the outset. On June 12, 1248, King Louis IX went to Saint-Denis where he received the pilgrim's pouch and staff and raised the oriflamme to signal that the royal army was on the march.

The Charlemagne window (bay 7), situated between the axial and

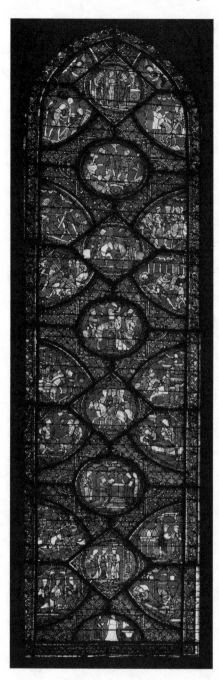

Charlemagne Window

the first radiating chapel in the northeastern part of the apse, celebrates the military victories of the emperor along with his translation of relics from Constantinople to the imperial seat at Aix-la-Chapelle, today's Aachen, Germany. From Aachen, as we know, the gift of a book, the *Celestial Hierarchies* attributed to Pseudo-Dionysius, went via Charlemagne's grandson Charles the Bald to Saint-Denis, as the holy tunic of the Virgin went to Chartres. The Charlemagne window acknowledges in its donor panels the guild of furriers, showing as it does a merchant holding up a garment, flecked with tracings of pelts, for the inspection of a client, while skins are draped over a table and hang on the wall. The scenes depicted in the panels above follow the narrative arc of several Latin and Old French works, combined and recombined in the glass designer's mind. These recount the emperor's fictive journey to the Middle East to aid his homologue, the emperor of Constantinople, along with his expedition to Spain to stop the despoiling of the tomb of Saint James at the pilgrimage site, still operative, of Saint James of Compostela.

The series begins in the lower right with the dream of the Byzantine emperor, brought by an angel, of Charlemagne's arrival bearing the oriflamme of France. Right from the start, and throughout, the French are recognizable by their lozenge-shaped shields and cylindrical helmets, while the enemy sport round shields and conical headgear. As we move up the quadrants and round panels, Charlemagne receives emissaries from the East and is welcomed in Constantinople where he fights the pagan foe. While in the Holy Land, according to the poet of an epic, *The Pilgrimage of Charlemagne to Jerusalem*, he asks the patriarch of Jerusalem to give him "some of your holy relics, which I shall take back to France, for I wish the country to be illuminated by them." The patriarch offered him Saint Simeon's arm, the head of Saint Lazarus, some of the blood of Saint Stephen, a piece of the shroud Jesus wore in the sepulchre, "one of the nails from his feet, the holy crown from his head, and the chalice which he blessed." Charles offered in return a pledge of friendship, as "feelings of joy and compassion welled up within him." These are significant relics, as fragments of the crown of thorns, Christ's shroud, and Saint Simeon's arm, the very limb which held Jesus at the Presentation in the Temple, were all claimed by the abbey church of Saint-Denis. Here, Chartres seems to be "piggy-backing," according to Stuart Whatling, on Saint-Denis to validate its own most valuable relic, the holy tunic.

The second quadrant on the right shows Charlemagne, who has traveled from Jerusalem to Constantinople, in the presence of the Byzantine emperor, who, with one hand on Charlemagne's shoulder and his arm outstretched, bestows upon him three reliquary boxes in the shape of miniature churches on an altar built upon columns which taper in floral capital friezes. In the full circle above, Charlemagne deposits in his capital a reliquary in the shape of a crown, presumably containing part of the crown of thorns, as two monks and a young man who is possibly his beloved nephew Roland look on. The identity of Roland is affirmed by the signal horn or "olifant," made from the tusk of an elephant, which hangs on the wall. The reliquaries seen in the panel below are now safely home and rest in niches between the pillars of the church behind him. The dome-shaped roof resembles, in distinction to a Gothic cathedral, Charlemagne's basilica at Aachen.

In the right quadrant above, Charlemagne is visited in his sleep by Saint James who, according to a Latin chronicle known as the *Pseudo-Turpin*, complains that his "body lies forgotten in Galicia, a place still shamefully oppressed by the Saracens." Charlemagne's dream, which needs no analysis, is nonetheless interpreted in the left-hand quadrant by two men, one of whom wears the hat associated with Jews and points upward to a purple-and-white band in the sky, which we know from literary sources is the Milky Way. Though weary of war, the emperor sets out on a Spanish expedition, shown in the round panel above. The historical Charlemagne participated in the reconquest of Muslim Spain in the last quarter of the eighth century. There, he prays before the city of Pamplona, known today more for the running of the bulls than for the eighth-century Muslim occupation, in preparation for attacking the city, whose walls, which "by God's concession and through the prayers of Saint James, fell as their foundations crumbled." In the round panel above, the emperor on horseback, finger raised in a gesture of command, directs hods carrying stones up a ladder and masons laying them in courses on top of a structure laced with flying buttresses in a portrayal of the building of a Gothic church in the stained glass of the queen of Gothic cathedrals.

The top of the Charlemagne crusade window depicts battles against the Saracen foe, including the iconic bifurcated image of the last stand of the hero Roland who, as part of the rear guard of the French army returning from Spain to France, finds himself trapped by the enemy in a tight pass in the Pyrenees. He attempts, on the left, to break his sword against a rock so it will not fall into pagan hands, and, on the right, blows a signal horn to summon the aid of his uncle Charlemagne. Though the fictional Roland was never portrayed as a saint, he is shown near the top of the bay with a red nimbus around his head as the hand of God descends from the top of the rondel to take his soul to heaven in a mixture of heroism and saintliness.

The top round panel of the Charlemagne window is shrouded in a mystery connected to the emperor's confession to Saint Giles, who founded the Abbey of Saint-Gilles-du-Gard, on the route home from Saint James of Compostela, though the historic Saint Giles died around 710 CE, almost forty years before Charlemagne's birth. James of Voragine recounts in *The Golden Legend*: "As they were speaking together of the things of the soul, the king begged the saint to pray for him because he had committed an enormous sin, which he durst not confess to anyone, not even to the saint himself." Charlemagne sits within the framing columns and arches of a church, his head bowed in a gesture of repentance. In the top right a scroll passes from the hands of an angel to those of Saint Giles who stands before an altar just as in James of Voragine's account. God sends a message "wheron was written the king's sin, Giles's prayer, and God's pardon." The cup bearing wine as well as the priest standing between Giles and Charlemagne indicate that this is a portrait of the celebrated Mass of Saint Giles (not the painting of the Mass of Saint Giles discussed above) associated with the revelation of the emperor's sin of having slept with his sister, from which coupling Roland, who is not a nephew but a son, was born, his death being an expiation of the sin of incest. Nor does the entwining of conquest and incest end with the Charlemagne window on the inside of the church. The Mass of Saint Giles appears in the sculptural program of the south facade of Chartres in the lower register of the four voussoirs above the right door.

CATHEDRALS AND CRUSADE

CRUSADE IS AT THE ORIGIN of the embarrassment of reliquary riches of Chartres. Though Charlemagne may have been personally sinful, he is forgiven in glass and sculpture on the inside and outside walls of the church, and he is the source of the holy tunic, the "gem and the glory of the city" (Jehan le Marchant), brought as booty from his fictitious expedition to the Middle East. Louis of Blois sent the head of Saint Anna back to his wife Catherine, who consigned it to the great reliquary chest behind the altar (see p. 134). Secular and religious heroism are staged all around the three deeply recessed porches of the south portal, which acknowledge the relationship between cathedral construction and war.

The jamb statue to the far left of the left door, a later addition to the original plan of the early thirteenth century, has been identified as Roland. Dressed in a coat of mail, the hero of epic holds a lance in his right hand, a shield covered with fleurs-de-lys in his right hand, a sword girded at his side. Saints Stephen, Clement, and Lawrence complete the series to the left of the door. Each is identifiable by the scene represented in stone below their feet: Stephen by a man in a Jewish hat, a member of the Sanhedrin court that condemned him to be stoned; Pope Clement, who was drowned in the Black Sea around 100 CE, by the receding of water and, according to James of Voragine, "a small house which the Lord had built in the fashion of a marble temple." Lawrence, usually associated with the grill on which he was tortured, is pictured here above a small devil who grabs by the neck the saint's torturer, the emperor Valerian, known for indulging in sorcery. On the right side of the door, the figures of Saints

Vincent, Denis, and Rusticus. In symmetry with Roland on the outer edge, Saint George, the slayer of dragons, is shown at the base of the wheel of swords on which he died. Portraits of martyrs and scenes of martyrdom limn the tympanum, which focuses upon the lapidation of Saint Stephen, to whom Christ in the upper register extends His benediction.

The central porch of the south portal of Chartres holds the Last Judgment reserved for the west facade in other cathedrals, the site of the end of the day, end of life, and the end of human time. The trumeau features a *Beau Dieu*, "Beautiful Christ," holding an ornate book, his feet on a lion and a dragon, the whole subtended by a sculpted base on which bakers carry large baskets of bread, donors in part or wholly of the sculptural program. Saints fill the jamb niches on either side of the door with Christ of the Last Judgment in the tympanum and the Resurrection of the Dead on the second level of the voussoirs. The saved and the damned process in opposite directions on the left and the right sides of the lintel, their march to heaven and hell spilling over to the first level of the voussoirs which, on the right, show particularly graphic examples of the devil seizing the souls of recognizable social types—a noble lady wearing a toque, a nun with her wimple, a moneylender with a purse around his neck, and a naked prostitute tossed over the back of a devil with donkey's ears. To the left, Abraham with the traditional three souls in a sling leads a procession of angels, each of which, in turn, bears a naked, socially indeterminate, figure to eternal salvation. A highly coded order of angels out of the *Celestial Hierarchies* of the Pseudo-Dionysius is arranged in the voussoirs around the tympanum: Seraphins or "burning ones," their hands aflame, on the right of the first ring, Cherubins on the left; seated Thrones wearing crowns and holding scepters around the second ring; crowned Dominations on the left of the third row, and Principalities, head uncovered, on the right; Powers standing and holding books on the left of the fourth row; and Virtues with lances standing on dragons on the right. Archangels and angels waving censers and holding candles in the fifth and outer ring complete the angelic choir.

In its most distinctive features, Chartres integrates more fully than any other cathedral the three orders of medieval society. "The community of the faithful is a single body, but the condition of society is threefold in order," Bishop Adalberon of Laon (d. 1030) wrote to King Robert II, the Pious, of France (d. 1031) sometime around 1020 in a letter that distinguished between those who pray, those who work, and those who fight. Devotion to prayer, extended to study, is written upon the west facade of the church in the spectacular depiction of the seven liberal arts around the door of the right portal. The contributions of serfs and peasants, "who," Adalberon continues, "provide money, clothes, and food, for the rest," is to be found among the Works of the Months. Extended to the urban trades that catered to pilgrims and that built the cathedral, manual labor looms large in the donor windows throughout. And the military mission, "the warriors and the protectors of the churches, the defenders of the people, both great and small," extended to cover the call to crusade, is featured in glass and stone both inside and outside of the cathedral, but nowhere more powerfully than on the south facade. This third entrance to the church is dominated by heroes and martyrs from the first centuries of Christianity, not only those who appear in the jamb statues on either side of the doors, in the tympana above the doors, and the surrounding voussoirs, but around the deep porches on either side. The outer pillars and the archways between the pillars and the doors are covered by an army of muscular Christians—musicians from the Apocalypse of Saint John, saints, confessors, martyrs, and powerful popes who serve as a reminder of the crusaders who enriched the cathedral and the martyrs who defended it. No one, however, was more aware of such an economy of salvation than Louis IX, the crusading king who staged his own sainthood in the theater of the Sainte-Chapelle to which we now turn.

CHAPTER

4

SAINTE-CHAPELLE
The King's Chapel

SAINTE-CHAPELLE.
IO BOULEVARD DU PALAIS, PARIS IE.

Access by subway (Cité) or by foot through courtyard of French Su-
preme Court. Begun ca. 1240, private chapel of King Louis IX to
house relics of the Passion, lower chapel where royal retinue prayed
known for the botanical specimens in capital friezes and upper cha-
pel renowned for its high sheets of stained glass, martyr medallions,
apostle statues, and reliquary tribune. Heavily damaged at the time
of the French Revolution, restored in the nineteenth century.

IN THE REALM OF RELICS: FROM
CONSTANTINOPLE TO PARIS

IN 1237, BALDWIN II, the fifth Latin emperor of Byzantium after the
crusader capture of Constantinople in 1204 and cousin of King Louis IX
of France, visited the West in search of cash. Things had not gone well
for the Western rulers of Byzantine Greece, once the richest empire in
the world. Reduced by that time primarily to the imperial city, Latin
Byzantium found itself besieged by Mongols, Turks, and dispossessed
Greeks. The failure of the Frankish crusaders to settle and maintain the
territories they had seized in the aborted fourth crusade, which failed
to achieve its goal of liberating Jerusalem from Muslim rule, left those
who remained with no choice other than to sell, like English aristocrats

fallen on hard times after the decline of the British Empire, the only capital they had left—that is, the few remaining relics that had not been pillaged and sent to the West in the immediate aftermath of the fall of the capital.

Baldwin "the Broke" proposed to Louis IX that he purchase the crown of thorns. Byzantine empress Irene (d. 803) was said to have given several thorns from the crown to Charlemagne at the end of the eighth century, though the crown itself, which had been preserved in the Basilica of Mount Zion in Jerusalem, reached Constantinople *in toto* somewhat mysteriously only after 1063 CE. "I ardently desire," Baldwin confided, "that this precious relic go to you, my cousin, my lord, and my benefactor, and to the kingdom of France, homeland of my parents." King Louis, who had inherited the throne at age twelve and who had reigned under the threat of rebellious barons from the outset, was only twenty-three at the time and saw such an offer as an act of divine intervention to strengthen his rule. Bishop Gauthier Cornut of Sens, who left an account of the purchase of the Passion relics, reports that "the king wisely recognized that this was a message from the Lord. And he was further gladdened because as the place to display this honor, God had chosen his France."

Negotiations surrounding Louis's purchase of the crown of thorns were complicated, but ended around Christmas 1238, when, in exchange for the sum of 135,000 pounds, Baldwin wrote a letter ordering the transfer of the crown to two Dominican emissaries dispatched by Louis. This was an enormous price, given that the annual budget of the realm was only 250,000 pounds. When Brother André and Brother Jacques of Longjumeau arrived in Constantinople, they discovered that the Byzantine need for money was such that Baldwin had offered the crown of thorns as collateral on a loan from Venetian bankers under the condition that, if it were not redeemed before the feast of Gervais and Protais (June 18), it would become the possession of Venice. The Venetians had long traded in relics, and those of Saint Mark's Basilica had been brought there from Alexandria, Egypt, at the beginning of the eleventh century as well as after the Venetian-led conquest of Constantinople in 1204. They agreed, however, to cede the crown of thorns to the French, under the condition that it stop in Venice on its way to France.

Winter was a perilous time to think of transporting such a valuable object by sea, and the threat of hijacking loomed large. The Greeks had, via spies, learned of the sale and intended to intercept it. The crown, however, following the same route as the head of John the Baptist a third of a century earlier (see pp. 202–7), arrived by ship in Venice where it was exhibited in Saint Mark's. Brother André stayed with it in Venice, while Brother Jacques returned to Paris to fetch the money. After further negotiations, the crown left Venice by land under the safe conduct of Louis IX and German emperor Frederick II. On August 9, 1239, Louis met the convoy with his mother, brothers, Archbishop Cornut, Archbishop Bernard of Auxerre, and many barons and knights at Villeneuve-l'Archevêque, seventy miles southeast of Paris. When they undid the seals placed there by the Latin barons of Constantinople and those attached by the Doge of Venice, there was a tremendous outpouring of emotion. "They rest transfixed before the sight of the lovingly desired object," Archbishop Cornut observes, "their devout spirits seized by such fervor that they believe they see before their eyes the Lord in person wearing in that instant the crown of thorns." Even before its arrival in Paris, the crown of thorns had produced its "relic effect" with the sensation among those who saw it of having been transported back through time to the Passion itself.

Having affixed their own seals, the king and his brother Robert, barefoot and wearing only tunics, carried the reliquary of wood, silver, and gold the twenty miles from Villeneuve-l'Archevêque to Sens, where it was exhibited in the cathedral of Saint-Étienne, and then by boat on the Yonne River to Paris where an immense crowd gathered to welcome "the living lord in His relic." The incredibly pious Louis IX, who saw himself as the leader not only of France but also of Western Christendom, organized a great celebration in which all the relics in the Paris region were brought to the Abbey of Saint-Antoine *extra muros* where they were arranged in a display surrounding the relic of relics, the crown of thorns. From Saint-Antoine, it was brought "as if it were the ark of the Lord," according to an anonymous witness, into the city where it was placed briefly in Saint-Nicolas, the chapel of the royal palace. There, Louis peeled off a few thorns to be distributed to the bishoprics of Arras, Amiens, Angers, Bouillac, Grenoble, Le Puy, and Reims, the power of the relic being entire in each of its barbs. The rest of the prize relic was moved to Saint-Denis for safe-keeping. The elaborately orchestrated ceremony by which the crown of thorns was received in France made King Louis the equivalent of the Byzantine emperors Constantine and

Heraclius, and, in some wild sense, their heir as the proud possessor of the relics that they had amassed.

Baldwin II's money troubles, however, continued after the sale of his prize relic, and in 1241 King Louis purchased the holy sponge with which the tormenters of Christ gave him vinegar to drink, a piece of the holy shroud, a swatch of the purple robe Pilate made Christ wear to mock his royalty, some of the linen from Christ's washing of the feet of the apostles, the iron of the holy lance with which Longinus pierced Christ's flank, a fragment of the sepulchral stone, a victory piece of the cross, which means it had actually touched Christ's shoulder, and, in a rare example of a relic from the Old Testament, the rod with which Moses struck the rock to produce water in the desert.

You may have wondered long before now about the authenticity of the relics tendered by Baldwin II to Louis for purchase for not inconsiderable sums of money. Any doubt you may have about their legitimacy might only be doubled by skepticism surrounding the historic reality of a man-god named Christ, His birth in the absence of biological conception, His capacity to heal the sick and raise the dead, His own death and resurrection, not to mention the specific biographical narratives of each of the Twelve Apostles or the writings of the Four Evangelists. And, yet, the question is not so much what we know or do not know about the historical figure of Jesus and those around Him, but what the medievals believed at the time of Louis's enormous investment of the resources of his realm in relics—the Louisiana Purchase of the High Middle Ages! You might consider that the price the French king was willing to pay for holy objects is prima facie evidence of his belief in their authenticity, the way that certain masterpieces associated with the vague category of human genius fetch enormous prices at today's auctions of fine art. Further evidence of the efficacy of relics lay in the miracle cures they occasioned in those who suffered bodily, in which I believe as wholly as in the remedy of any psychosomatic disorder, or in the favorable outcome of events for rulers who appealed to them in times of collective crisis. Again, the outcome is a function of the depth of initial belief, the criteria and parameters of which change over time.

THE SAINTE-CHAPELLE

T HE SITE OF THE royal palace only a few hundred yards from Notre-Dame Paris on the Île de la Cité may first have been occupied by Gallo-Roman and Merovingian castles. Robert II, the Pious (d. 1031), king of the Franks, rebuilt a palace at the beginning of the eleventh century as did Philip Augustus (d. 1223) at the beginning of the thirteenth. Philip's grandson Louis IX lived between his palace at Vincennes, on the eastern outskirts of Paris, and a residence which stands on the site of the current Palace of Justice, which served as a royal residence until Charles V moved to the Louvre in the late 1300s.

Louis IX was a great builder. He was the driving force behind the construction of a military port at Aigues-Mortes on the Mediterranean from which he set out on the seventh crusade and a fort at Jaffa once he had arrived in the Holy Land. The future saint was especially interested in pious and charitable works. He built hospitals at Pontoise and Compiègne, abbey churches at Maubuisson and Royaumont, a priory at Nogent, and, in Paris, a hospice—the Quinze-Vingts—for the blind, a convent for beguines at Vauvert, and a student residence in the Latin Quarter near the nascent Collège de Sorbonne.

Soon after the arrival of the second batch of precious objects in 1241, Louis decided that Saint-Nicolas was not a grand enough home for the sizeable collection of relics he had amassed. His decision to build a new chapel attached to the royal residence received the blessing of Pope Innocent IV in 1244, indicating that construction was already underway. And not just any construction, for the Pope used in his bull the phrase *opere superante materiam*, "the workmanship surpassing the material," which is the phrase used by Ovid to describe the gold portals made by Vulcan for the Palace of Apollo, and refers to artistic work of great "brilliance and intrinsic value." In January 1246 Louis endowed a college of canons as keepers of the relics and of the liturgical regimen of the private shrine within the royal compound alongside the Palace of Justice and the Chamber of Accounts, the legal and economic arms of monarchy fixed within the heart of Paris. Built with extreme rapidity at a cost of forty thousand pounds, plus another one hundred thousand pounds for the elaborate reliquary structure behind the altar, the Sainte-Chapelle was consecrated on April 26, 1248, two months before King

Louis departed for what turned out to be six disastrous years of crusade, in the course of which he was taken prisoner and ransomed, and the Christian army captured or destroyed. This may seem like a psychically incoherent act on Louis's part, yet the crusader spirit is so inscribed in the Sainte-Chapelle, and the Sainte-Chapelle is so designed to bring the experience of the crusades to Paris, as to make them two faces of the king's elaborate staging of his own sainthood.

The idea for the Sainte-Chapelle, even the name, originated in the East where the crusaders who had sacked Constantinople in 1204 reported having seen the Holy Chapel. The knight participant and chronicler of the fourth crusade Robert de Clari's description of the Boukoleon Palace, where the relics of the Passion were kept before they were sent to France, defines an esthetics of fullness and sets a high bar for architectural extravagance: "there was not a hinge nor a band nor any other part such as is usually made of iron that was not all of silver, and there was no column that was not of jasper or porphyry or some other rich precious stone. . . . Within this chapel were found many rich relics. One found there two pieces of the True Cross as large as the leg of a man. . . , and one found there the blessed crown with which He was crowned, which was made of reeds with thorns as sharp as the points of daggers."

The Sainte-Chapelle is not a pilgrimage church designed to serve the needs of both a permanent congregation and passing pilgrims: thus, the lack of ambulatory aisles and radiating chapels. In fact, it is not a cathedral, the seat of a bishop with defined spaces to separate the clergy from the flock of faithful, but a slim high church built within the confines of the city, appearing from the outside even to be somewhat cramped. The Sainte-Chapelle is a palace chapel, serving less as a Bible for the poor than as a theological theater for the king and his retinue.

King Louis's private shrine is organized structurally like no other Gothic building on such a monumental scale. Though it is as high, say, as the cathedral of Noyon and as wide as that of Laon, the Sainte-Chapelle appears to be of only modest size. This is a shrine that speculates on "the elegance of scale," in the phrase of Robert Branner, and not on the immensity of space. It radiates an intimacy in which the human body does not feel dwarfed or lost in the cavernous volume of a nave, choir, and double side aisles. There is no crypt, but an upper and a lower chapel that gives the impression of a crypt without the burden of protecting relics or of burial. There are no flying buttresses, but an extremely high and solid base, which slopes off at the level of the vaults of the lower and the walls of the upper chapel, providing for solid buttressing via the horizontal solidity of the whole. The problem of the lateral thrust of the wide vaults is handled by a series of chains stretching across their upper side and by another set of iron links around the perimeter of the building, barely visible in the seams of the sheets of stained glass, and through the vertical masonry window mullions. Though the Sainte-Chapelle is situated along an east-west axis, there is no entrance or dramatic presentation along the west facade, no jamb statues or gallery of kings in the king's house of prayer. Instead, coming from the palace, the royal family entered through a long north portico affixed to a covered porch at the level of the upper chapel; or, from the reign of Louis XII (d. 1515) on, up a staircase, since dismantled, on the south side. Today, you can also reach the upper chapel through winding stairwells at both corners of the west wall.

THE LOWER CHAPEL

As a private palace chapel designed to serve the needs of the king and his household, the Sainte-Chapelle is divided socially as well as spatially. The lower chapel was designed for Louis's domestic retinue, which was not inconsiderable. In addition to the officers who managed his personal property and government, the chancellor, marshals, legal and political advisors, butler, and the stewards of his estates, the king regularly kept fifty-to-sixty servants who were part of his immediate entourage—five stable squires, two smiths, three stable-boys, cooks in the kitchen, a sauce-cook and someone to blow the bellows to keep the kitchen fires burning, a pantler who provided bread, and two others in charge of linen, not to mention those who served at table. The king employed a carter, ushers, a chancellery staff of clerks, pages, runners, even a wax-warmer at the ready when documents needed to be sealed, all of whom prayed downstairs.

The lower chapel possesses many of the elements of design—stained glass windows, quatrelobe arches along the walls, columns from which spring ribs and vaults you have seen in other churches. Yet, all are so foreshortened as to give the impression of a truncated Gothic cathedral. Though the ceiling reaches a maximum of twenty-one feet, much of the internal volume is taken up by the coattails of the vaults which coalesce into bundles of ribs at a height not much greater than that of the average human being all along the external walls as well as up and down the nave, making for side aisles only seven feet wide.

As you enter the lower chapel, you may experience claustrophobia intensified by the hovering vaults and by a relative lack of light, the product both of the smallness of the windows and the dark red and blue paint covering every surface of this low-slung, low-lit, mildly exotic space. The lower chapel was ravaged by a flood in 1689 and by abuse and neglect after the Revolution, but those who restored it in the middle of the nineteenth century did so according to recent discoveries by archeologists that classical and medieval masonry was painted and in fact often highly colored. The lower chapel of the Sainte-Chapelle is a polychromic tour de force. Your eye may wander quickly across painted column bases, columns, walls, and ceiling which are blanketed by gold fleurs-de-lys and Castile castles, the insignias of Louis and his mother Blanche of Castile, against royal blue and red backgrounds. You may look lightly at the gold heraldic lions rampant and wing-spread eagles on the outer walls up to the level of the faux wainscoting, and, beyond that, stars sprinkled upon the same red field as below. The heavy outlines of the gilded moldings of the trilobe arches, the gilding above and all around the windows, on the thick sheaves of ribs emanating from the columns and crossing the ceiling where they meet at gold shield bosses, and the floral carvings at the top of each column are, however, worthy of your attention and a closer look.

NATURE ON DISPLAY

Many of the columns at Saint-Denis, Notre-Dame Paris, or Chartres are capped by floral patterns, and other cathedrals—Amiens, for example—display long leafy bands outside and inside the church, but nothing matches the approximately one hundred natural specimens on the capital friezes of Louis's lower chapel, of which no two are alike. Together, they represent a cornucopia of botanical specimens, flowers and plants joined to stems that seem to grow out of the columns that appear as the trunks of trees. Some are indigenous to France and some exotic. Specialists in bio-art history have identified the umbellifers (plants lacking permanent wooden stem) and ranunculus, the leaf of the maple, oak, fig, vine, holly, ivy, hawthorn, and rose; acorns and grapes, figs, raspberries, and walnuts. If you like visual puzzles, you might search among the capital friezes for small animals—lizards and tiny birds—which lurk in the elaborate scroll-and-vine work growing there.

The botanical garden of the lower chapel is part of the encyclopedic spirit of the Age of Cathedrals, the observation and collection of natural phenomena in a world which came increasingly to value nature and natural philosophy. Louis IX was a patron of Vincent of Beauvais whose *Speculum naturale* ("Mirror of Nature") was a compendium of natural science in the middle of the thirteenth century. Thomas Aquinas, whose *Summa Theologica* was written during the last decade of King Louis's life, was interested in the necessary but not sufficient material causes of natural phenomena. Both espoused the systematic organization of such knowledge along the lines visible in the lower chapel of the Sainte-Chapelle, whose aim, alongside the larger Gothic cathedrals, is a total work of art—architecture, painting and decoration, stained glass, and sculpture combined.

THE UPPER CHAPEL

THOUGH ABBOT SUGER LEFT an account of the building of Saint-Denis along with his image in the sculpture and stained glass of the first Gothic cathedral, we have no idea what his role in the actual design of the church might have been. Similarly, the building trades are amply represented at Chartres, yet the master mason and sculptors, the carpenters and glassmakers, are anonymous. The Sainte-Chapelle, in contrast, is the product of the vision of one man, a royal commission by the king, whose powerful mother also participated in the overall plan. Thus, the unity, simplicity, and directness of a structure that exhibits none of the complex, fleeting, relative perspectives of Gothic churches partitioned on the inside between nave and aisles, choir and ambulatory, arcades, tribunes, triforia, and clerestory. The Sainte-Chapelle is a great open space whose dazzling effects were felt even by medieval observers. The theologian and political theorist Jean de Jandun, writing in 1323, was so struck by the transparent windows, the stone-studded altars, the jewel-encrusted shrines, and the gilded statues of the Sainte-Chapelle that he declared this house of prayer to possess "such a degree of beauty that on entering one would think oneself transported to heaven and with reason one might imagine oneself taken into one of the most beautiful mansions

Upper Chapel

of paradise." Indeed, to enter the upper chapel of this great house of glass is to experience the effects of light and lightness as nowhere else. Stained glass windows have displaced masonry walls, and the high vaults are held aloft by slim columns running from the floor to that place four-fifths up the wall where they spring from gilded sheaves into the radiating ribs that crisscross the star-filled blue ceiling. The Sainte-Chapelle, a "super-shrine turned outside-in," makes up for a lack of decoration on the outside with an upper sanctuary that bursts with color and whose every surface, from floor to ceiling and in myriad media, reveals the intent of the most skilled painters and sculptors, metal, glass, and wood-workers, enamelers and tilers to refine their materials into an elaborate decorated wonderland.

THE RELICS WINDOW

THE UPPER CHAPEL of the Sainte-Chapelle abides as a celebration of relics and the realm. And this from the start. Directly across from the exit of the winding stairway from the lower level into the main hall, an entire bay of stained glass on the southwest corner is devoted to the ancient and recent history of the relics of the Passion. The Charlemagne window of Chartres may depict the emperor's acquisition of relics in the East and their deposit at Aix-la-Chapelle. But the 168 individual images of this signature window of Louis's palatine chapel recount visually the prehistory of the relics in Jerusalem, the difficult negotiations surrounding their purchase by the French king, their long journey from Constantinople to Venice, and from Venice to Paris. Like a play with two acts, the whole of this highly restored bay is divided into two halves, the lower part of which begins on the left with the emperor Constantine's dispatch of his mother Helena to Jerusalem to seek the relics of the Passion. The closeness of mothers and sons may be reflected in the double dedication of the Sainte-Chapelle. Unlike the cathedrals at Paris, Chartres, Amiens, and Reims, which are consecrated wholly in the name of Mary, only the lower sanctuary of the Sainte-Chapelle is devoted to the Mother of God, the upper chapel, to her Son.

King Louis was exceedingly close to his mother. Blanche of Castile was a formidable personality who not only fended off the rebellious barons who tried to wrest the crown from her son in the years of his minority after her husband Louis VIII's death, but who served as regent when her son was on crusade. Jean de Joinville, who accompanied Louis to the Middle East and left an intimate portrait of the king, recounts that even in the royal residence at Pointoise, Louis and his wife Marguerite de Provence arranged to meet in the spiral staircase between their respective bedrooms and that they had stationed ushers who "would knock on the door with their staffs" when they saw the queen mother approaching. "The king would run to his chamber to ensure that his mother would find him there," and "the ushers outside Queen Margaret's chamber did the same." Such bedroom farce did not, however, prevent the royal couple's producing thirteen children!

Joinville's anecdote in *The Life of Saint Louis* sensitizes us both to mother-son relations as well as to historically heroic women in the stained glass of the Sainte-Chapelle. Much of the relics window, which consists of alternating quatrelobes depicting single narrative scenes and lozenges divided between two scenes, is modern and not medieval. The fields between quatrelobes and lozenges are laced with miniature castles and fleurs-de-lys, the emblems of Blanche and Louis that extend the enmeshing of mother and son the entire length of the bay.

The relics window is meant to be read from bottom to top and back and forth—from left to right and then from right to left—as in the boustrophedonic writing of certain ancient texts copied alternately in opposite directions. In the bottom row of quatrelobes, Helena arrives in Jerusalem, makes inquiry about the cross among Jews who present her not with one, but with three crosses. Not knowing which is the True Cross, she cleverly tests them by holding all three in front of the corpse of a dead man, who, in the phrase of James of Voragine (d. 1298) in *The Golden Legend*, "instantly came to life." Having identified the True Cross, Helena then asked the Jews to help her find the holy nails, which, after a successful search, she brought with the cross back to Constantinople. The lower half of the second lozenge from the bottom narrates the destruction of Jerusalem by the seventh-century Persian king Khosrow II (d. 628), shown carrying off vases filled with relics. The Byzantine emperor Heraclius (d. 641), in turn, captured the Persian capital, returned to Jerusalem with what remained of the cross, and eventually transported it to Constantinople. As in the authentication of a valuable work of art by tracing its provenance, the lower part of the relics window offers an account of how the relics of the Passion arrived in the Byzantine capital from the site of the Passion in Jerusalem.

The lower half of the third lozenge from the bottom shows King

Relics Window: Purchase of Relics, Transport from Venice,
Presentation to King Louis IX (© Painton Cowen)

Louis dispatching Brothers André and Jacques to fetch the crown of thorns. From right to left, the royal emissaries travel first to Constantinople, then accompany the relic, lashed to the back of a horse, to Venice, where, in scenes that are no longer shown in sequence, they complete the purchase. In the upper half of the lozenge, the precious object was brought back to France where it was exposed, in the scene of astonishment described by Archbishop Cornut (see p. 153), to Louis and his retinue at Villeneuve-l'Archevêque. The king and his brother Robert process with the crown into the town of Sens, where it was exhibited. Then, joined by Blanche, the procession continued to Paris, where, in multiple scenes of ostentation, it was placed on an altar. One depicts the arrival of the second batch of relics in 1241 where Louis is seen holding the True Cross. "In the middle of universal joy . . . ," in the phrase of the English chronicler Matthew of Paris, "the king, his face bathed in tears, raised the cross in the air, and all the prelates who were there raised with strong voice a hymn: 'Here is the cross of the Lord.'" The upper halves of the top row of lozenges show the construction and the consecration of the Sainte-Chapelle, in what art historians call a mise-en-abyme, the portrait of an object containing the image of itself in what amounts to an infinite regress. Indeed, the portrayal of the building of the Sainte-Chapelle should, theoretically, include that portion of the relics window that depicts the process of building the church. The very top of this highly narrative bay consists of one large and two smaller rosettes with scenes of adoration of the relics in the chapel itself.

THE MEDALLIONS OF MARTYRS

SAINTE-CHAPELLE WAS DESIGNED as a giant reliquary to house the holy objects that Louis had amassed. Even the outside, which lacks decoration, dramatizes the crown of thorns. The top of the apse, seen from the ground, presents as a great spiky crest, a crown of protruding gargoyles set in pairs as if they were giant thorns on the helmet of the church. Inside, the showcasing of Louis's treasure in the relics window continues at eye level around the entire shrine. Unlike most cathedrals, which celebrate the saints in glass and sculpture, the Sainte-Chapelle features images of the torments of forty-four martyrs in quatrelobe medallions set in gilded decorated arcades throughout the room. Decoration which simulates an "arcade effect" takes the place of the arcades and

Spiky Crest

side aisles found in other Gothic churches. The quatrelobes, in groups of three between the major pillars, are set at the top of broken arches and just below trilobe moldings which are themselves resting on columns terminating in floral capital friezes like smaller versions of the botanical displays in the lower chapel (see p. 158). The columns are somewhat detached from the wall, a sign that textiles may originally have been suspended there.

At present, faux curtains realistically painted on the background between the pillars so as to show a sag between the points at which they are attached, pleats which make the cloth appear to fall naturally to the floor, and exotic animals like those woven into Byzantine silks render a "textile effect," the creation of modern restorers. The upper edges of the broken arches are limned with delicately worked displays of various botanical specimens. Sitting atop the very point, fantastic little beasts—dragons, basiliks, and grillos—confront each other from opposite sides of the arch. The triangular spaces between the arches are filled with angels popping from the clouds and bearing gifts—crowns and censers—in their hands. The whole is framed at the upper edge by a running linear band of gilded molding worked with a combination of domestic and exotic leaves.

The medallions which limn the Sainte-Chapelle were partially painted on the wall, with backgrounds chiseled directly into the stone, and partially composed of shards of painted glass set into mortar, which creates the effect of a mosaic or of enamel work. They were heavily damaged in the Revolution of 1789 and also by storage units installed in the upper chapel, covering the medallions, the simulated arcades, and up to two meters of stained glass. Between 1803 and 1837, the Sainte-Chapelle was used as an archive for the overflow of documents from the Palace of Justice next door. Some of the original lower glass was removed and went to Alexandre Lenoir's Museum of French Monuments, and from there to the Cluny Museum of the Middle Ages where it can still be seen today. Other panels were sold off to English amateurs seeking stained glass for their castles. In 1804 and 1808, a dealer from Norwich, John Christopher Hampp, ran public sales of parts of windows he had amassed in France and Flanders, which is how windows from the Sainte-Chapelle ended up in churches in Twycross, Wilton, and Canterbury. About half of the painted medallions were restored as part of the overall restoration undertaken in the middle of the nineteenth century.

On the basis of drawings made at the outset of the rehabilitation of the Sainte-Chapelle beginning in the 1830s, a small number of the martyrs of the medallions are recognizable by the names that were once painted on the outer rims of the quatrelobes. Some twenty-five of the forty-four can be identified by their tortures or manner of death: Hippolytus, by drawing and quartering; Sebastian, by an impaling of

Medallion

arrows; Agatha, by the severing of her breasts; John the Baptist, along with Denis, by beheading.

The principle of selection of the martyrs in the dados of the Sainte-Chapelle is somewhat of a mystery, as is that of their arrangement. Some, like Blasius, Eugenius, Quintinus, Godograndos, and Agapitus, are obscure, while others—John the Baptist, Sebastian, Lawrence, Stephen, and Thomas Becket—are much more common in the cathedrals of northern France. Popes are grouped along the southern wall, while the few women who figure among the medallions appear on the northern side. Just on the other side of the medieval prayer screen between the second and third bay of the Sainte-Chapelle, a niche set in the wall on the left facing the altar was reserved for the prayers of the king, that on the right, for the queen. Since these were set devotional spaces, it is no accident that King Louis sat facing Saint Denis, the patron saint of France, while Queen Margaret sat facing her namesake, Saint Margaret. William of Auvergne, bishop of Paris during the time the Sainte-Chapelle was being built, once preached a sermon in the queen's presence about Saint Margaret in which he pointed out that she "can be glorified in God because she is married to God as to a husband. . . . If to have the king of France for a husband is such an honor, how much greater a one is it to have the King of Glory?"

The royal niches occupy fully two of the spaces devoted to each medallion and are crowned by an elaborate rounded arch whose upper rim displays ten angels with censers ascending to a relief of God the Father holding the cruciform orb of the world on Louis's side and Christ holding a book on that of Queen Margaret. Each of the walls is pierced by a stained glass window with fleurs-de-lys bordered by castles on the north and castles bordered by fleurs-de-lys on the south. The walls are painted with fleurs-de-lys on the king's side and castles on that of the queen. Again, one can only imagine how Queen Margaret might have felt sitting opposite her husband in a reserved space of prayer blanketed by the insignia of her mother-in-law, Blanche of Castile.

On one account of the eclectic assembly of martyrs in the medallions of the Sainte-Chapelle, there is a common thread: these are all saints whose relics belonged to one or another of the churches of Paris in the first half of the thirteenth century. They were, thus, part of the gathering of relics at the Abbey of Saint-Antoine upon the arrival of the crown of thorns at the outskirts of Paris in 1239. Their strategic arrangement surrounding the crown at that unique event is thus reproduced symbolically in the array of images depicting the martyrdom that turned human beings into relics in the first place. Their presence is a reunion of sorts, a regrouping around the permanent home of the crown of thorns, and an embracing link between the relics window, which displays a visual record of its journey from Constantinople to Paris—including the convocation of relics at Saint-Antoine—and the monumental reliquary tribune at the east end of Louis's shrine.

THE RELIQUARY TRIBUNE

To some extent churches are always reliquaries, the possession of relics the substance of their glory, honor, riches, and prestige. Conversely, the boxes that contain relics are often designed as miniature churches. A reliquary box from the second half of the thirteenth century, which once held the remains of three beheaded saints—Maxien, Lucien, and Julien—is, in fact, a miniature version of the Sainte-Chapelle in whose treasury it once resided, though now it can be seen in the Cluny Museum of the Middle Ages. Louis's upper chapel inserts yet another layer between reliquary boxes in the shape of a church and the church itself, and this by way of the reliquary platform behind the altar in the curve of the apse—an enlarged ciborium or baldachin, a canopy or covering supported by columns, freestanding in the sanctuary. Carried on eight pillars, with three broken arches separated at the top by trilobes on either side of a wider, higher, broken arch, the lattice which cloisters the reliquary tribune from the rest of the church functions like a stage in a theater to dramatize the instruments of the Passion, mounted in the platform accessed by a wooden staircase on either side. Six angels floating upward through clouds on the inner edge of the middle arch bear a vividly spiked crown of thorns as if they were both delivering and reminding us of the importance of the prized sacred object in the great golden box above.

The reliquary tribune is designed as a miniature version of a single bay, seen from both inside and outside, of the Sainte-Chapelle. The frontal perspective from the ground reveals the type of gable with oculus that could be part of the transept of a Gothic cathedral. The cross roof structure is topped at either end with a finial in the shape of a miniature shrine which adds weight and stability to the buttress of a real cathe-

Reliquary Tribune

dral. The finials of Louis's reliquary tribune are genuine mini-cathedrals
with a three-portal facade, towers with spires, and broken arches with
lancet windows and an oculus on the west side. In the center, a larger
version of the front finials serves as a central spire like that on the roof
of the Sainte-Chapelle or Notre-Dame Paris. All the spires as well as
the frontal gable are crested by fancy fleurs-de-lys. Looking up into the
reliquary tribune, you will see that the trilobe in the upper part of the
open arch continues the clover-like pattern in the arcades around the
church. The ceiling, complete with gilded ribs and shield boss, repro-

duces in miniature the ceiling of the upper chapel with its gold stars on a field of blue. The reliquary tribune of the Sainte-Chapelle is a dollhouse of a church.

The imbrication of smaller forms within larger ones, within larger ones still, the reliquary box within the reliquary stage, within the larger architectural structure, is one of the principles of Gothic design, and works to abolish time, or to transform time into space. If smaller things, which have the same form as larger things, can be contained within them in some version of an infinite regress, then the present might be contained within the past. Louis and all who worshipped before the tribune of the relics participated in the aura of Old Testament and Christian history in a great enfolding of time upon itself.

JERUSALEM ON THE SEINE

THE FRENCH KING may have translated the relics of the Passion from Constantinople to Paris, as Constantine brought them from Jerusalem to Constantinople, yet the elaborate structure in which they rest reproduces a sacred space with roots reaching, via kings David and Solomon, all the way back to Moses, who received the ark of the covenant, a great gold chest which housed the tablets of the Law. Louis manufactured a relic house designed to resemble the Old Testament Tabernacle as part of a new "spiritual kinship" between Jerusalem and Paris. Within the Sainte-Chapelle, a new Temple on the Mount, the structure at the east end of the upper chapel, duplicated the Throne of Solomon with its porch of justice, "the tent of testimony," in the phrase of Saint Stephen: "Our ancestors had the tent of testimony in the wilderness, as God directed when he spoke to Moses. . . . And it was there until the time of David, who found favor with God and asked that he might find a dwelling place for the house of Jacob. But it was Solomon who built a house for him" (Acts 7:44–47).

It may seem like a singular lack of humility for a man destined to be a saint, but Louis IX of France, expressing himself through architecture, sought to place himself in the line of King David. Like David, who had a larger vision for his kingdom than that of his predecessor Saul and made a new capital in Jerusalem, Louis sought to expand the royal domain with Paris at its center. As David "and all the house of Israel brought the ark of the covenant of the Lord with joyful shouting, and with sound of

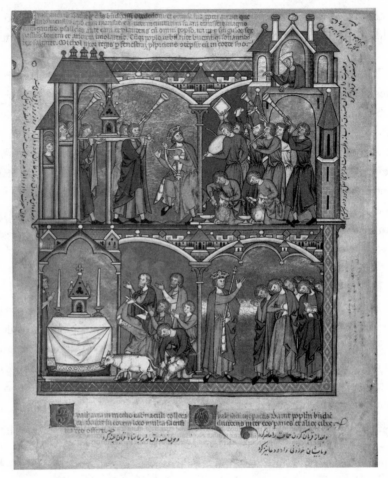

David and the Ark (The Morgan Library & Museum / Art Resource, NY)

trumpet" (Second Kings 6:15) into his new city, so Louis commissioned a reproduction of the ark of the covenant for the Sainte-Chapelle. Any doubt about his intent is dispelled by comparing the manuscript illumination of David bringing the ark into Jerusalem in the Morgan Bible (MS 638, folio 39v), copied in the very decade the Sainte-Chapelle was built, with Louis's reliquary tribune. The Old Testament structure on the parchment page is capped by a fleur-de-lys, in a wild anachronism, as the lily was not associated with any French king before Clovis (d. 511). Moreover, in the lower half of the illumination, the ark sits in the city of Jerusalem on the altar of a schematic church with pointed gables and finials under a trilobe Gothic arch that resembles nothing so much as the architectural frame at the east end of the Sainte-Chapelle.

The reproduction in Paris of the temple on the mount containing the ark of the covenant is a sign of the extent to which France of the thirteenth century laid claim to the legacy that once belonged to Jerusalem, Byzantium, and Rome. Nicholas Mesarites, sacristan of the Boukoleon Palace in Constantinople, on which the Sainte-Chapelle was modeled, declared it "a second Sinai, a new Bethlehem, a second Jordan, a new Jerusalem." King Louis continued the westward path of a manifest spiritual destiny in which Paris picked up where Constantinople left off. Already in the twelfth century, we find in literature a motif known as the *translatio studii*, a move westward of intellectual life, from Ancient Greece, to Rome, to western Europe. The first French writer of Old French Romance, Chrétien de Troyes (d. ca. 1191), begins his chivalric tale *Cligès* with an evocation of the classical past: "Our books have taught us that learning first flourished in Greece; then to Rome came chivalry and the sum of knowledge, which now has come to France. . . . God merely lent it to the others: no one speaks any more of the Greeks or Romans; their fame has grown silent and their glowing ember has gone out." The westward move of knowledge implied, of course, an analogous transfer of power, *translatio imperii*, to Paris, where royalty and theology combined in the personage of the king who became a saint, the first step in the evolution of monarchy that culminated in the seventeenth century with Louis XIV, the Sun King.

Saint Louis may not have been capable of articulating the motifs of the *translatio studii et imperii* that swirled in the culture around him, but he and his counselors sensed the usefulness of the *translatio Sacratissimae Passionis instrumentorum*, the "transfer of the Holy instruments of the Passion" in the making of the French state a new "sacred landscape" and Holy Land. According to Archbishop Gauthier Cornut of Sens, "Just as our Lord Jesus Christ chose the Land of promise to show the mysteries of his redemption, . . . he chose our France in particular . . . because of the transfer worked by our Lord and Redeemer from the region of Greece, which is close to the East, to France which borders on the West, the instruments of his most Holy Passion." At the dedication of the Sainte-Chapelle, the Archbishop noted that "there can be no doubt that . . . the true Solomon, the peacemaker, proceeds to a second incarnation." The relics that Louis assembled made him the heir to the emperor of Rome, a new Constantine whose cross of victory he protected, even a new Moses with the rod that made the King of France the head of a chosen people. He was the successor of the kings of Israel, part of an alliance, seen also in the jamb statues of priests, patriarchs, and kings at Saint-Denis, Notre-Dame, and Chartres, between ancient and medieval kingship.

THE APOSTLE STATUES

IN THE UPPER CHAPEL, twelve statues of the apostles stand on piers, their backs against the shafts, a pedestal under their feet, and canopies over their heads. Like the kings of the gallery of kings of Notre-Dame Paris (see p. 69), the apostle pier statues of the Sainte-Chapelle underwent rough treatment in the aftermath of the Revolution. In the course of their removal in 1797 when the Sainte-Chapelle was converted into an archival storeroom, two fell and were shattered. The other ten made their way to Alexandre Lenoir's Museum of French Monuments and were, with one exception, transferred to churches at Saint-Denis, Cre-

Apostle Statues

teil, and Mont-Valérien with their high colored polychromy still relatively intact. The four that went to Mont-Valérien were, again like
the kings of Notre-Dame, decapitated and buried in the Revolution of
1830. So, when Félix Duban and Jean-Baptiste-Antoine Lassus began the
restoration of the Sainte-Chapelle in 1836, they faced the task of reas-
sembling what remained of the original apostle statues. Retrieving and
disinterring those they could, they managed to rescue six of the twelve
and to recreate on the basis of drawings and fragments the others in a
remarkable rescue of medieval artifacts. The pieces that could not be salvaged are now part of the permanent collection of the Cluny Museum
of the Middle Ages, the thirteenth-century paint still visible on their
battered bodies and clothes.

For their exactness of detail, classical heads, the deep folds cut in their
garments, the pier apostles of Sainte-Chapelle are some of the major
works of medieval sculpture. These "spiritual pillars of the church," in
the phrase Abbot Suger used to describe the choir of Saint-Denis, stand
guard in the upper chapel. When among them, you may experience the
eerie feeling that they are watching you. Indeed, they keep watch over
the relics reassembled in Paris as artifacts from the events in which the
apostles actually participated as they are relived in the daily rituals to
which the statues, again, bear witness. As a group, their placement at
equidistant intervals, aligned with the piers, anchors and balances the
space between and all around them. They are looking at you, their heads
turned down. Try as you may, there is no place to turn, no place to hide,
no place in which you might escape the view of these powerful representatives of the original church. Freed from the strictures of attach-
ment to a column, as in the case of the jamb figures that flank the portals
of most Gothic cathedrals, they are poised to step forward and move
around the room.

The apostle statues present with hyperrealistic detail. Their faces are
painted in dark flesh tones, their beards rendered as realistically as the
folds of their garments, which in places reproduce the faux fabric on the
chapel walls. The hems of their robes are encrusted with precious stones.
Each bears a monstrance in one hand, and some hold a staff in the other,
while others gesture with upturned palm, fingers against the chest, a
clenched fist even. These figures are in motion, their fine featured faces
are full of expression that is individual, personal, deeply emotional.
Peter, keys in hand and a cross pressed against his chest, stands behind the

reliquary arches to the left of the tribune, while Paul, holding a sword, is to the right. Both stare with fixed gaze, their faces full of sadness for what they have seen and with sympathy for the viewer. The bigger-than-life apostle statues of the Sainte-Chapelle are more like figures in a wax museum than the sober sculptures around the doors and along the high galleries of Gothic cathedrals. They are so radiant, present, and alive as to reinforce the feeling that Louis has brought Jerusalem, visible in the canopies of the Holy City above each of their heads, to Paris. The bare feet visible under some of the hems of their apostolic robes suggest that these sentries of the Sainte-Chapelle have travelled from the Middle East to Paris without their shoes.

Between Peter and Paul and above the reliquary tribune stained glass images of the Passion hover over the very objects and figures which were part of the drama depicted in the window at the east end of the upper chapel. The lower quadrants of the fifty-four panels of this fifteen-meter bay are modern and show angels carrying the instruments of the Passion—nails, the point of the lance, the cross, and the crown of thorns, though they are largely hidden from view by the reliquary stage. The story of Judas's betrayal and of Christ before Pilate fills the lower section up to the point at which the agonies of the Passion are shown in the second row of full square panels, the flagellation on the left, with Christ tied to what looks like a column in a Gothic church with a floral capital frieze in the middle of a broken arch, His flail-bearing tormenters under similar arches and between columns on either side. To the right, six of these place the crown of thorns on Christ's head in what is the culminating moment of the Passion in the making and meaning of the Sainte-Chapelle.

The morning light passing through the image of the crown of thorns in the Passion window hits the very object it represents. One could not imagine a more powerful fusion between the sign of a thing and the thing itself, a melding that Saint Augustine considered the goal of all communication and of religious striving. "We all seek," according to Augustine, "a certain resemblance in our ways of signifying such that the signs themselves reproduce, to the extent to which it is possible, the thing signified." That moment—a return of Christ the Word to the Father who spoke the words of Creation—coincides with the sacrament, performed at the altar just beyond the reliquary where the image of the crown of thorns, passing through the Passion window, coincides with

Christ Crowned with Crown of Thorns (© Painton Cowen)

the crown itself. As the blood and bread become the body of Christ at the eucharistic moment of transubstantiation, the past of the Crucifixion is blended with the present in a great uplifting abolition of earthliness that Augustine described as an "extreme nearness of the feeling of eternity." This may seem a little abstract, but it is, finally, not so far from the pleasure we experience when we express ourselves accurately or encounter others who do; and it explains the delight we feel when art captures aptly—whether in images, words, or sounds, whether literally or metaphorically—the world around us. Art and theology blend in the medieval cathedral in such a way that even those who do not believe in the efficacy of grace might nonetheless experience some of the magic belonging to an esthetic loss of self.

THE STAINED GLASS
OF SAINTE-CHAPELLE

THE STAINED GLASS OF Sainte-Chapelle is a world unto itself. It is now more accessible than in the past via a software application for smartphones and tablets. If you install it before your visit (see p. 321), you can point to any panel up and down these high sheets of glass, and it will identify what you are looking at amid one of the largest ensembles of glass anywhere. The windows of Louis's palatine chapel cover more than 6,500 square feet, of which two-thirds is original and the other third restored in the nineteenth century, some 1,134 narrative scenes, of which 720 are authentically medieval. The windows differ from those found in other Gothic cathedrals because of the absence of local and even universal saints and of secular subjects like the signs of the zodiac and the Works of the Months. It could be that the king and nobles who prayed there were not directly involved in agriculture nor did the royal chapel serve parishioners from the surrounding countryside. Under instructions from their royal patrons, as distinct from the canons who mapped out the windows in other cathedrals, whoever designed the overall layout as well as the specific scenes—and we shall never know their names—aspired to universal biblical history of which Louis's enormous architectural reliquary is the culmination.

Even within a single set of windows, there are choices to be made, and the glass panels of Sainte-Chapelle are heavily inflected by the presence of women, no doubt due to the influence of Blanche upon King Louis. In the story of the Crucifixion and Resurrection, two panels of the Passion window show women at the tomb, three feature Mary Magdalene to whom Christ appears and who alerts the apostles, four quadrants just under the uppermost full squares depict women and apostles looking upward. And what do they see? Not Christ resurrected, but little rondels with yellow castles against a background of gules or red, the heraldic sign of Blanche of Castile, which alternates all up and down the window in filler segments of glass between the main scenes of the Passion with fleurs-de-lys on a field of blue, the device of her son Louis, in a great mixing of mother and son with the most sacred story of the Christian Bible.

The program of windows that fills the upper chapel culminates over the altar with the Passion surrounded on both sides and along the walls of the nave by a vast unfolding of the Hebrew and Christian Bibles which situates the Redemption as, in the phrase of Louis Grodecki, "the center-piece in the history of the world." If, upon entering, one encounters on the southwest corner the most recent events in human history, the translation of relics and the building of the Sainte-Chapelle, on the northwest, we find the story of the creation of the world along with that of Joseph in a total of ninety-one historiated panels, which were heavily damaged at the time of the construction of the Palace of Justice on which it abuts, and thus are also heavily restored.

GENESIS

THE BOTTOM TWO ROWS of round and oblong frames of the Creation window present a detailed visual account of the events contained in Genesis 1:4–8. The panels, meant to be read across all four lancets, depict the creation of the heavens and the earth, the separation of the waters, the coming into being of the planets, moon, sun, and stars, fish and birds, four-footed beasts and reptiles, Adam, who names the animals, the emergence of Eve from his side, God's injunction not to eat of the Tree of Knowledge, the Fall and expulsion from paradise, the clothing of Adam and Eve, the sacrifices of Cain and Abel, and Cain's murder of his brother. Moving up the Genesis bay, we find, as at Chartres, the story of Noah, the construction and destruction of the tower of Babel, God's covenant with Abraham, Abraham's willingness to sacrifice Isaac, the marriage of Isaac and Rebecca, the birth and birthright of Esau and Jacob, and Jacob's struggle with the angel (Genesis 6:13–32:24). The top three rows, two oblong and one round, recount the story of Joseph and his brothers, his time in Egypt as an interpreter of dreams, and his reunion with his father Jacob (Genesis 37:5–46:8). As in the Passion window, rondels with yellow castles on a red field and fleurs-de-lys against a blue field link the oblong panels all up and down the Genesis window, signaling the entwining of Louis and his mother at the beginning of time and the creation of the world.

MOSES AND SAINT LOUIS

FOLLOWING THE ORDER OF the Hebrew Bible, the four lancets in the bay to the right of the Genesis window present a visual rendering of the story of Exodus in 121 quatrelobe quadrants and square panels perched obliquely like diamonds on end. Of these, fully one hundred are devoted to the young Moses and the preparation to leave Egypt, the plagues, the passage across the Red Sea, wanderings in the desert, the reception of the tablets of the Law, and the episode of the worship of the golden calf. The depiction of the ten plagues which God inflicts upon the Egyptians in order to convince Pharaoh to free the Israelites from bondage is particularly vivid. The affliction of frogs shows three of Pharaoh's counselors raising their hands in desperation while yellow, purple, and green frogs leap all over their bodies; the plague of thirst shows them with tongues hanging out of their open mouths; that of flies shows Pharaoh and his counselors with pockmarks on their faces. The slaying of the first-born children of the Egyptians dramatizes an angel, sword in hand, before a crowd of parents bent over in grief.

So, too, the drowning of Pharaoh's army is a masterpiece of chaos, the entire diamond filled with blue-and-red wavy lines for the Red Sea, between which are interspersed bodies, one human head still wearing a crown and another a helmet, the head of a horse, and the wheels of a chariot—the detritus of war. Speculation as to why the liberation of the Jews from bondage in Egypt is depicted in such copious vivid detail leads me to think that King Louis IX, on the eve of crusade to liberate Jerusalem from the Muslims who had recaptured the city in 1244, somehow assimilated the Mamluks, who controlled Egypt at the time, with the oppressive pharaoh of Genesis 5:5–8. What could be more tempting for the king who would be a saint than to imagine himself in the role of Moses? History, however, did not turn out as Louis had hoped, and his defeat outside of Cairo at the Battle of Al Mansurah where his

Pharaoh's Army Drowned, Exodus Window (© Painton Cowen)

brother died, the Battle of Fariskur where his army was annihilated and he suffered the humiliation of his own capture and a case of royal dysentery, all conspired to make it seem as if the plagues were inflicted upon the would-be liberators and not the thirteenth-century avatars of the ancient pharaohs.

The representation of the Exodus of the Israelites from Egypt focuses on several objects with particular meaning for King Louis and the Sainte-Chapelle. In the second row of the right lancet, God gives a rod to Moses, and, in the fourth row on the middle right, Moses strikes the rock of Horeb with the very rod that figures among the relics in Louis's collection. Unlike the stained glass image of the crown of thorns, however, through which the morning light might hit the thing itself, relatively little light penetrates the north sheets of windows which are not in the direct line of sight of the grand reliquary case which reproduces the ark of the covenant referenced in the Exodus window. The two top diamonds in the right lancets feature the tabernacle, empty on the left and occupied by Moses sitting with God on the right. The quatrelobe quadrant above the latter depicts the altar of the tabernacle, on which is placed in a round dish "a whole ram for a burnt offering" (Exodus 29:17). The image is so similar to that of the crown of thorns at Sens in the relics window as to reinforce the assimilation of the Old Testament ark of the covenant and the reliquary tribune in which the crown is kept behind the altar.

The Exodus window is, of course, Moses's window, and Moses is portrayed not only as the liberator of the Israelites but also as the bringer of the Law, which also has special meaning for Louis IX. No less than eight panels show him with the Ten Commandments, beginning with that in the next-to-the-top-row middle left lancet in which God bestows upon Moses two tablets on which are written the words "LEGE DOMINI" [sic]. In succeeding scenes, Moses, enraged by the idolatrous behavior of the Israelites in his absence, breaks the tablets and receives a second set, which he guards closely to his person. Moses clutches them as he descends Mount Sinai, stands with his brother Aaron, faces the people whom he leads, and sits with God in the tabernacle.

The tablets of the Law are, along with horns protruding from his head, Moses's emblems in the stained glass of Gothic cathedrals. This physiognomic anomaly stems from the mistranslation of the Hebrew word *qāran*, meaning "shining" or "emitting rays," as *cornuta* in the Latin

Vulgate version of the Bible: "And when Moses came down from the Mount Sinai, he held the two tables of the testimony, and he knew not that his face was horned from the conversation with the Lord" (Exodus 34:29). Though the most celebrated example of horned Moses is that of Michelangelo from the second decade of the sixteenth century, the vexed elision from Moses to the Jewish people has been a source of the mistaken belief right down to the present day that Jews have horns.

As we shall see (p. 185), Louis IX was no friend of the Jews, but he was a peacemaker between his barons—those of Brittany, Navarre, and Champagne—as well as between France and England. Above all, he was known as an advocate of justice and a man of laws. In what was one of the most important legal decrees of the Middle Ages, Louis prohibited the old feudal judicial procedure of trial by battle or combat, *deo judicium*, to be replaced by civil procedures still recognizably our own. "We forbid battles throughout our domain in all disputes," an ordinance of the late 1250s reads, "and instead of battles, we put proof by witness and charter." Well into the twentieth century members of the French aristocracy claimed the right to settle their quarrels among themselves, as attested by the practice of dueling in the early morning in the Bois de Boulogne. Louis, however, mandated the procedure of inquest, "proof by witness and charter," which came increasingly to define the means by which legal matters were resolved under a monarchy increasingly interested in the state monopoly of violence. Inquest involved the collection of the material facts surrounding a case, its organization into a dossier, debate between plaintiff and defendant in a court, which might include at its highest level, the Parliament of Paris, the place where one speaks instead of fighting—and which was situated directly next to the Sainte-Chapelle.

Louis was famous for his accessibility and fairness, confirmed in the iconic image of justice rendered under the oak tree of Vincennes. "During the summer he often went and sat in the woods at Vincennes after Mass," Joinville relates. "He would lean against an oak tree and have us sit down around him. All those who had matters to be dealt with came and talked to him, without the interference of the ushers or anyone else. He himself would ask, 'Is there anyone here with a case to settle?' " Louis's return from the crusade in 1254 was marked by a general judicial reform, a royal decree that all his judicial officers—"*baillis*, viscounts, *prévôts*, mayors and all others"—should not only deal fairly with all people, regardless of social status or wealth, but that they should administer justice in accordance with the laws, "the usages and customs," of the realm. The principle of fairness characterizes the *Life of Saint Louis*, and justice accompanied him even on his deathbed where he urged his son, above all, to rule as a just sovereign. "Uphold the good customs of your kingdom and abolish the bad." Louis, like Moses, was an advocate of the written law. The body of his legal prescriptions, known as the *Etablissements Saint Louis*, were collected shortly after his death and represent one of the first systematic attempts to rationalize a body of laws and procedures not in the mode of the traditional customary codes, but in that of the old Roman statutory law as it was revived in the High Middle Ages.

KINGS AND CROWNS

To the right of the Exodus window, the Book of Numbers, which continues the story of the Israelites wandering in the desert, is most notable for the number of scenes involving the crowning of the princes of Israel. No less than twenty panels in the lower section depict corona-

Moses Lifts Ark of the Covenant, Book of Numbers Window
(© Painton Cowen)

tions, culminating in that of Aaron and Moses in the second row of the right lancet. Again, you can see in the Numbers window images of the ark of the covenant transported on an ox cart across the desert, elevated by warriors, including Moses, whose horns stick through the coat of mail covering his head, and situated in the tabernacle on an altar, as is its reproduction in the reliquary tribune of the Sainte-Chapelle. Interestingly in another image, dominated by a large menorah in the middle foreground, a book can be seen in front of the ark, in what is an anachronistic substitution of the Christian codex of the Bible for what should have been the scroll of the Hebrew text. On a second altar to the right of the menorah, a jeweled crown capped by a fleur-de-lys situates the royal insignia of the Capetian monarchy, Louis's own logo, firmly amid the kings of Judah. This represents an astonishing collapse of historical perspective, made no less so by the hundreds of fleurs-de-lys that fill the blue spaces, punctuated by rondels with yellow castles on red, between the narrative panels of the Numbers window. Because of its repetitive nature the Numbers window does not figure among the distinguished bays of Sainte-Chapelle. Yet, it does affirm themes seen elsewhere and that link it to the making and meaning of the upper chapel as well as to the affirmation of kingship at the core of King Louis's version of the Gothic enterprise. And it introduces among its higher sections the theme of pious warfare prevalent in other bays of the upper chapel, always in the background of Louis as a crusader king.

To the right of Numbers, the so-called Deuteronomy and Joshua window depicts the preparation of the Israelites to enter the land of Canaan, with special emphasis, again, upon the law, coronation, the ark of the covenant, and military conquest. In the bottom panel of the left lancets, God speaks to Moses, who, in the panel to the right, sits with the tablets on his lap before a gathering of the people of Israel, while God hovers overhead. In the second row from the bottom, second lancet to the left, Moses, having designated as his successor Joshua, who wears the crown of a French king, places a scroll in the hands of the new leader of the Israelites with the words "IOSUE POPULUS." To the right, Moses places the scroll in the ark of the covenant, two broken arches with a larger one featuring a gable in the middle that resembles the reliquary platform in the apse. A series of images of the ark running across the north side of the upper chapel serves, like the relics window on the other side, as a visual provenance which guarantees the authenticity of the tribune at the east end of the room. The rest of the Deuteronomy Joshua window, which depicts the fall of Jericho, the slaughter of its inhabitants, and the victorious campaign against the Amorites, is in line with the triumphalist crusader rhetoric of Louis's own military ambitions in the ancient land of Canaan.

A double lancet to the right of the Deuteronomy Joshua window is devoted to the Book of Judges and the difficult relationship of the Israelites, once in Canaan, with God. It is capped at top by images of Samson, the last of the judges, who managed the Israelites before the advent of kings. Samson demonstrates his strength by slaying a lion with his bare hands and by single-handed combat against the Philistines with the jaw-bone of a donkey. After Delilah cuts his hair, his eyes are gouged, he is forced to turn a mill, and the temple of Dagon is destroyed.

ISAIAH, IDOLATRY, AND THE
DEMONIZATION OF MUSLIMS AND JEWS

IN THE NORTHEAST CURVE of the apse, a double lancet captures the Book of Isaiah on the left side and Isaiah's dream of the Tree of Jesse on the right. Isaiah, as the last of the prophets of the Old Testament and an evangelist in germ, signals the swerve of the apse of the Sainte-Chapelle from the Hebrew to the Christian Bible, which will culminate in the axis with the Passion, the central event of Christian history. In some large sense the entirety of the north wall of glass has been a preparation for the Passion and a meditation on God's plan for the destiny of Jerusalem. His intention to manifest Himself in the line of David dominates the windows of the apse, which, along with those of the nave, are highly inflected, by choice and fashioning of subject, to coincide with the culmination of contemporaneous history in the reign of Louis IX—and, to some extent, his mother. Between Louis's purchase of the relics in 1239 and his departure on crusade in 1248, the building of the Sainte-Chapelle in the astonishingly short period of less than a decade inserts the local and punctual interests of mid-thirteenth-century France—middle or human time—into the sweep of history from the creation of the world to its end, figured in the rose of the west wall (see p. 196).

The Isaiah window as a point of turning between the Hebrew and Christian Bibles, as between the nave and the apse, is seen in the choice

Mahomet Detail, Isaiah Window (© Painton Cowen)

of themes from the Book of Isaiah rooted in both testaments. Thus, at the very bottom, an oblique diamond panel pitched to the past and to the unruliness of the Israelites, a scene of idolatry referring to Isaiah 1:4: "Woe to the sinful nation, a people laden with iniquity, a wicked seed, ungracious children: they have forsaken the Lord, they have blasphemed the Holy One of Israel, they are gone away backwards." While two figures worship a golden idol in human form, one hand on his chest and the other on his genitals, Isaiah towers behind and above them with a figure pointing upward toward an inscription "YSAIAS PRO[FET]." Below the feet of the retrograde Israelites, the letters "MA.META" stand for "MAHOMETA" in a wild anachronism, since Isaiah lived in eighth century BCE, while the prophet Muhammad was not born until around 570 CE.

Such a temporal elision is aimed at demonizing Muslims on the eve of King Louis's departure to recapture Jerusalem, which had fallen to the Ayyubid Sultanate, a Sunni dynasty, in 1244, and at justifying war against non-Christians. The Isaiah depiction of idolatry echoes a panel at the top of the Numbers window in which the Israelites worship a golden idol on an altar and two panels in the Joshua window, one of which shows Israelites before a similar statue and the other of which shows the idol worshipers being punished by clubbing. The conflation of Muslims and Jews is of a piece with the temporal elision of the life of Isaiah with the setbacks of the Latin rulers of Jerusalem in the first half of the thirteenth century. Though he imagined himself a peacemaker in foreign affairs, a fair judge of all who resided within his kingdom, and notoriously generous to the poor, King Louis IX was no friend of the Jews. Following what was known as the Disputation of Paris in 1240, in which French rabbis were called to defend the Talmud against allegations of blasphemy against Christianity, a great number of Hebrew books were publicly burned in Paris. Louis's most famous biographer Jean de Joinville recounts that the king, "hearing the story of a knight who interrupted a debate between Jews and Christians by striking the former's spokesman, said, 'a layman, whenever he hears the Christian religion abused, should not attempt to defend its tenets, except with his sword, and that he should thrust into the scoundrel's belly as far as it will enter.'" Joinville's report is in the line of the earlier observation of William of Chartres, writing to make the case for Louis's sainthood, that "he so loathed the Jews, people hateful to God and man, that he could not look at them," refused to take their money, and banished them from France, "lest it be further befouled by their filth."

Looking forward to the New Testament, the vision of Isaiah, prophetic of the birth of Christ, begins about two thirds of the way up the Isaiah window where the red-nimbed prophet holds on his arm the baby Jesus with a full beard. The diamond panel immediately above Isaiah's visual prophecy illustrates the way in which his words were understood to refer to the Annunciation of the angel Gabriel to Mary: "Therefore the Lord himself shall give you a sign. Behold a virgin shall conceive, and bear a son and his name shall be called Emmanuel" (Isaiah 7:14). The right lancet displays a Tree of Jesse, with a sleeping Isaiah on the bottom and fourteen generations of kings culminating in the Virgin and Christ at the top of an elongated but otherwise unremarkable genealogical series. With the exception of Jesse's son King David, the kings are not only anonymous but are also for the most part copied from just three different facial patterns, one of which was also used for the figure of the Virgin; the twenty-eight prophets present similarly undifferentiated groups, with the exception of the ninth prophet from the bottom on the left who is, according to the scroll unfurled between his two hands, no other than Isaiah himself—the dreamer in the dream.

THE TWO JOHNS

BETWEEN THE ISAIAH AND the Passion windows, a double lancet is devoted to Saint John the Evangelist, author of the Apocalypse which dominates the rose window on the west wall, and the Infancy of Christ, which picks up where the Isaiah window left off, that is, with scenes of the Annunciation, Visitation, and Nativity, the common tableaux of Herod and the Kings, the Visit of the Magi, Massacre of the Innocents, and the Flight of Jesus, Mary, and Joseph into Egypt. On the other side of the Passion window, a double lancet depicts on the left important scenes from the life of Saint John the Baptist, the precursor, who, according to Mark and Matthew, was foretold by Isaiah and who, in turn, foretells the arrival of Christ: "And in those days cometh John the Baptist preaching in the desert of Judea. And saying: Do penance: for the kingdom of heaven is at hand. For this is he that was spoken of by Isaias the prophet" (Matthew 3:1–3). Thus, about halfway up the left side, we see John baptizing Christ in the Jordan River, and, in the top panels, the events preceding John's death. Holding the two tablets of the Law, John reprimands Herod for violating the seventh commandment, "Thou shall not commit adultery," for having seduced his brother-in-law's wife Herodias. In the second diamond from the top, John is thrown into prison, while, just above, Salome is shown to dance so acrobatically at Herod's feast that she is literally doubled over, her head touching her feet. In the top diamond the executioner, sword raised, is ready to behead John, while a servant, arms extended, waits to receive the precursor's head on a plate.

The story of Daniel—his captivity at the Babylonian court of King Nebudchanezzar, dream interpretation, and time spent among the lions—is aligned with the story of John the Baptist and belongs to the series of Hebrew prophets that ring the axis Passion window. A double lancet devoted to Ezekiel makes the definitive turn of the apse in the direction of the southern bays of the nave. To the right a lancet dedicated to the prophet Jeremiah culminates at the top with the fall of Jerusalem—"Thus saith the Lord: Behold I will deliver this city into the hands of the king of Babylon, and he shall burn it with fire" (Jeremiah 34:2)—which had special meaning on the eve of King Louis's departure on crusade with the intention of reconquering the Holy City. Paired with Jeremiah is the story of Tobit and his son Tobias, who was held in the Middle Ages as a paragon of the faithful husband. The upper part of the lancet focuses upon the marriage feast of Tobias and Sarah, completing a ring of marriages around the tops of the stained glass windows of the upper chapel, from that of Joseph in the Exodus window, to that of Ruth and Boaz in the upper tracery of the Joshua bay, to that of Tobias, to whom, according to his wife Marguerite, Louis prayed three days before consummating his own marriage.

The focus upon marriage prepares the heroically feminine bays of the south side of the upper chapel. The north side of the nave is dominated by Old Testament patriarchs, prophets, judges, warriors, and kings. Few women appear among the powerful men under whose crownings and conquests Louis sat in the alcove reserved for his devotions. Nor are those women who are included in the glass on the north side necessarily shown in the most attractive light or in the most flattering episodes of their life story. Moses's sister Miriam, for example, is shown "white as snow as with a leprosy" (Numbers 12:10) for having taken part in the murmurings against Moses among the Israelites in the desert, but there is no portrait of her beneficent rescue of her infant brother from the bulrushes nor of her dancing joyously with timbrels once the Israelites reach the other side of the Red Sea. Unidentified Hebrew women are shown hiding their children from the soldiers who carry out Pharaoh's order to kill the male "children of Israel," and they walk in the crowd of those crossing out of Egypt. But aside from marginal visual mentions of Ruth and Deborah, who, in the Judges bay, "sat under a palm tree . . . : and the children of Israel came up to her for all judgment" (Judges 4:5), there are no active women, leading ladies, in the glass of the north wall. Deborah rendering judgment under the palm tree must simply have been irresistible to Louis IX as a forerunner of his sitting in judgment under the oak tree at Vincennes.

STRONG WOMEN: JUDITH, ESTHER, AND BLANCHE OF CASTILE

Two heroic women, each the chief protagonist of an independent book among the canonical texts of the Hebrew Bible, dominate the eastern half of the south wall, which is cinched in the lower part of the relics window by the story of Helena's enterprising retrieval of relics. The story of Judith, who rescues the Israelites from the oppression of the vengeful Assyrian King Nebudchanezzar, is related in forty panels that highlight the fierce courage of the young widow. The bottom of the Judith window emphasizes the cruelty of Holofernes, the general dispatched by Nebudchanezzar to subdue the nations that have refused to submit to him. In a series of panels in the lower part of the bay, Holofernes is shown practicing techniques of warfare that may not have changed since the Hellenistic era—ca. 135–78 BCE—when the Book of Judith was written, but are nonetheless contemporaneous with Saint Louis. The Assyrian soldiers in pursuit of their enemy wear coats of mail, carry lozenged-shaped shields, and wield banners that are distinctly medieval. According to the techniques of medieval siege craft, they raze the harvest in fields and cut off the water supply to towns that capitulate with the iconic gesture of surrender, the rendering of keys at the city gates closer in appearance to those of the thirteenth century than to those of the centuries before Christ.

Judith's slaying of Holofernes occupies fully ten panels which emphasize, through the glass master's choice among the myriad scenes from the deuterocanonical text, not only the heroine's bravery but also the cool-headed care with which she prepares the deed. Thus, we see Judith in consultation with the elders of the besieged city of Bethulia. They have decided to surrender if aid does not arrive in five days and advise Judith, who has summoned them to counsel, against "murmuring against the Lord" (Judith 8:24) as was the wont of the Israelites— remember the leprosy of Miriam!—in the desert. Having hatched a plan, she makes them promise not to inquire into what she is doing. She prepares to depart, as her servant pours liquid into a small barrel, which may signal the wine with which to inebriate Holofernes. She kneels before an altar in a panel (sixth oval on the left) with a banner on top: "CI:PRIE:JUDIT:D[I]EU:QUELE:PUIST ENGINIER," "Here Judith prays that she might, . . ." and the word engi[g]nier in Old French is tricky. It derives from the Latin "genius," the male spirit of a family, which came in the late Middle Ages, before passing into English, to refer to the disposition or natural talent of an individual. Used as a verb in the thirteenth century, enginier means "to do something artfully," "to invent," "to machinate," "to use all the intelligence or means at one's disposal," "to find a way of doing something difficult." It lies at the root of the modern English and French "engineer"/ingéneur, and, in

Judith Inebriates Holofernes, Slayes Holofernes, Judith Window
(© Painton Cowen)

a semantic spinoff, *enginier* also means "to trick" and, when speaking of a woman, "to seduce."

The figure of Judith captures all the semantic resonance of the Old French term enginier, the difficulty, the ruse, the seduction, all part of her difficult mission. She enters the Assyrian camp, meets Holofernes, and, then, in a dilation of the drama of the murder, bathes at night and grooms herself in a scene with particular resonance for a woman widowed three-and-a-half years earlier and who has lived until then in seclusion. In the eighth oval from the bottom on the far left, Judith and Holofernes, surrounded by attentive servants, toast each other at the feast at which the Assyrian general drinks so much that, having fallen asleep, the heroine, in the oval just to the right of the banquet, is able to slay him with his own sword, as her servant, in a departure from the biblical text, watches anxiously at the foot of the bed. Still holding Holofernes's sword, she exhibits the severed head in a gruesome illustration of the Book of Judith 13:19: "Behold the head of Holofernes the general of the army of the Assyrians, and behold his canopy, wherein he lay in his drunkenness, where the Lord our God slew him by the hand of a woman." In the aftermath of the death of Holofernes, the liberated children of Israel massacre the Assyrians and loot the occupiers' camp.

There is some debate as to where exactly the city of Bethulia is located, or even whether or not it is another name for Jerusalem. This much, however, is certain: on the eve of the seventh crusade, the story of the liberation of a city situated somewhere in the Holy Land and occupied by Assyrians, again anachronistically and vaguely associated with Muslims, refers to Louis's pending departure for the Middle East with the goal of liberating the Holy City. Like the Renaissance paintings of the Nativity with an Italian hill town in the background, the Judith window tells the tale of events that supposedly occurred in sixth-century Palestine. Yet, they are hugely topical. The dress, headgear, weaponry, architecture, interior design, right down to the crosshatched pattern of the tablecloth at Holofernes's feast, belong to France of the thirteenth century.

The story of Judith, the courageous woman who saves her people from destruction, resonates so strongly with that of Blanche of Castile that it is hard to imagine that the Queen mother did not have a hand in fashioning the Judith window. The suggestion would not necessarily have had to be direct. The desire of a glass painter to please his patron, known for her powerful personality and willingness to intervene in affairs of state, might have led naturally to a design stressing the cool courage of the biblical heroine. Like Judith, Blanche was a widow who managed to protect the young Louis IX, crowned at the tender age of twelve after his father's untimely death, from a clique of rebellious barons which sought to place Pierre Mauclerc upon the throne. (This is the same Pierre Mauclerc who donated the south rose window at Chartres and whose image at the bottom of the lancets sits opposite the north rose which was the gift of Louis IX and Blanche). Returning from the coronation ceremony at Reims while the coalition sought to test the queen, a foreigner, Blanche arranged for the people of Paris to meet her and her son on the outskirts of the city, which avoided a crisis until Count Thibaut IV of Champagne, whom Blanche had cultivated and whom the gossips claimed was her lover, arrived with a force of three hundred knights to quell the rebellion. Blanche served as regent during Louis's minority and in his absence, and in the four and a half years between the king's departure and her own death in 1252, she sat in the alcove on the women's side of the Sainte-Chapelle under the stained glass cycles of Judith and Queen Esther, two heroic women whose beneficent deeds saved their people, as Blanche had rescued the kingdom of France.

QUEEN ESTHER

IF THE STORY OF Judith is one of invasion and occupation by a foreign foe, that of Esther is one of court culture with resonance for the king, queen, and retinue of nobles and functionaries surrounding Louis and his mother. The lived quality of this tale of obedience and disobedience, envy, rivalry, and intrigue amongst the retinue of Persian king Ahasuerus would have been all the more vivid for the royal court of mid-thirteenth-century France because the Book of Esther is alone among the books of the Hebrew Bible not to feature the intervention of God in the affairs of human beings. Though the narrative thread of the 129 panels of the Esther window, the fullest of the narrative programs of the Sainte-Chapelle, is difficult in places to follow, the viewer should nonetheless stop before this significant rendering of King Ahasuerus's repudiation of his wife and taking of Esther, the plotting of courtiers against the king, Haman's appointment as governor, his anger at Esther's uncle Mordecai and condemnation of the Jews, which is

Esther at a Banquet, Esther Window (© Painton Cowen)

reversed by Esther's artful domestic diplomacy, Mordecai's triumph, and Haman's execution.

The story of Esther is to some large degree a story of banquets, and this is where the Esther window begins in the bottom left four panels, with the banquet that Ahasuerus offers the people of the capital city of Sushan and which lasted for 180 days. When, after a prolongation of another seven days, the king sends for his wife Vashti, "with the crown set upon her head, to shew her beauty to all the people" (Esther 1:11) and she refuses to come, Ahasuerus meets with his advisors and decides to choose another queen. His counselor Mordecai, who has raised his brother's orphaned daughter Esther, brings her before the king, who is smitten. In the middle left of the second row of oval and half-oval panels, Ahasuerus places a crown upon the head of his new queen. As elsewhere, crowns are an essential prop within the Esther window, which turns around a power struggle at the highest level of the Persian court. Here, too, the kings and queens of the ancient world wear crowns topped by the fleurs-de-lys of the kings and queens of France, and even more specifically the very crown worn in manuscript and sculptural portraits of Louis IX.

In a subplot which fills the third row of ovals from the bottom and the left half of the fourth row, Mordecai, who has discovered the plot of two courtiers to kill the king, transmits this information to Esther who informs the potential victim. Ahasuerus summons the conspirators and has them beaten, imprisoned, and hanged. Louis and Blanche might have been moved by Ahasuerus's discovery of a scheme against the king, which no doubt reminded them of the machinations of the conspirators in the early years of their reign. Throughout the 1230s, and really until his victory at the Battle of Taillebourg (1242) over a coalition of barons from the region of Poitiers allied with King Henry III of England, the French king was beset by a series of intrigues and open rebellions against such a young monarch and his foreign mother.

THE WRITING LESSON

IN A UNIQUE MOMENT in the vast sea of stained glass of the upper chapel, a protagonist in the myriad dramas of Old Testament history makes a written record of the events in which he has participated. An oval in the middle right of the fourth row of the Esther window shows Ahasuerus depositing in the royal archives the recorded testimony of Mordecai's service to the crown. The significance of such a scene of writing cannot be underestimated. The Sainte-Chapelle is connected to the Parliament of Paris, the supreme court of France, where, beginning in the twelfth century, the recording and orderly preservation of judicial decisions was an important catalyst to the transformation of a system of judgment based on memory and ordeal into one based upon the written procedure of inquest and records of precedent. It is ironic, in light of King Ahasuerus's archiving of Mordecai's loyal deed, that the lower panels of the windows were destroyed in 1803 when the upper chapel was transformed into a storage depot for the overflow of archived documents from the court on which it abuts.

The visual verbosity of the Esther window is nowhere more evident than in the ten scenes at the very right of the fourth and all along the fifth row of ovals in which Ahasuerus appoints Haman as his governor. The people of Sushan prostrate themselves before him, with the exception of Mordecai, who, as a Jew, refuses to bow down. This is the point at which Haman decides to kill "all the nation of the Jews that were in the kingdom of Ahasuerus," and consults the lots to determine "on what day and what month the nation of the Jews should be destroyed." In a second scene of writing in the middle left of row six, a scribe records Haman's order in a visible rendering of the Book of Esther 3:12–13: "And the king's scribes were called . . . and they wrote, as Aman had commanded, to all the king's lieutenants, and to the judges of the provinces, and of divers nations, as every nation could read, and hear according to their different languages, in the name of king Ashuerus: and the letters, sealed with his ring, were sent by the king's messengers to all provinces." The transcription of the edict, its translation into different languages, authentication with a seal, and distribution to the provinces are all in keeping with the procedures of the Parisian royal chancellery, which was responsible for the control of official documents, including letters. They reflect the daily practices of the circle of officialdom of the French court and represent an important element of state building in medieval France.

Meanwhile, Mordecai sends word of the fate of the Jews to Esther who arranges and hosts a banquet, while Haman prepares the scaffold on which to execute Mordecai. Ahasuerus, however, is unable to sleep and "and he commanded the histories and chronicles of former times be brought him. And when they were reading them before him, [2] They came to that place where it was written, how Mardochai had discovered the treason of Bagathan and Thares the eunuchs, who sought to kill king Assuerus" (Esther 6:1–2). It is the written word that saves Mordecai, who is not hanged by Haman but rewarded by Ahasuerus. At a second feast, illuminated in the upper part of the window, Esther, who reveals to her husband for the first time that she is Jewish, also uncovers Haman's plot, which leads to the execution of the treacherous governor on the gibbet he had prepared for Mordecai who replaces him as viceroy and issues new edicts to spare the Jews of the kingdom: "Then the king's scribes and secretaries were called . . . and letters were written, as Mardochai had a mind, to the Jews, and to the governors, and to the deputies, and to the judges, who were rulers over the hundred and twenty-seven provinces, from India even to Ethiopia" (Esther 8:9).

Ahasuerus authorizes the vengeance of the Jews, who, dressed as medieval knights wearing coats of mail and wielding heavy swords, are shown in the top rows of the Esther window destroying those who would have destroyed them. At the pinnacle on the middle right, in a scene bordered, as is the entire Esther window, by interlaced castles of

Castile and fleurs-de-lys, the heroine and her uncle dictate to a scribe two letters, one recording the events recounted verbally in the Book of Esther and visually in the Esther window, and a "second epistle," in order that these days, which are called Purim, the "day of lots" because of the lots that were thrown into the urn, "shall never be forgot," but "established as a festival for the time to come" (Esther 9:28–29). There is some indication that Esther's message was received and read, as a figure at ten thirty in the outer lobe of the small rose above the whole is shown reading a scroll, possibly delivered by the messenger before him, the Book of Esther, known in Hebrew as the "Megillah," being one of the five scrolls of the Hebrew Bible. In a wild anachronism, not visible to spectators below, this scroll is sealed by nothing more nor less than Louis's own insignia—the fleur-de-lys!

Between the Esther and the relics window on the south side of the nave a large bay displays a selection of scenes from the four Books of Kings. Given the enormity of the biblical narratives, which cover the reigns of Samuel, Saul, David, and Solomon, the material selected is, again, revelatory of the concerns of the French monarchy. The Kings window summarizes many of the themes found elsewhere in the windows of the upper chapel. The lower panels narrate the birth of Samuel and the struggle between the Jews and the Philistines in which the ark of the covenant is key. The Philistines who capture the ark find themselves beset by plagues: "And while they were carrying it about, the hand of the Lord came upon every city with an exceeding great slaughter" (I Kings 5:9). The destruction of the idols is featured in the Kings window, and, as elsewhere, is used to justify Louis's crusade against the Muslims in the Middle East. So, too, the question of succession, which dominates the Books of Kings and marks the transition from the period of Judges to the monarchy, plays a significant role on the south side of Louis's palatine chapel. In a scene among the lower panels, Samuel, under pressure to unify the tribes of Israel, anoints Saul as king. And though Samuel as prophet, priest, and judge, was not himself a king, he wears the crown and holds the scepter, both, again, capped with the fleurs-de-lys of the King of France.

Louis IX's focus upon the Book of Kings is deeply rooted in the history of France in the centuries preceding his reign and in his own ambitions not only for crusader conquest abroad, but for the development of state institutions at home. The history of the monarchy in the century and a half preceding the reign of Louis is one of gradual state expansion and formation. Beginning with Philip I (d. 1108), French monarchs, like the tribal leaders of Judah, recuperated the lands and rights that had escheated to local feudal lords in the period following the dissolution of the Carolingian Empire after Charlemagne's death in 814 CE. The expansion of the royal domain, especially under Philip Augustus (d. 1223) and his grandson Louis IX, was accompanied by the rationalization of the French state, the development of the institutions of civil government—social, economic, judicial, and political—that explains Louis's identification with the transition depicted in the Book of Kings from tribal to monarchic rule. Chief among these, of course, is state "monopoly of the legitimate use of physical force" or violence, in the phrase of Max Weber, which, as we have seen (p. 115), motivated Louis's outlawing of the independent resolution of legal disputes via judicial duels or by private warfare.

It is easy to imagine that King Louis must have delighted in the institutional scenes of writing—records kept and decrees dispatched to distant parts of the realm—depicted in the Esther window. How much more, then, must he have resonated with the biblical example of state building in Samuel's creation of kingship, at God's behest, based upon military might: "This will be the right of the king that shall reign over you: He will take your sons, and put them in his chariots, and will make them his horsemen, and his running footmen, to run before his chariots" (I Kings 8:11). Samuel removes Saul when he disobeys God's command in a campaign against King Amalec and anoints David, whose conquests— the slaying of Goliath and victory over the Philistines—occupy a large portion of the middle panels of the Kings window. Louis responded most fully, however, to the narrative contained in 2 Kings 5–6 of David's conquest of Jerusalem, the entrance of the ark of the covenant into the city, and the building of the first temple by David's son Solomon. Indeed, the Sainte-Chapelle not only reproduced the ark of the tabernacle, but housed the relics pictured in the window just to the right of the Kings window in the heart of the fixed capital of a new Jerusalem on the Seine.

THE WEST ROSE AND FINAL THINGS

THE NORTHEASTERN CORNER of the Sainte-Chapelle depicts the creation of the world, and the eastern curve of the apse, the central event of human history, the Passion of Christ. The western wall, under which one enters and over which the sun sets, is dominated by a spectacular rendering of the end of time as contained in the Apocalypse of Saint John. This great burst of light and color is from a different period altogether, having been reworked, masonry and glass, in the late fifteenth century. The west rose reflects not so much the radiating Gothic style of Chartres and Notre-Dame, with their large rose windows whose spindly stone bars radiate like the spokes of a wheel, as the flamboyant Gothic of the late Middle Ages, with its flowing entwined double curves that make it seem as if flames were shooting from the core. The curvy tracery of the west wall contrasts with the more precise and geometric composition of the other windows. The tonality of its color stands out among all the glass of Louis's chapel. In the place of the strong reds and blues of the apse and nave, the Sainte-Chapelle apocalypse displays pale blues, off-whites, and luminous bright yellows which only entered the palate of medieval stained glass in the fourteenth century with the introduction of silver stain, a combination of pipe clay mixed with silver nitrate or silver sulfide, which enabled greater control of the coloring process.

Oculus, West Rose Window
(© Painton Cowen)

New Jerusalem, West Rose Window
(© Painton Cowen)

The great west rose of the Sainte-Chapelle contains as literal a rendering of the Apocalypse of Saint John as one might imagine, beginning at the center oculus with an image of Christ of the Last Judgment, a sword in His mouth, surrounded by seven candlesticks, seven stars, and the seven churches of Asia to which John's revelation is addressed:

And I turned to see the voice that spoke with me. And being turned, I saw seven golden candlesticks: [13] And in the midst of the seven golden candlesticks, one like to the Son of man, clothed with a garment down to the feet, and girt about the paps with a golden girdle. [14] And his head and his hairs were white as white wool and as snow. And his eyes were as a flame of fire: . . . [16] And he had in his right hand seven stars. And from his mouth came out a sharp two-edged sword. (Apocalypse 1:12–16)

At Christ's right foot, John kneels prostrate, his hands joined in prayer like Suger on the west facade of Saint-Denis. Twenty-four white-robed elders of the Apocalypse sit on stools in the petal-shaped cluster above Christ. Each holds a harp and wears on his head a golden crown, bearing, of course, the fleur-de-lys, no longer primarily the heraldic sign of Louis IX, but a symbol of all of France. Above the elders, another image of Christ holds the "book written within and without, sealed with seven seals" (5:1) and opened by "the Lamb with seven horns and seven eyes."

Visionary figures associated with the Apocalypse of John spew forth like flames from the central oculus as an opening of the seals, an unfolding of the book, in a furious imagining of what the end of the world will look and feel like. Some thematic order of John's Book is preserved in the opening of the seven seals, the sounding of the seven trumpets, the emptying of the seven vials of the wrath of God. However, gone from the west rose is any semblance of narrative order, as in the biblical stories of the other windows. Instead, a delirious display of feral images, each from the Revelation of John, but scattered all about and separated from each other by thick stone tracery, make for a great grotesque whirlwind of visual terror. Some of the horror is humanized: the horsemen in the first cluster of petals below the oculus, a figure of death carrying a javelin in one hand and a tangle of vipers in the other, emerges from a huge green Hell's mouth, a dragon with a penetrating red eye. On the outer rim at eight thirty, the whore of Babylon rides a beast with seven heads and ten horns, "having a golden cup in her hand, full of the abominations and filthiness of her fornication" (17:4). Some of the horror resides in a mix of nature and man, as in the terrifying image in the outer cluster of petals at noon of "locusts that were like unto horses," with the tails of scorpions, "And on their heads were . . . crowns like gold: and their faces were as the faces of men. [8] And they had hair as the hair of women, and their teeth were as lions" (9:7–8). Figures that represent an upturning or cessation of nature join those that are, in the medieval phrase, "against nature": the earthquake that accompanies the opening of the sixth seal, the natural disasters following the sounding of the seven trumpets, signal a collapse of the heavens with darkening of the sun, moon, and stars, and mountains on fire.

Amid all the images of terror that will accompany the end of human time, the world depicted there is still that of the late Middle Ages, with, perhaps, a slight Germanic cast in the pudgy brutish bodies, angular faces with large chins, and carved profiles lacking in the grace of the drawn figures of the stained glass in the rest of the upper chapel. The dress, headgear and hair style; the arms and armor, lances, bows and arrows; the horses and riders, their saddles, reins, caparisons, stirrups, and spurs; and especially the architecture, round-towered castles, Gothic chapels, city walls, and middle-class Parisian houses are all inspired by the contemporaneous culture of France. One image, in particular, holds special meaning for Louis's palace church. The representation of the New Jerusalem, situated in the outer cluster of petals at nine thirty, is a visualization of the description of the Heavenly City in John 21:10–24, with its twelve gates guarded by twelve angels, twelve foundations "with the twelve names of the twelve apostles of the lamb" and adorned "with all manner of precious stones." Yet, it is also an idealized depiction of fifteenth-century Paris with its defensive crenelated walls, turreted gates and buildings with arrow slits for windows, and decorated Gothic churches, one of which might have been the Sainte-Chapelle itself, in a great conjunction of Saint Louis's chapel of glass and John's vision of "the glory of God, and the light thereof like to a precious stone, as to the jasper stone even as crystal."

In a cycle that takes us from the creation of the world, through Christ's Passion, the arrival of relics in Paris, and the Last Judgment, the stained glass of the Sainte-Chapelle dramatizes the whole of human history—past, present, and future. King Louis was a keen dramatist, and his palatine chapel, with its reliquary stage, was only one of the theaters in which he staged his own sainthood. The king was known for his humility. In a saintly stunt reminiscent of Christ's washing the feet of his disciples, Louis publicly washed the feet of the poor of Paris whom he also invited to eat at his table in the royal palace. His courage in the crusade which he organized and financed, and in the course of which he endured sickness and captivity, made for ready comparison with the suffering and humiliated Christ. You may think it mawkish or improbable, but Louis even staged his own saintly death. Having again embarked on crusade in 1270, the king took sick in Tunis on his way to the Holy Land. When it became clear that he might not survive, he donned a hair shirt and lay down "on a bed of ashes spread out in the shape of a cross" and died "at the same hour at which the Lord Jesus Christ . . . expired on the cross," in the phrase of Geoffrey of Beaulieu, one of his early biographers.

As per the medieval mortuary custom for royals or nobles, Louis's innards were removed. His body was boiled to separate the flesh from the bones, the heart and intestines sent to Palermo where they remained in the cathedral of Monreale close to his brother Charles of Anjou, King of Sicily. Louis's bones were transported in a long cortege from Tunis to Calabria in southern Italy, and then to Rome, Florence, Milan, across the Mont Cenis Pass to Lyon, Troyes, Paris and, finally, Saint Denis where they rested among the kings of France whose remains he had dramatically apportioned according to dynasty while he was still alive. In 1306, Louis's head and some of his bones were translated to the Sainte-Chapelle, and his jawbone at least ended up in the treasury of

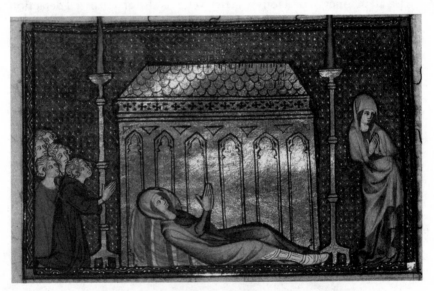

Emmelot de Chaumont from Miracles of Saint Louis,
Guillaume de Saint Pathus (Paris, BnF, Français 5716 f.298)

Notre-Dame where you can still see in the treasury a reproduction of the reliquary in the shape of a bust of the royal saint.

Almost immediately after his death, contact with the body of the deceased king occasioned miracles which were the sign of sainthood. In one such episode, Emmelot of Chaumont, a twenty-eight-year-old woman, came with two companions to Saint-Denis where she took lodging at the house of Emmeline la Charronne on a Sunday. On Monday she did all the tasks that healthy women do—fetching water, baking bread, and making beds; but on Tuesday night around midnight she was struck in the right thigh, leg, and foot by an ailment which prevented her from walking. One of the women with whom Emmelot came to Saint-Denis and her host Emmeline began to touch the afflicted leg, which was observed to be redder than the other one and had no sensation. They tried poking the leg with a needle and placing her foot in the fireplace, all to no avail. Emmelot begged to be taken to the tomb of King Louis, whose help she had invoked, promising, if cured, to go on a pilgrimage for him and only to eat once a day. Emmelot's friends put her on a stretcher and carried her to the church in front of Saint Louis's tomb. She returned to her host's house on crutches, dragging her leg and foot behind her. Emmelot kept returning to the tomb until, one Holy Sunday of the Passion, she was finally cured. In fulfillment of her vow, she made a pilgrimage to Boulogne-sur-Mer, a distance of 130 miles, then returned to Saint-Denis where she worked as a domestic servant until her death.

Louis's bones worked so many miraculous cures at Saint-Denis—sixty-three all told—that Pope Martin IV, under pressure from Charles of Anjou, who had lobbied for his election to the papacy, began an official inquiry which lasted from May 1282 to March 1283 and called 330 witnesses to Louis's saintliness. That inquiry, in the phrase of Pope Boniface VIII, who supervised Louis's canonization in 1297, produced more documents "than a single ass could carry." King Louis had at last fulfilled his deepest desire in all he said or did: he had become a relic lying amid the relics he had amassed in the Sainte-Chapelle where the architectural and artistic aura of the building, art having replaced religion, can still be felt long after the bones have disappeared.

We turn now to Amiens cathedral and its beginning in the long journey in 1206 of another relic—the head of John the Baptist—from Constantinople to France.

AMIENS
The Parthenon of Cathedrals

NOTRE-DAME D'AMIENS. PLACE NOTRE-DAME,
AMIENS, 75 MILES NORTH OF PARIS,
LARGEST CATHEDRAL IN FRANCE
(260,000 CUBIC YARDS), BEGUN 1220 CE.

Access via train from Paris's Gare du Nord and a ten-minute walk from the Amiens train station, turn right on the Boulevard d'Alsace Lorraine, then left on the rue Gloriette to the rue Cormont. Treasury houses the face relic of John the Baptist. Amiens is known for an abundance of sculpture, the dramatization of local saints, the quatrefoils all along the west facade, the elaborately carved wooden stalls in the choir.

· · · · · ·

JOHN THE BAPTIST HEADS TO AMIENS

ON THE EVENING OF September 8, 1206, Walon de Sarton, a minor cleric who had participated in the crusader capture of Constantinople in April 1204, made an astonishing discovery. As a canon of the church of Saint George Mangana along the water at the southeastern part of the city, he should have participated in the vespers service. But he had just returned from military maneuvers as part of the effort to secure control of the countryside wrested from the Byzantine or Greek leaders after the French and German knights who had participated in the fourth crusade had failed to reach their original goal of recapturing the

Muslim-controlled city of Jerusalem and had turned upon the Christian city of Constantinople instead. Walon had not had time to shave or to tonsure his hair. This was no small matter. A Church council held at Toulouse in 1119 prescribed excommunication for any cleric who, "like a layman, allowed hair and beard to grow." The current Pope Alexander III decreed that the churchman with excessively long hair or beard was to be shorn, by force if necessary. So, Walon hesitated to enter the choir with his fellow clerics. In an alcove between the main altar and a building "where," according to his own testimony, "no living creature lived," a former pleasure palace of emperors, he had hoped to recite his prayers discreetly when his eyes fell upon a window stuffed with straw and other stray matter. Someone clearly had wanted to hide something but had neither the time nor the materials to seal the opening with mortar. In the pillaging of the Byzantine capital, there had been many such attempts to conceal precious secular and religious objects from the avid French and Venetian raiders. Removing the straw, Walon found a vase containing the remains of a finger and an arm, with other objects further in the recess.

Reaching beyond the vase, he felt two leather pouches, and, opening them, two large silver plates. In the safety of his room, he looked at the two silver dishes and noticed that each contained fragments of writing in Greek. On one, the inscription, "ΑΓΙΟΣ ΓΕΟΡΓΙΟΣ," and, on the other, "ΑΓΙΟΣ ΙΟΑΝΝΗΣ ΠΡΟΔΡΟΜΟΣ." Neither understanding Greek nor wanting to ask anyone for help, for fear of revealing what he had found, Walon wandered from church to church in Constantinople until he came upon images with similar letters. Imagine his surprise at learning that his discovery of the evening of September 8 was none other than the heads of Saint George and of Saint John the Baptist, as indicated by the word "ΠΡΟΔΡΟΜΟΣ," "Precursor." John, whose own birth was shrouded in mystery, proclaimed the arrival of Christ whom he baptized in the River Jordan before himself meeting a violent death at the hands of King Herod. The Gospels of Luke, Mark, and Matthew contain the story of John's rebuke of King Herod for having put aside his legitimate wife and taken his brother's wife, Herodias, who was angry at the reproach and repeatedly sought revenge. In the course of a banquet in or around the year 30 CE, Herod was captivated by the dancing of Herodias's daughter Salome and offered her the reward of her choice. Salome, consulting her mother, asked for the head of John the Baptist, who was already in Herod's prison, on a platter. In the cycle of the life of Christ, there is no more important figure than John the Baptist, no more sacred object than the head that had announced in real time the coming of the Messiah.

Holding the two sacred sacks in his hands, Walon faced a dilemma. In order to avoid the disorder of wild pillaging and to ensure equal distribution of booty, the crusaders had in the month before their successful assault upon the richest city in the world sworn an oath that liturgical objects—relics, crosses, icons, platters, and other vessels—should be placed in a common stockpile to be distributed under the supervision of Bishop Garnier of Troyes according to the "quality and merit" of individual knights, squires, and clerics. Not all had complied, of course. As one of the leaders of the fourth crusade and its most vivid chronicler, Marshal of Champagne Geoffrey Villehardouin, noted, "Some were honest in presenting their spoils, others deceitful," risking excommunication by the Pope or even execution: "a good number were hanged."

Walon had at the outset been one of the good ones. Having come into possession of the head of Saint Christopher, the arm of Saint Eleuthere, and the relics of several "other joyous saints," he returned them to the general store and received nothing in return. He must have known that others had fewer scruples than he did and that they had provided for themselves the kind of generous homecoming that the heads of Saints George and John the Baptist might afford him. He might even have witnessed the defilement of holy objects in the most sacred of places, the church of Hagia Sophia, built by the Emperor Justinian in the sixth century as the cathedral of Constantinople and the largest and most elaborate building on earth. So great was the haul that the marauding crusaders, in the words of Niketas Choniates, the aristocratic former imperial secretary, brought into "the very sanctuary of the temple itself mules and asses with pack saddles; some of these, unable to keep their feet on the smoothly polished marble floors, slipped and were pierced by knives so that the excrement from the bowels and the spilled blood defiled the sacred floor." All who were there remarked upon the extraordinary quantity of church possessions that were looted in the aftermath of 1204.

Given the extraordinary nature of his discovery, Walon made a decision. Separating the smaller bejeweled plates, which contained portions of the heads of Saints George and John the Baptist, from the larger silver plates on which they were mounted, he crossed the commercial districts formerly occupied by the Genoese, Amalfitan, and Pisan traders in Constantinople, to the Venetian quarter, which had dominated trade between Byzantium and the West since the Conquest. There Walon sold the fungible portion of his findings. He now had enough money for the journey home, and the smaller size of the bundles he would be carrying made the relics easier to hide. But Walon apparently felt guilty, and so he vowed to dedicate to pious works any money in excess of what would be needed for travel back to Picardie.

On September 30, 1206, with sacred loot under each arm, Walon headed for one of the Venetian-controlled harbors between the city wall and the Golden Horn. As he emerged from the city gate, he could see the warehouses and shops, the money-changing stalls and the taverns along the "steps" between the wall and the water. On one side of the deep curved port, he observed ships loading and unloading their commercial goods; on the other, the shipbuilding yard and the enclosure reserved for the manufacture of oars. On the far shore of the inlet, Walon caught a last glimpse of the Galata tower which, until the arrival of the crusaders in Constantinople, had been the place from which the iron chain across the harbor was controlled and was the first structure to fall under crusader attack.

When Walon boarded the ship for Venice, he was not traveling alone. His companion, a fellow cleric named Wibert, had been the chaplain of Aleaumes de Fontaines, a knight who had participated in the sacking of Constantinople but who had died in Greece in 1205. Wibert, too, was carrying relics back to a church near Amiens, the Abbey of Longpré. Walon's and Wibert's ship, one of the mixed genre combining sails with rowers, not a ship designed for the open seas, but for island and coastal hopping, sailed through the Sea of Marmara and the Dardanelles. Having alighted for only one night at the island and coastal natural ports along the way, the travelers to Venice probably spent several days on Crete while the crew rested, merchants on board bought wheat, wine, cheese, and wool, and sold spices picked up in Constantinople. The boat was no doubt reloaded with grain, oil, meat, eggs, dried fish, and especially with barrels of water for the trip against adverse winds and currents around the Peloponnesian peninsula and up the Adriatic. The voyage, managed until then mostly under sail, would now periodically require the manpower of rowers, and rowing required hydration.

Walon's ship hugged the Balkan coast up the Adriatic, which was much more favorable than the Italian side, the lee shore toward which ships were naturally blown. The travelers reached Venice thirty days after setting out from Constantinople. They had made good time. The distance between the two ports is 1169 nautical miles, which meant that they had travelled thirty-nine miles per day. The average October day in the region provided twelve hours of sunlight, which put their average speed at a little over three miles per hour, perhaps even a little more, considering layovers in major trading and supply ports.

The port of Venice bustled with the trading and military energy of its newfound empire which stretched all along the route that Walon and Wibert had traveled. They were anxious to begin their overland journey to Picardie. Once ferried from Venice to the mainland, they retraced the route they had taken almost five years earlier. Crossing the Veneto and Lombardy, they arrived around the middle of the month of November in Piacenza, where crusaders from the North as well as from the West had originally assembled on their way to Venice in 1202. They pushed on to Asti, Chieri, and Turin, then to Susa at the foot of the mountains where they traversed into what is now France via the Mont-Cenis pass.

The returning crusaders headed north and, skirting the Lac du Bourget, turned west to the towns of Belley and Saint Rambert, currently Saint-Rambert-en-Bugey where Walon reports that they were robbed, losing some of jewels they had brought from Constantinople but not the holy head. They crossed the Ain river and then the Saône, probably at the bridge at Chalon-sur-Saône, which took them through rich wine country, past Beaune, Nuits-Saint-Georges, Vosne-Romanée, Chambolle-Musigny, and Gevrey-Chambertin, to Dijon, and from Dijon to Châtillon-sur-Seine, and on to Troyes. It was a day's ride to Noyon, then to Roye, and another day to Beaufort-en-Santerre where Walon sent word to his uncle Pierre de Sarton of his return bearing one of the most sacred and prestigious relics ever to arrive in the West.

Pierre, a canon of the cathedral of Amiens, alerted Bishop Richard de Gerberoy, who sent a delegation to meet Walon at Beaufort, some twelve miles from the center of the city. On December 17, 1206, an assembly of clergy and representatives of all the various constituencies of Amiens accompanied Walon to the gates of town. There, they were met, according to the returning clerical hero, by the bishop, "dressed pontifically, and by the all the clergy, followed by a great rush of townspeople who, with all imaginable demonstrations of joy, broke out into hymns,

Walon de Sarton Arrives at Amiens (© Painton Cowen)

canticles, and other prayers, all sung in honor of the Precursor. . . ." The head of Saint John the Baptist, having been taken out of hiding in Constantinople, smuggled by ship to Venice, and then overland along the most frequented trade routes of Europe, arrived at last in Amiens. As seen in this quatrefoil relief, Bishop Gerberoy took the sacred head of Saint John the Baptist in his hands and carried it into the church of Saint Firmin where it remained until the building of the great cathedral that still stands today.

AUTHENTICITY OF THE HEAD RELIC

You MAY WONDER ABOUT the authenticity of the head relic of John the Baptist, and you are not alone. The process of authentication began almost as soon as it arrived in Amiens. In the weeks and months following Walon's return, he was deposed by Bishop Richard de Gerberoy who recorded in Latin the official testimony of his astonishing find and journey from Constantinople to Amiens; and though that testimony has been lost, it exists either wholly or in part via a French translation published in 1609 by a canon of the cathedral, Robert Viseur. Such testimony, known as a "translation," was not unusual, but rather served as part of the procedure for the legitimation of a relic which moved from one place to another without a sealed letter as a guarantee of provenance.

In Christian orthodoxy, sainthood is inextricably entwined with miracles, which account in the first instance for the power of relics—the relic effect, and thus, as we saw in the case of Louis IX, their authenticity (see p. 201). John's head occasioned many miracles, and, in particular, cures of what was known in the Middle Ages as the "sickness of Saint John," or epilepsy. By analogy with Salome's frenetic dance before Herod, epileptics were the "dancers of Saint John," whose attacks were reported to become more frequent as Saint John's Day (June 24) approached and to be cured by contact with the face relic. The head of John the Baptist intervened not only in the lives of those who suffered from epilepsy, but in great affairs of state. King Charles VII (d. 1461) prayed to the relic to aid him in his struggle against the English in the Hundred Years' War, and his success in recapturing Normandy in the 1440s is attributed by some to an intervention by the Saint, in appreciation of which the king retrofitted the reliquary with jewels.

A visual account of the beheading of Saint John at Herod's feast along with images of its journey from Palestine to Constantinople and then to Amiens is contained in a series of high relief tableaux and quatrefoils on the north side of the wall around the choir. There John is seen denouncing Herod for committing adultery with his brother's wife and is taken prisoner for his temerity before the king. The king, seated at table in the background, speaks with Herodias, while Salome, having danced, "demanded the head of John the Baptist." In a third tableau the executioner holds the saint's severed head in one hand, a sword in the other. The image is well placed, for the stairway leading to the room in which the face relic of John the Baptist was kept until the French Revolution was situated just on the other side of the ambulatory across from the gruesome scene of decapitation, which becomes only worse in the final carving of the series.

The tableau on the far left depicts Herodias, dagger in hand, stabbing the forehead of John the Baptist as Salome faints with a look of horror upon her face. Close examination of the face relic, which is still visible in the cathedral treasury, reveals a hole just above the left eyebrow, forensic evidence of the reality of the relic. The eighteenth-century Bollandists' *Acta Sanctorum*, considered to be authoritative when it comes to the lives of the saints, alludes to Herodias's vengeful anger after John the Bap-

Head of John the Baptist Stabbed by Herodias

tist's death, more precisely, to her piercing his tongue with her comb and his eyebrow with a knife—*ita impegiste etiam cuspidem cultri in super-cilium Sancti* ("thus she drove the point of a knife into the eyebrow of the Saint"). The legend of Herodias's stabbing of the dead head of John the Baptist resurfaced when what was believed to be the actual platter upon which the head was served was offered as a gift by Pope Innocent VIII to the city of Genoa where it now resides. The platter, embellished around 1300 with a gold and enamel head of the Saint, shows a wound over the right and not over the left eye, indicating that the artist knew the story but had not seen the holy head in Amiens.

Head of John the Baptist (© Maile Hutterer)

The attempt to authenticate the face relic of Amiens culminated in a scientific study conducted in 1959 by the director of the Musée de l'Homme, the anthropologist Henri Victor Vallois, and a commission hired by the diocese, consisting of medical experts—a pharmacist, a radiologist, a surgeon, and a specialist in diseases of the mouth. Using radiographic and photographic imaging, the forensic team concluded that the small protrusion of the eyebrows and of the space between the eyes "are characteristics of the male sex." The absence of teeth make it hard to assess the age of the original bearer of the face, but the fact that the sockets are fully developed and that certain of them show slight wear around the edges is in keeping with an adult "between 25 and 40 years old." The morphology of the head is "europoïde," that is, Caucasian, and neither "négroïde" nor "mongoloïde." In what appears a holdover from the nineteenth-century practice of phrenology and of the racial stereotyping characteristic of the early social sciences, the examiners state that in ancient Palestine before Christianity there were two very different racial types: Mediterranean, with a "smaller and narrower head (like today's Bedouins), and "type arménoïde," with a fuller head (like today's Lebanese and Armenians). Given the small dimensions of the Amiens head and the development of the eyebrow arches, the scientific team notes that "if indeed this piece comes from Palestine, it corresponds to the former type."

Like coroners performing an autopsy as part of a criminal investigation, the experts assembled by the Musée de l'Homme note that there can be no doubt that the hole above the left eyebrow is the result of a "violent trauma with a sharp instrument." The absence of any evidence of scarring or of even a rough change in the bone, indicates further that it is "a port-mortem lesion."

As to the age of the specimen, the forensic team infers that it seems to be older than the bones from "our Middle Ages" and less ancient than human remains from the Mesolithic era or the middle part of the Stone Age. Without the benefit of carbon dating, which was not part of the evaluation, they localize the piece as being between 1,000 and 2,000–2,500 years old. The overall conclusion of such an analysis cannot, of course, be affirmative, as there is no positive way to link the face relic of Amiens to Saint John the Baptist, if, indeed, such a person actually ever existed. And, so, the committee's determination, which neither confirms nor denies the authenticity of the relic, corresponds most closely to the philosophical principle of noncontradiction. "The examination of the whole of the case permits us to affirm that none of the elements examined is of a nature to nullify the authenticity of this relic, considering the notions of historical traditions."

A NEW CATHEDRAL
IN THE GOTHIC STYLE

REGARDLESS OF ITS REALITY, the arrival of the head of John the Baptist in Amiens coincided with the construction of a new cathedral in the Gothic style. As elsewhere, the story of building is one of fires. The town was destroyed by flames in the twelfth century, and a Romanesque cathedral was built between 1137 and 1152. That church was devastated in 1218 by another fire, like that of Chartres in 1194, of dubious origin. Amiens had gained enormous prestige with the arrival of the face relic of Saint John in 1206, yet a cathedral in the old Romanesque style was not sufficiently forward-looking in light of the new Gothic churches begun in Paris in 1163, Soissons in 1176, Chartres in 1194, and Reims in 1211. There was tremendous pressure to rebuild, and the laying of the equivalent of a cornerstone, a masonry block on the southern transept with the outline of a Dutch trowel, only two years after the fire of 1218, indicates a welcome readiness of funds, communal will, and urban initiative, all coordinated in this initial phase by two bishops—Évrard de Fouilly (d. 1222), described on his tombstone on the south part of the nave as "He who provided for the people, who laid the foundations of this edifice, to whose care the city was entrusted," and Geoffroy d'Eu (d. 1236), who lies on the north side, on a "humble bed, in preparation for a lesser or an equal one for us all." The enterprising builder-bishops negotiated a complicated plan for the urban renewal of thirteenth-century Amiens. The collegial school of Saint Firmin the Confessor and the hospital or Hôtel Dieu were displaced in order to align the towers of the new cathedral along the old Roman road between Senlis and the port of Boulogne.

A metal plaque at the center of the labyrinth in the nave of Notre-Dame d'Amiens—one of only two, along with that of Chartres— provides the names of the architects or master masons who supervised the work and attests to its rapidity: "In the year of grace one thousand two hundred and twenty was the work herein first begun. At that time Evrard was the blessed bishop of this bishopric and Louis King of France, who was the son of Philip the Wise (Philip Augustus). The one who was master builder was Master Robert, whose surname was Luzarches. It was Master Thomas de Cormont after him, and after him, his son Master Renaud who had these letters placed here, in the year of Incarnation 1300, minus 12 (1288)." Because of the speed with which first the transept, then the nave and apse, were completed, conditions favoring unity of design and execution, Amiens is considered by some to be the most perfect of French cathedrals—"the Parthenon of Gothic architecture," in the phrase of Eugène Emmanuel Viollet-le-Duc, who contributed to its restoration in the 1850s. Notre-Dame d'Amiens is also the biggest cathedral of the thirteenth century—475 feet long, 230 feet wide through the transept, and 140 feet high under the vaults of the nave. Only Beauvais, at 158 feet, is higher, but was never completed beyond the transept crossing and choir.

FINANCING "THE WORKS"

Amiens had always been prosperous. A great Roman provincial city, it served as a supply link to legions stationed in Britain, and, at its height, might even have had twice the population of Lutetia, Roman Paris. Caesar and his army spent the winter of 54 BCE there—among the Gallic tribe of the Ambiani—on his return to Rome from his second expedition to Britain. A hub of trade on the river Somme between the English Channel, the fairs of Champagne, the city of Lyon, and Italian markets, Amiens flourished. The city, situated in the middle of a rich grain belt, was an industrial center for the manufacture of arms and other metal implements used for agriculture, textiles, and fine woolen cloth. Amiens was especially known for its production of blue woad dye, acknowledged in the dedication of the chapel of Saint Nicholas on the north side of the nave, several stained glass windows, and a sculpture showing woad merchants with a sack full of their merchandise on the southern exterior wall of the cathedral—all the gifts of local woaders. The woad, wool, spices, alum, fish, cereals, and wine that were traded or passed through the city enriched the bishop who controlled the tolls on river traffic.

Though the town of Amiens was incorporated as a commune in the early twelfth century, which placed its citizens under the protection of the King of France, there is no evidence of monarchy's direct involvement in the building of the Gothic church, which was financed by the bishops of the diocese, who, in addition to the tolls on river traffic, received considerable income from taxes for the administration of justice and from their rural estates in the surrounding countryside. Bourgeois enriched by manufacture and trade, and about forty local seigneurial families, many with ties to the canons of the cathedral, all contributed generously.

The arrival of the head of John the Baptist in Amiens in 1206 enriched the Picard city of approximately 20,000 inhabitants even further. With it, Amiens became one of the central pilgrimage sites in western Europe, and pilgrims, like today's tourists, meant money spent on food, lodging, and other necessities of travel. So, too, pilgrims favored the church with pious donations for miracle cures or, on a more regular basis, for time off either for themselves or their ancestors from the pains of purgatory

according to an elaborate system of indulgences developed in the thirteenth century for turning the afterlife into a source of profit.

A MEDIEVAL FUND-RAISING SERMON

W E ARE EXTREMELY LUCKY to possess an actual appeal for funds
to build or to finish the cathedral of Amiens in the shape of a sermon
preached not in Latin for the clergy, but in French for a lay audience
either in the church itself or, more likely, in the surrounding countryside
as part of a parade of relics, one of which may have been the famous face
relic, through the outlying parishes of the diocese. The listeners, whom
the priest admits at the outset were few, consisted of the wealthy landholders of the area, though those who worked the land were excused
from work that day.

With the rhetorical skill of a seasoned orator, the itinerant priest
urged his listeners to make a pilgrimage to the mother church in Amiens
and to give alms. He warned his audience of the tortures that await those
who arrive in purgatory without having obtained pardon for the wrong
they have done while on earth.

Calculation of the time for purgation of sins in the afterlife was based
upon the number of derelictions: "Our Lord Jesus Christ has set a pen-
alty for each sin, according to which is uglier and more foul than the
other; . . . some for ten years; others for twenty years; still others for
sixty, or for a hundred, two hundred, three hundred, five hundred, one
thousand, two thousand years." The sinner might, however, reduce his
or her time in purgatory by seeking the pardon—and here the speaker
plays upon the Old French *pardonner* ("to pardon") and *par donner* ("by
giving")—obtained by pious donation, penance, or confession. Lest
there be any question of the terms of the exchange, the preacher cajoled
his audience, "Listen carefully; I shall speak gently to you: I tell you
that by giving you are pardoned, and by pardon you have God." Nor is
there any doubt about the destiny of donated funds. The preacher speaks
of the initial phase of cathedral building when "the first squared stone
of this church was laid and the first children were baptized and reborn
in the holy fonts," and he urges alms for the completion of "the work."

The priest traveling with relics participated in one of the great theological innovations of the High Middle Ages, the remapping of the afterlife to accommodate purgatory as a territory for the expiation of earthly

sins. The wholly bad will go to Hell, the wholly good, that is, the saints, will go to paradise, but those who are neither wholly good nor wholly bad will suffer in purgatory according to the degree of their personal guilt before reaching that place of heavenly delight. Purgatory made for a tailoring of the afterlife to the moral worth of the individual as well as for supple negotiations about the length of an individual's sojourn there. Pious donations might lessen one's sentence or that of one's ancestors, in what amounts to a great equivalence of time and money characterized by Jacques Le Goff as the "bureaucratization of the afterlife." The terms of such an equivalence are clear. "Know truly that to all the benefactors of the church my Lady, Saint Mary of Amiens," the preacher promised, "sends 140 days of true pardon to mitigate the vivid penance that you must do in the cruel fire of purgatory." The tariff may seem high, especially if one were required to redeem hundreds of years of anticipated torture. Yet, the skilled orator claims, the offer is comparatively generous. Saints Peter and Andrew "gave up all that they had, both quick and dead, for pardon." For the wealthy landholders of the environs of Amiens, the chance to purchase paradise with money and not with one's life must have seemed like a bargain.

AN ABUNDANCE OF SCULPTURE

FROM THE SQUARE IN front of the cathedral, Amiens appears to be the most ornate of cathedrals. Life-size figures are suspended in midair along the four buttresses on the outer edge of three deeply recessed portals. The portals themselves are lined with jamb statues and a profusion of smaller figures in the tympana and voussoirs. Foliated half-rings line the underside of the broken arches at the edge of the porches, and crocketed nubs cap the straight edges of the pointed gables. Bas reliefs wind like a ribbon in and out of the portals and buttresses which taper at several levels all up and down the face of the west facade. The buttresses support elaborate pinnacles, miniature churches with open arches between columns, towers, and spires limned with filagree, themselves crowned with stone lilies. At the midpoint, similarly decorated pinnacles coincide with the gallery of kings. Each pinnacle houses a royal figure, while the thick arches above their heads are rimmed with garlands of fig leaves separated by the grotesque heads of beasts that leer out like gargoyles without down spouts. At their top the buttresses support four

West Facade

elongated tabernacles with intricate gabled roofs and figures between their decorated columns. Trefoils and quatrefoils in tracery, some in open arches and others against the background of solid wall, dot the fancy face of the cathedral.

The west facade of Amiens is defined vertically by three zones, two under the north and south towers and one in the middle section which houses the rose window and the open-work bridge between them. Compared to other cathedrals, the towers do not extend very far above the body of the cathedral. Horizontally, four distinct layers separate the porch level from that of the tribune and the gallery of kings. These are naturally partitioned from the rose and belfries, which in their turn lie below the level of the bells. The overall effect is one of lacy openness—in the broken arches just above and behind the portals, in the slim-columned open arcades between the porches and the gallery of kings, in the belfries through which the sky is visible, in the balustrade and open-arched canopy of the bridge, and in the spindly lattice fence above the bridge almost at the height of the towers. Wherever one looks there is an abundance of decorated stone all up and down and across this great wedding cake of a cathedral.

Every Gothic cathedral is to some extent a total work of art, combining as it does architecture, sculpture, and stained glass along with one element no longer present as it was in the Middle Ages: music—the chanting of prayers at regular intervals by the canons responsible for maintaining the divine hours: matins at around 2:00 a.m., Lauds at 5:00, Prime at 6:00, Terce at 9:00, Sext at noon, None at 3:00 p.m., Vespers at 6:00, and Compline or Night Prayer before bed at 7:00 p.m. Unless one is lucky enough to attend a concert on one of the great reverberating organs of Notre-Dame Paris or Chartres or to attend mass accompanied by chant, Gothic cathedrals are now for the most part sadly silent.

The diverse artistic media that go into the design of a Gothic cathedral do not always contribute equally to the esthetics of a particular church. In the Sainte-Chapelle, for example, spectacular glass overwhelms the important but modest sculpture inside Louis's shrine and more than makes up for a lack of figurative stonework on the exterior walls. Amiens, however, is all about sculpture. The abundance of worked stone all over the west facade and the southern transept portal compensates for the relative paucity of surviving stained glass on the inside. As in the realm of music, however, the elaborate stone carving is not what it once was, and the silence of today's cathedrals is joined by the cool monochrome statuary. Every nook and cranny of the sculpted ensemble of Amiens—the jamb statues between the portals, the trumeaux or posts between doors, tympana or triangular spaces above the doors, and the voussoirs which rim the tympana—was once painted in vivid colors, only bits and pieces of which still remain visible today.

Some of the thematic elements of the west facade of Amiens resemble those of other cathedrals, and some were even copied from earlier churches. The trumeau and tympanum of the middle portal, the larger-than-life apostles on either side, the wise and foolish virgins on the door jambs, medallions of the virtues and vices under the jamb statues so closely follow the sculptural program of Notre-Dame Paris that those who sought to restore the Parisian church in the nineteenth century—especially the central statue of Christ as *Beau Dieu*—turned to Amiens for guidance. Other elements, however, are unique to the provincial city, which may even have sought to express its prosperity and independence via the richness of the west facade of the largest of the major Gothic cathedrals. Saint-Denis was the royal necropolis; Notre-Dame Paris, the central church in the capital of the realm; Chartres, the direct benefi-ciary of monarchic support for the northern transept; Sainte Chapelle, the king's palatine chapel; and Reims, the coronation site of French rul-ers from the eleventh century to the anointing of Charles X in 1825. Alone among its rivals, Notre-Dame Amiens was built outside the orbit of the king of France and without royal patronage, though a side chapel was dedicated to Louis IX a decade after his canonization in 1297.

The cathedral of Amiens expresses at once a will to exceed its rivals in external opulence, to be like the competitors in maintaining with variants the required components of Gothic style, and to be entirely unique in its integration of local elements found nowhere else among the churches of northern France. Chief among these is the integration of local saints, nearby geographic locales, and the everyday experience of those who lived in the surrounding countryside in the north por-tal of the west facade and in the entrance of the southern transept. In distinction to the universal saints found elsewhere, inside and outside of the church, the north portal of the west facade is dedicated to saints connected directly to the town and whose bodies or body parts were held in the cathedral. It is not impossible that their relics were among those paraded by the itinerant preacher on his fund-raising journey through the region. The left jamb statues feature Saint Honoré (d. 600), seventh bishop of Amiens and patron saint of bakers, to whom the southern transept is also dedicated, and who is here accompanied by an angel. To the left of Honoré, two decapitated saints, Acheul and Ache, hold their own heads. They are separated by a second angel holding a scroll from Saint Ulphe or Ulphia, an eighth-century female hermit saint, who founded a local religious community. Following the life pat-tern of many virgin saints, Ulphe declined several offers of marriage, insisting that she would have no spouse other than Jesus Christ. When her parents attempted to impose a secular life upon her, she simulated madness, running half-naked through the streets. Ulphe abandoned her father's house in Amiens and sought solitude in the wilderness, where she fell asleep by a spring. The Virgin appeared to Ulphe in a dream, splendid in light, holding the infant Jesus, who told her to establish a house where other women might follow her example, for which she lived on in the memory of the inhabitants of the region. To the right of the door, stand Saint Firmin the Confessor, Saints Domice, Salvius, and either Fuscien, Warle, and Luxor or Fuscien, Victoric, and Gentien, who were martyred in the third century. All are little known and some without written biographies by which to know them.

THE SIGNATURE QUATREFOILS

In what is the most complete calendar of any we have seen, a series of quatrefoil bas reliefs beneath the jambs of the north portal are the signature framing device of the lower register of the west facade. They exhibit the familiar signs of the zodiac in the top row and the Works of the Months on the bottom. The cycle moves on the left from Sagittarius (November/December), represented by a man planting winter wheat under Saint Honoré, to Cancer (June/July) over a man with a haymaker; and, on the right, from Capricorn (December/January) and a man killing a pig under Saint Firmin the Confessor, to Gemini (May/June) as lovers holding hands and a man sitting in a garden listening for the sound of birds on the trees under Saint Luxor. To those who entered the cathedral under the gaze of local saints and who might live in the agricultural belt around Amiens, the rural Works of the Months might have the special effect of making the cathedral seem familiar without the heavy moral pressure of the vices and virtues in the quatrefoils around the central portal or the theological weight of the biblical figures around the south entrance.

FINDING FIRMIN

The trumeau of the north portal features the standing figure of Saint Firmin the Martyr (d. 303), credited with bringing Christianity to the area, the first bishop of the city, as distinct from his successor Saint

Firmin the Confessor. Firmin, originally from Pamplona, Spain, holds in his left hand the bishop's crozier with which he crushes his persecutor, the Roman governor Sebastianus who imprisoned and executed him in the late third century. In the lintel above Firmin's head, six bishops, each wearing his miter and holding a book or a crozier, flank an ornate reliquary box on top of a decorated altar, both miniature versions of the church itself. The contents of the box, without doubt the saint's remains, were, until the French Revolution, kept in a similar reliquary behind the main altar of the cathedral.

The carved narrative frieze on the upper lintel and tympanum of the Saint Firmin portal are unique in that they refer not to biblical history nor to the end of time and the Last Judgment, but to an actual event which occurred along the spectrum of human time, at a precise moment and place, and which left a written record. The *Acta Sanctorum*,

North Portal, West Facade

an authoritative account of saints' lives, contains an account of Bishop Salve's search in the seventh century for Firmin's remains: "Since people did not know where the body of Christ's holy martyr lay, thanks to the instructions of the Holy Spirit, [Bishop Salvius] came to the place where Christ's martyr lay and, raising his eyes to heaven, with indescribable terror he saw as if a ray of light coming from a lofty throne lighting the place where Saint Firmin lay. Grateful for this sign of divine mercy, he began quickly and very reverently to dig. . . ." The length of the top of the upper lintel is covered by the swervy lines of a sky that vibrates with energy and meaning and from which a ray, twisted like a rope, descends in the middle of a crowd of no less than ten figures. In addition to Bishop Salvius, who, without removing his miter, digs with a spade in one hand and blesses onlookers with the other, two men also stand with shovels at the ready. The carver has taken care to include at least one woman, identifiable by her wimple and her delicate hands clasped in prayer, and both bearded older men and unbearded youths in the group searching for Firmin's body, which rises from a decorated sarcophagus, pitched diagonally along the full breadth of the crowd. On his head Firmin still wears the bishop's miter after three centuries underground.

The scene of invention is not only visual, but olfactory as well. As Saint Salvius opened the tomb, "the odor that emanated was so sweet and alluring, it was as if all kinds of colors and scents were crushed together and the countryside was alive with the beauty of various flowers. He [Salvius] raised him up from the tomb and set out for the city [of Amiens], the people bearing the holy martyr." The odor of Firmin's sanctity spread so widely, in fact, that a man named Simon who resided in the nearby town of Beaugency and who suffered from leprosy, opened his window and was miraculously cured. Out of gratitude, Simon travelled to Amiens where he gifted the church with considerable wealth, including the chateau of Beaugency. Firmin's sweet smell spread through the countryside. On either side of the scene of the invention of the relics, intricately carved representations of cities, with churches, bells, and towers feature, on the far left, the figure of a woman looking from city ramparts at crowds of people emerging, according to the *Acta Sanctorum*, from the nearby cities of Thérouanne, Cambrai, Noyon, and Beauvais. Again, the carver is remarkably anxious to include citizens of both sexes and of all ages. Of the three women who leave the city on the left, one carries a baby, as does the woman in the mixed crowd just to the left of the scene of discovery. Among those who leave home just to the right of Firmin's head, one woman holds a young child by the hand. The bearded man next to her carries a small child on his shoulder. Citizens who emerge from the city on the right kneel in prayer in what might be the most elaborate scenes of intimacy with the common people of any of the cathedrals we have seen.

The discovery of the remains of Saint Firmin occurred on January 13, and, as the *Acta Sanctorum* reports, it was accompanied by miraculous natural phenomena: "As the venerable Bishop Salvius . . . raised Firmin from his tomb, the substance of all the elements was changed, and such a boiling heat came into the world that all the people present, stupified and in a state of ecstacy, were amazed." The tympanum above the scene of discovery depicts the procession of relics back to Amiens with the startling details of a rebirth of nature in the middle of winter and miracle cures along the way. Tree branches in the lower left corner are shown conspicuously ladened with leaves. On the right, youths at the entrance to Amiens hang garlands to decorate the gates of the city. One of their number has taken off his tunic which he places on the ground, in keeping with the textual description: "Crowds of people rushed up on the way, throwing their clothes on the road." The male figure on the left of the tympanum has removed his shirt which he carries, bare-armed, on a stick slung over his shoulder. The sprig of leaves which he holds in the other hand along with the leafy garland around his head have led some to identify this youth with the Green Man, a pagan symbol of fertility, and there is evidence that, up until the eighteenth century, each year on January 13, the clergy of Amiens dressed in green, strewed ivy on the floor, and burned incense redolent of the odor emanating from the exhumation of Firmin in order to celebrate the entry of his relics into the cathedral. The great band of sculpted leaves that runs all around the inside of the cathedral at the base of the triforium, exactly halfway up the interior wall, may be the architectural embodiment of the garland on the head of the Green Man. Within the color scheme inside and outside the cathedral, both were likely painted a vivid green.

The historical color, social mix, details of architecture and dress, even the bodily sensations of heat and smell on a January 13 at the beginning of the seventh century lend the miraculous discovery and translation of the relics of Saint Firmin a realism that is rare in the depiction of medieval religious subjects, one that is not open to the kind of figural interpretation appropriate elsewhere. Nothing in the Hebrew or Christian Bible prefigures the events depicted in the north portal of the west facade, nor are they filled with meaning for the salvation of mankind. They are deeply rooted in the history of Amiens, and the depth of their roots in local lore can be appreciated by comparison to similar scenes in the life of another home hero, Honoré, the patron saint of bakers, which are nonetheless framed by the world historical stage of both the Hebrew and Christian Bibles.

THE SOUTHERN PORTAL
OF SAINT HONORÉ

THE SOUTHERN TRANSEPT ENTRANCE, which you reach by walking around the right side of the cathedral along the rue Cormont, is known as the portal of Saint Honoré or of the Golden Virgin because of the trumeau statue that is one of the jewels of thirteenth-century sculpture. Wearing a crown decorated with fleurs-de-lys and a long tunic over a gown that falls to the ground in graceful folds, the Virgin Mother holds Jesus, who himself cuddles in His hands a round object like a globe. Mother and Child look glowingly at each other. The expression on Mary's face, her almond-shaped eyes, are an early example of that

Honoré Portal Tympanum, South Entrance

slightly cloying sweet look characteristic of the virgins and angels of high Gothic sculpture, her body pitched at that hip-shot angle with full weight on her left leg, a function of maintaining upright posture while balancing a child at her side. The sculpture currently in place is not the original, which stands inside the south transept, having been removed in 1980 to prevent further damage from the elements. Nor is it clear that when the southern transept portal was erected in the mid-1230s the virgin statue was in the place where its reproduction now stands. The bas reliefs on the base of the trumeau display generic scenes of priests, bishops, and holy women, while the trumeau on the northern transept portal features Saint Honoré with scenes of the Annunciation and the Nativity at its base. At some point, either between the planning of north and south transept entrances and their actual construction or in a late medieval retrofitting, the two portal trumeaus were reversed. Further evidence for such a rethinking of design lies in the way in which the Virgin's crown and three angels, suspended in midair under an elabo-rate architectural canopy, hold the nimbus on which green paint is still visible behind her head, which interrupts the vine and scroll floral band running along the base of the lower lintel.

The lower lintel is separated from the tympanum by its height, by the decorated columns on either side, by its rectilinear refusal of the curve of a true tympanum, and by a thick band of fig leaves, miniature gables, and towers. It contains a remarkable display of the twelve apostles, who, bearded and wearing similar dress, are, with two exceptions, indistin-guishable from one another: to the right of the architectural canopy above the Virgin's head, Saint James the Major, patron saint of Spain, is distinguished by his hat and pilgrim's staff. Standing next to him, John, the young apostle, is identifiable by his lack of beard and his rounded youthful face. They are the only pair facing the viewer. All the others, in pairs, are engaged in animated conversation and turned toward their interlocutor. The fervor of their words is suggested by their body lan-guage: heads pitched toward their partner, as if to listen more intently, to question, or to acknowledge consent; arms extended or folded to the chest; hands that point either at the figure before them or at themselves. The subject of discussion is rendered by the books they hold in their hands, or, as in the case of the couple on the far right, the scroll unfurled between them. Both the scroll, associated with the prophets of the Old Testament, as distinct from the book which Christ even as a child holds in His hands, and the skullcap on the head of the lone apostle shown in full profile are indications of their status as Jews.

The tympanum of the southern transept portal is dedicated to the story of Saint Honoré, seventh bishop of Amiens at the end of the sixth century. According to hagiographic legend, he was reluctant to assume the title of bishop until a flow of oil miraculously appeared upon his forehead, a sign of divine election. The miracle is represented as a thick cloth-like gush of liquid not unlike the image of the ray of light that signals to Saint Salvius the location of the grave of Saint Firmin on the north portal of the west facade. It emanates from the wall behind Saint Honoré who is seated at the far left of the lower lintel of the true tympanum. Both are awkward, as the difficulty of depicting a ray of light or a stream of oil is more obvious in sculpture than in painting.

The first miracle of Saint Honoré is witnessed by eight figures. One administers to Honoré while his fellow holds the bishop's crozier in one hand and a book in the other. The others discuss in pairs like the apostles below them what we can only assume to be the designation from on high of the new bishop. An altar with a chalice and a low retable capped by a cross separate the tableau of Honoré's election from the scene on the right hand side of the lower lintel in which the installed bishop, sitting under a trilobe arch that is at once a church and a castle, points with one finger to a book on a reading stand and looks at the scene on his left (our right) which is the miraculous discovery, according to legend, of the bodies of three local saints—Fuscien, Victoric, and Gentien. By a sub-miracle, the voice of Lucipin, the priest who located the bodies and who is here shown pickaxe in hand, could be heard several kilometers away in a parallel to the saintly odor of Firmin spreading throughout the countryside. Both the flowering of trees surrounding the sarcophagi and the potential presence of these three saints among the jamb figures on the right side of the Saint Firmin portal tie the scene on the Saint Honoré entrance to that on the north porch of the west facade.

The middle lintel of the tympanum shows Saint Honoré celebrating mass with what appears to be the hand of God emerging with a wafer from a cloud behind the retable of the altar. In the right tableau the saint cures a blind woman whose eyes he touches with the edge of the cloth which he raises from the altar, while, behind the blind woman, a lame man, bearing a crutch in one hand and holding a dog on a leash in the other, waits his turn. A procession of the relics of Saint

Honoré to Amiens fills the top lintel, which is the only one not divided into two tableaux. Led by three choirboys, two of whom bear crosses, those who accompany the reliquary box are portrayed in some detail. Of the adult figures on the left, one holds a frame-like object which could be a reliquary of the flat Byzantine type, a staurothek. The figure on his left carries an arm reliquary, that is, a case in the shape of an arm with two fingers extended at the top, which contains a piece or the whole of the humerus, ulna, or radius bone of a saint. As he goes along, the figure between the small reliquaries and the large casket-like box exhibits the pages of an open book. Beneath the main reliquary three kneeling figures seeking to be cured reach up to touch the vessel containing the remains of Saint Honoré. The crowd which follows is remarkable in its diversity, consisting as it does of a Jew, identifiable, again, by his hat, a black man, and three women, one of whom holds a child by the hand. The triangle of the tympanum is dominated by a crucifix between Mary and John who are themselves flanked by censing angels. Since the bottom of the cross practically touches Saint Honoré's reliquary box, it has been suggested that the two scenes refer to the legend according to which the crucifix atop the prayer screen in the church of Saint Firmin the Confessor, which preceded the cathedral of Amiens, actually inclined toward the saint's remains when they passed by.

The co-presence of the apostles who bear witness to events which occurred in the late sixth century and afterwards has the effect of collapsing time, of bringing the story of Saint Honoré alive in the here-and-now. How much more dramatic must it have seemed to the medieval viewer when accompanied by a clerical guide to embellish the narrative as today's guides seek to elicit the attention of tourists with accounts of the lives and miracles of saints. The attention to material culture in the tympanum of the Honoré portal—the depiction of the retable or altar, the crutch and seeing-eye dog, the arm reliquary and the pick-axe, the diversity of the crowd of onlookers—bring into vivid relief the everyday life of common people in the thirteenth century. History is a dialogue with the dead, and this glimpse of a distant world, like a realistic diorama in a museum, leaves me, for one, both humbled and in awe of the miraculous power of images to revive those who have died, art, again, being our version of religion.

THE SOUTHERN JAMBS:
CLERICS AMID THE CARNIVAL

THE JAMB STATUES OF angels and clerics on either side of the southern transept entrance are not distinguished examples of Gothic sculpture. There is, in fact, something monotonous about these rotund, neckless, stiff bodies coupled with a downward gaze that renders them lifeless. The corbels on which they stand are, moreover, clumsy, nothing more than flat or rough-hewn slabs on top of architectural models. Beneath the column figures, however, a series of small carvings which loom just over the heads of those who enter provide a source of interest that the main statues lack. The cleric on the far left is that of a crouching African holding a bowl between his legs. To his left (our right) two wrestling youths are engaged in what appears to be painful combat. The angel closest to the left door stands on two birds which, were they smaller, could be pigeons, but in reality are more like birds of prey. To the right of the entrance, two scenes of bear baiting dilute the seriousness of the jamb figures with a hint of carnival or street fair. Beneath the angel a soldier, and beneath the cleric a peasant, who carries a child on his back, both beat captive animals with a stick. The cleric to the right stands atop a long-eared devil, while that on the outer edge of the group is supported by a crouching man who also appears to be laughing wildly. The corbel carvings around the southern transept portal are a source of curiosity without connection to the rest of the artistic program. They are sculptural doodlings akin to the marginal grotesques in medieval manuscripts, meant, it has been suggested by Stephen Murray, "to appeal to a popular audience." Yet, the southern portal, which gave upon the cloister by which the canons, many of them from local noble families, entered the cathedral was not accessible to the general population which came to church via the doors on the western facade.

THE SPIRITUAL HISTORY OF MANKIND

THE VOUSSOIRS OF THE Saint Honoré portal are distinguished by the detail of the carving and by the specificity and range of subjects depicted in four rows around the tympanum. Unlike the generic angels, elders of the Apocalypse, prophets, and kings that limn cathedral entrances elsewhere, including those of the west facade at Amiens, the fifty-four small statues arched above the southern transept are identifiable and organized in such a way as to offer the clerics who entered there a condensed experience of the spiritual history of mankind. With the exception of the angels bearing censers and crowns in the first tier, the scenes in the three outer rows are drawn from the Old and New Testaments. They represent a compendium of scriptural knowledge meant not to inspire those who approach the church with the stakes of salvation or damnation, but to remind them of what they already know. Less a bible for the illiterate than a celebration of learning, this is an entrance for intellectuals, and here is what you might see there.

In its outer rim the voussoir of the Saint Honoré portal self-consciously frames the glory of a textual tradition with images of books and of reading and writing. At the lower left, Luke, identifiable by the ox which protrudes from the wall behind him like a hunting trophy, sits at his writing desk, his hand poised midair as if to indicate the thoughts in his mind before committing them to parchment. In an analogous position on the right lower corner, Mark gazes, pen in hand, at the lion over his shoulder. At eleven o'clock on the left side, John, identifiable by the eagle that emerges from a cloud in the wall behind him, raises his hand to his cheek in a gesture of deep thought, contemplating the scroll spread out on his lap. On the right outer rim at two o'clock Matthew writes on a tablet beneath the figure of a winged man with a hand on his shoulder, so close as to seem to whisper in his ear. Almost every figure between the four evangelists—a woman holding a raised vessel like one of the wise virgins above Luke, James the Major wearing a shell on his shoulder above John, Paul at one o'clock on the right, or the foolish virgin with down-turned vessel above Mark—holds a book in his or her hands. One figure in particular, the queen identifiable by the crown she wears at top left, is captured in the act of reading, her left hand pointing to a passage in the book before her, while her right hand turns the page.

Looking at the pattern of finely sculpted figures from both Jewish and Christian traditions, you can observe in the second and third rims of the voussoir—between the inner row of angels and the outer row of evangelists and apostles—scenes from the Old Testament or from the Hebrew canon of Prophets. Like all sculpture which captures a moment in the larger arc of a story, the voussoir portraits depict particular episodes in the life of a biblical figure, and they do so with impressive realism. The details of material culture—weapons, tools, furniture, and dress—may belong more to thirteenth-century France than to ancient Judea, yet they still translate visually the words of the ancient text, and they are vividly animated, filled with actions and gestures candidly caught in medias res. Beginning at the beginning, Adam, dressed in skins at the bottom of the second row, is visualized working the earth, his left foot firmly planted on the ground, his right foot pressed upon a spade. With all the digging that goes on above the portals of Amiens, it is hard not to think that Adam's spade work is related to the unearthing of the bodies of Saints Firmin, Fuscien, Victoric, and Gentien. Above Adam, Noah turns an awl in the fashioning of the ark whose layered siding he straddles. Melchizedek stands above Noah, his arms outstretched with the offering of bread and wine to Abraham, as in Genesis 14:18–20. And above Melchizedek, the scene of the sacrifice of Isaac by Abraham is represented in astonishingly compressed detail which is worth a closer look. The moment shown is that just before the planned offering, as the father, the pommel sword of a medieval knight in one hand and the hair of his young son in the other, is interrupted by an angel projected from a cloud with one hand staying the patriarch's blade and the other pointing to the ram caught in the brambles below. Above the drama of the Akedah, Isaac blesses Jacob; and above that, Jacob blesses the children of Joseph. At the top of the left arch, Job is depicted barefoot on the dung heap scratching his sores with a shard.

Moses holding a tablet of the Law in one hand and the bronze serpent atop a pole on the other stands at the crest of the right arch, while below him, his brother Aaron, identifiable by the jeweled breastplate he wears, bears a flowering rod, the sign of his election. Below Aaron, Samuel anoints a young David, while below David, the Judgment of David's son Solomon presents another of the animated packed carvings like that of the sacrifice of Isaac, and which is of special interest if your time at Amiens is limited. With the legs of a wriggling baby in one hand and a raised sword in the other, Solomon is beseeched by the two women claiming a child, their hands folded in prayer. Below Solomon, Judith holds a sword in her right hand and the head of Holofernes in the left, while below Judith, Judah Maccabee in the garb of a medieval knight stands with his sword over his shoulder and a lozenge-shaped shield bearing the image of a lion, emblem of the tribe of Judah. At the bottom right of the second row of the voussoir, John the Baptist, dressed in skins like Adam in an analogous place at the bottom left, holds a disk bearing the Lamb of God to indicate that Christ is the new Adam.

The third tier of the voussoir displays sixteen representational scenes from the lives of the twelve minor and four major prophets in the order in which they appear in the biblical text, beginning with Hosea at the bottom left. Of special note at ten thirty on the left, Jonah is pictured emerging from the whale, one leg still in the giant fish's mouth and the other on its belly. The sculpted sketch above Jonah offers a rare glimpse of a medieval forge. Micah, swords and lances stacked against the wall behind him, wields an adze in a literal depiction of his prophecy of universal peace: "and they shall beat their swords into ploughshares, and their spears into spades: nation shall not take sword against nation: neither shall they learn war anymore" (Micah 4:3).

In two scenes of great violence, both part of the apocrypha associated with the prophets, Jeremiah is stoned to death at the top left of the third voussoir ring, while Isaiah is sawed in half on the right. Below Isaiah, Ezekiel finds himself before the closed east door of the temple. "And the Lord said to me: This gate shall be shut, it shall not be opened, and no man shall pass through it: because the Lord the God of Israel hath entered in by it, and it shall be shut" (Ezekiel 44:2). In a return to the minor prophets, Nahum sits below Ezekiel as witness to a pair of legs cut off at the knees with bare feet poised upon a bulging mass like a hill, the whole a literal rendering of God's curse of the king of Nineveh: "Behold upon the mountains the feet of him that bringeth good tidings" (Nahum 1:15). The carving below Nahum, at two o'clock, is one of the most dramatic of the entire series, depicting as it does an angel caught in mid-flight as he transports the prophet Habakkuk, his body pitched forward with one foot off the ground, to feed Daniel in the lion's den: "And the angel of the Lord took him by the top of his head, and set him in Babylon, over the den, in the force of his spirit" (Daniel 14:35).

The large array of sculpted vignettes from the lives of Old Testament figures, prophets, evangelists, and apostles all around the tympanum of the southern portal of Amiens bears witness to the power of art to capture and compress even so vast a sweep as between Adam and Christ. The representation of large things, people, and events in miniature exerts a fascination upon the viewer who senses the energy beneath the abbreviated scenes of larger lives and life stories. To pass beneath the Saint Honoré portal is to experience in compact form, in condensed measure, the spiritual history of mankind, unpacked more expansively, but no more powerfully, all across the porches of the west facade.

PROPHETS OF THE WEST FACADE

AMIENS IS DISTINGUISHED BY the heavy buttresses that protrude on either side and between the three main entrances on the west side, and they, in turn, stand out because of the vertical statues that line not only the deep porches but also face outward all along the front of the church. The figures attached frontally to the buttresses along with those attached obliquely to the corners are the very same minor prophets, from Hosea to Malachi, displayed in the same order as in the third voussoir of the Saint Honoré portal. The major prophets occupy the outermost edges of the wider central porch such that, were one to collapse inward the entire frontispiece of the cathedral, the rim of prophets—major on top with minor all around—would reproduce something like the archivolt of the prophets around the entrance on the south side. Though the prophets, minor or major, resemble each other and are marked as prophets by the emblematic scrolls they hold, we know their identities at Amiens because of another distinctive feature of design, the delicate images in the double row of quatrefoils beneath each vertical statue and above the band of floral design that runs like a cloth curtain between the quatrefoils and the ground. The oblique prophet statues on the edges of the buttresses are annotated by two sets of quatrefoils, one facing outward and the other lining the outmost inner edge of the porch. Some reproduce the same images as on the Saint Honoré voussoir, and others elaborate upon what is to be found at the southern entrance.

The top quatrefoil under Jonah, who faces forward in the middle of the buttress to the right of the central portal, again features the prophet "vomited" from the whale, though this time he emerges fully clothed with hands gesturing as if to prophesy, as he soon will, the destruction of Nineveh.

Micah, set obliquely to the left of Jonah, as you face the cathedral, is shown in even greater detail on the upper and lower inner quatrefoils than in the southern voussoir. There you can see the prophet and his apprentice working on anvils as they beat swords into plowshares and spears into spades. Intact swords rest against the back wall of the workshop, shards of broken weapons are strewn on the floor, and a forge

Central Portal Right Quatrelobes,
Detail Micah

complete with a bellows mechanism deepens the glimpse into a medieval foundry. The highlighting of metalwork has significance for the
building of the cathedral as well as for the rural economy of Amiens.
Metal workers provided essential components of Gothic design, from
the hinges and braces for doors, to interior grillwork, to the "H" rib-
bons of lead between painted pieces of stained glass and the metal bars
supporting windows, to the hidden braces by which stones in the outer
wall were aligned and held in place, to, as we shall see (p. 244), the enormous chain of "Spanish iron" installed at the end of the fifteenth century
around the circumference of the triforium at Amiens. Amiens prospered
in the twelfth and thirteenth centuries in part because of the development

of metallurgy in Picardy. In contrast to the bread belt around Chartres, the vineyards around Reims, or the cityscape of Notre-Dame Paris and the Sainte-Chapelle, medieval Amiens was a center for the manufacture of metal tools for the efficient working of the land. In the relative peace between the end of the chaos of the feudal period and the middle of the fourteenth century, when the Hundred Years' War began to affect the region, the swords in and around Amiens may literally have been beaten into plowshares and spears into spades.

The quatrefoils under Habakkuk, whose bigger-than-life statue is frontally situated in the middle of the buttress between the central and northern porches, are remarkable in their detail. They refer to the action begun in the Saint Honoré voussoir where an angel seizes the prophet by the hair to bring him to Daniel in the lion's den. Here, Habakkuk is shown handing food to Daniel who caresses a lion on the neck with his right hand and another under the mane with his left. A third lion gnaws a bone at Daniel's feet, bones and a skull strewn on the ground as reminders of the danger of cohabiting with large felines.

EVE AND MARY ON THE SOUTH PORTAL

THE SOUTH PORTAL OF the west facade, or portal of the Mother of God, is so-named because of the presence of the Virgin, here crowned as the queen of Heaven, and because the drama of the virgin birth dominates the jambs on either side along with the death and assumption of the Virgin in the upper reaches of the tympanum. You may notice that in the trumeau Mary holds Jesus with an upright posture unlike that of the hip-shot Golden Virgin of the southern entrance. This is because her weight is distributed equally on her two feet which crush a serpent with the head of a woman, a reference to Mary's redemption of Eve's part in the Fall which is represented in six tableaux, each enclosed in an architectural frame, at the base of the high statue. Here you should be prepared to move around the bottom of the trumeau, as on the top right, God creates Adam who stands on the rough clods of earth from which he came, while, on the left, God draws Eve by the arm out of the side of her sleeping husband. In the middle right, God, waving a long finger of admonition, warns the first couple not to eat of the tree of good and evil, which is represented schematically behind them; moving to the left, Eve hands the forbidden fruit to Adam, who takes it in

Virgin (South) Portal, Trumeau Base, West Facade

one hand and, choking, grabs his throat with the other. The serpent, in the guise of a woman, looks on, its tail curled around the tree. On the bottom right, the angel Gabriel issues the first couple out of the garden of Eden, and, on the left, they are pictured wearing skirts of skin, Eve with a spindle and strand of yarn stretched across her bare chest, while Adam digs with another of the spades of Amiens, the bottom half of which is missing.

THE INFANCY JAMBS

THE JAMB FIGURES ON the right of the Mother of God portal appear in familiar groups of two connected to the birth of Jesus: first, the

Annunciation of the Angel Gabriel to Mary who holds the book she has been reading in her left hand, while she gestures acceptance with the palm of her right hand; next, the Visitation of Mary and Elizabeth, mother of John the Baptist; finally, the Presentation of the Infant Jesus in the Temple. Mary hands the child to Simeon who waits with a cloth draped over his extended arms. The four quatrefoils beneath each pair of column statues elaborate upon the lives of the larger figures. Under the Presentation in the Temple, for example, the holy family is seen fleeing into Egypt where the idols, as per Isaiah 19:1, fall dramatically: "Behold the Lord will ascend upon a swift cloud, and will enter into Egypt, and the idols of Egypt shall be moved at his presence, and the heart of Egypt shall melt in the midst thereof." On the bottom left, Jesus debates with the doctors, and, on the right, Joseph and Mary, who holds Jesus by the hand, return to Nazareth. You may remember these from the lintel of the southern portal of Notre-Dame Paris, with which Amiens has a special relation, as well as from the Infancy glass programs of Saint-Denis, Chartres, and the Sainte-Chapelle. Their persistence teaches us much about the way medieval visual artists worked to render set scenes in the early life of Jesus in different media, and to different effect. In the case of the lintel of Notre-Dame, we can follow the narrative like a panorama through the various stages of the larger story. The glass renderings present with a certain simultaneity, as our eyes can take in the whole in a single visual sweep; and we are forced to impose order upon the story from left to right or right to left and up and down the larger panel. The Infancy jambs of Amiens, however, both because of their closeness and their bigger-than-life size, are designed to impress us. They transport us through time and space to the actual events. They are the source of an immediate dramatic effect distinct from the esthetic distance we experience before both small statuary and even the grandest sheets of colored glass.

The figures on the left of the south door continue the pairings of the right, with the three magi, unique as a grouping of full jamb statues, and Herod in discussion with the wise men before dispatching them "to diligently inquire after the child" (Matthew 2:7). The quatrefoils beneath Herod and the third magi show the king speaking with his counselors, the Massacre of the Innocents on the top, and, on the bottom, Herod ordering his men to burn the boats of the magi whom he thinks have betrayed him. The lower right shows the actual burning of the boats.

The outer pair of large statues continues the theme of wisdom with the figures of Solomon and the queen of Sheba. The quatrefoil under Solomon depicts him in majesty on his throne and, on the bottom, in prayer. The smaller images under Sheba depict the banquet at which the Queen, in the course of her visit to Solomon, "came to try him with hard questions"; below, the wise king gestures broadly with his hands, instructing his pupil who "said to the king: The report is true, which I heard in my own country, Concerning thy words, and concerning thy wisdom" (3 Kings, 10:1, 6–7).

The lintel above the head of the Virgin features four seated patriarchs pointing to passages from the scrolls unfurled on their laps. Between them, the ark of the covenant, which resided in the inner sanctum of Solomon's temple, is rendered schematically under miniature decorated columns, an exposed ribbed interior vault, trilobe arch and gable, towers, lance arches, and the tracery of a Gothic church. Moses, identified, again, by the horns on his head, holds the tablets of the Law to the left of the ark, while his brother Aaron, wearing his breastplate and holding a flowering rod, which are his emblems, sits to the right. Three traditional scenes of the dormition of the Virgin—the gathering of the apostles at the time of Mary's death, her transport by angels which lift her out of her sarcophagus, and Mary sitting at the right hand of Jesus—fill the tympanum of the south portal, while angels hover on both sides of the first ring of the voussoir. An abundant Tree of Jesse, twenty-six kings entwined in two rows of sculpted interlace follow the genealogical line from Jesse to Jesus. Thus Mary's origin, alongside her end, frames the area above the portal of the Mother of God.

LE BEAU DIEU

THE CENTRAL PORCH OF the west facade of Amiens, heavily restored in the middle of the nineteenth century, is noted less for its originality than for its depth and for the stellar summarizing and convening of the components of a Last Judgment portal as originally articulated elsewhere. The Christ of the trumeau, book in one hand while the other is raised in prayer, bespeaks a serenity for which this rendering is known as the *Beau Dieu* or "Beautiful God." His feet rest on a lion and an asp, as in Psalm 90:13, "Thou shalt walk upon the asp and the basilisk: and thou shalt trample under foot the lion and the dragon." The royal figure in the architectural frame at eye level has been identified with less than full certainty as King Solomon, the leafy design between them, as an instantiation of the Parable of the True Vine, a sorting before the Last Judgment, from John 15:1–2: "I am the true vine. . . . Every branch in me that beareth not fruit, he will take away: and every one that beareth fruit, he will purge it, that it may bring forth more fruit." The wise and foolish virgins flank the door jambs with full-size column statues of the apostles. Each bears either the emblem associated with them or an object connected to their martyrdom, beginning on the right with Peter and the keys to paradise, and, on the left, Paul, identifiable by his high forehead and the sword with which he was beheaded.

Accompanying the apostles on both sides are the major prophets, again seen as having foretold that to which the apostles bear witness. On the left, Ezekiel, holding a round case for a scroll, appears as an old man with a beard. In the quatrefoils beneath him, the prophet experiences his vision of a "wheel in the midst of a wheel," along with the rebuilding of the temple, figured by a man holding a plumb line in front of a massive, high, multi-towered structure, one of many images of architectural activity on the exterior walls of Amiens: "behold a man, whose appearance was like the appearance of brass, with a line of flax in his hand, and a measuring reed in his hand . . ." (Ezekiel 1:16; 40:3). To the left of Ezekiel, beardless Daniel stands holding an unfurled scroll, while, beneath, he emerges from the lion's den in the top quatrefoil and is seen in the lower frame at Belshazzar's feast at which the handwriting on the wall foretells the king's demise. On the right, Isaiah, closest to the apostles, is shown in the top quatrefoil looking up at God sitting on a throne surrounded by angels, next to a structure resembling medieval images of Solomon's temple that we encountered in the reliquary stage of the Sainte-Chapelle (see p. 168). Below, Isaiah, a scroll between his hands, is purified by one of the seraphim who places a live coal to his "unclean lips" (Isaiah 6:1–2, 7). Jeremiah stands to the right of Isaiah and, in the quatrefoil directly beneath his feat, using another of the spades of Amiens, follows God's command to bury a girdle "by the Euphrates," only to dig it up after several days to find that it has rotted, as the "great pride of Jerusalem," in the divine phrase, shall rot.

The quatrefoils under the apostles display, as at Notre-Dame Paris, a series of moral distinctions, with allegories of virtues on top and concrete examples of vices on the bottom. Some are remarkably graphic, filled with details that allow us to imagine narratives of good and bad behavior. Thus, to the right of Christ, under Peter, a medieval knight in armor sits defiantly with a sword in one hand and a shield bearing the image of a lion, like that of Judah Maccabee on the voussoir of the Saint Honoré portal, in the other. He is the incarnation of bravery, while a beardless youth below, startled by a rabbit jumping out of the bushes, drops his sword and flees. At the end of the row of apostles on the right, the quatrefoil on the top shows a king caressing the head of a dog emerging from the wall beside him, both symbols of loyalty, while, on the bottom, a disloyal cleric sneaks out of the church behind him, his duplicity signaled by his bare feet and the socks and shoes which fall from his hand as if he has stolen away from the monastery without wishing to be heard or seen. Under Paul, to the left of the door, a woman holds a shield with a cross on top of a chalice, the allegorical figure of religious faith, while, below, a man bows before a statue in an obvious act of idolatry. Under James the Major, the third apostle statue from the left door, the figure of charity holds in one hand a shield with a sheep, the symbol of selfless giving, and, with the other, she gives a cloak to a beggar. Beneath this figure of charity, a man seated at his desk counting his money embodies miserliness.

THE LAST JUDGMENT AT AMIENS

THE FULLNESS OF AMIENS sculpture is nowhere more dramatic than in the tympanum above the *Beau Dieu*. Again, the theme is not original but the figures are masterfully executed in their essential parts. An abundance of detail makes the central portal unsurpassed among renderings of the Last Judgment of Christ. On the lower lintel the number of resurrected souls emerging from their graves, some thirty all told, including one figure emerging from a cauldron, transmit a great sense of stunned chaos. Men and women of all stations, some clothed and some nude, one tonsured like a monk and another wearing a king's crown, arise to two angels sounding trumpets at either end of the disordered array.

The bodies of the resurrected are strewn in all directions. Some look heavenward, their hands in prayer. Some look out at the viewer, as if to say, "It could be you." Still others are too busy crawling out from underground to look anywhere but down. Many are contorted in postures so impossible to maintain that the whole is like a candid snapshot of the end

Central Portal Tympanum, West Facade

of time. Archangel Michael's scales, placed between the mass of undifferentiated humans before they have been judged, contains a lamb from whose back emerges a banner in the pan of the righteous and the head of a demon in the pan of the damned which a little cheating devil attempts to lower with his extraordinarily long extended arm. Allegorical figures of the synagogue, a woman with her head lowered in disgrace, and the church, a woman holding an unfurled scroll with her crowned head held high, sit beneath the devil's head and the Lamb of God. The lower lintel is bordered top and bottom by a wide spiraliform floral pattern that repeats the garland motif around the head of the Green Man in the northern portal as well as that encircling the interior of the church just below the triforium. Again, the bordering bands of the lintel were no doubt painted green when the polychromy of the west facade was still intact.

The orderliness of the upper lintel is striking in contrast with the chaos below and is both visual and rhythmic. The bodies of the saved and the damned march to their separate destinies in fixed double rows. Their separate ranks and the motion of their limbs—a little more serried among those marching to heaven and a little less tidy among those headed to hell—conveys the cadence of a military parade. The souls of the saved, who are also clothed, are shepherded by an angel moving to Christ's right (our left) and crowned by an angel at the door to paradise, represented as a small church. At the entrance, Saint Peter stands holding the keys to heaven in one hand and pointing the way to paradise with the other. The first soul to enter, his tonsured head captured in the process of being crowned, is, according to art historian Stephen Murray, Saint Francis of Assisi, recognizable by his triple-knotted belt and the cloth covering his hands. Francis habitually hid the stigmata which had appeared there two years prior to his death in 1226, just around the time of the construction of the west facade at Amiens. Hovering above this orderly procession, a row of angels, their bodies all turned to the left as if to indicate the direction of the procession, carry crowns to bestow upon the saved. To Christ's left (our right), a hairy, horned demon prods a row of condemned souls, some of whose genitals are exposed, toward an enormous gaping hell's mouth which still shows traces of reptilian dark paint. Among them, a king wearing his crown, a bishop with his crozier, and a moneylender with a bag around his neck are all identifiable in their earthly incarnation. Angels whose bodies are turned in the direction of the Leviathan wield flaming swords above the naked and the damned.

The triangular space at the top of the tympanum features Christ in majesty, the stigmata visible on his upturned hands, surrounded by Mary and John along with angels bearing the instruments of the passion—cross and crown of thorns on the left, and nails and lance on the right. The paint still visible on His face, and especially His eyes, make for a terrifying intensity that looks in judgment upon all who see the all-seeing figure under the architectural canopy of the heavenly city. It is impossible to stand there without thinking, "He is looking at me!" At the top of the tympanum, Christ reappears with double-edged swords extending from his mouth and holding a scroll in each hand. An angel on the left holds a disk in his hand with an image of the sun, while an angel on the right holds the moon, together signifying the obscuring of the earth's sources of light with the apparition of celestial Jerusalem that will accompany the Second Coming. In one of the deepest and most elaborate set of voussoirs around the tympanum of any Gothic cathedral, the central portal of Amiens features angels on both sides of the first ring and angels bearing souls in the shape of small human beings in the second. The next three rows are filled with saints, and the sixth, with old men of the Apocalypse holding cithers and vases. Two additional bands of small carvings, separated from the voussoirs by arcs of solid masonry, belong theoretically to the porch and exhibit a Tree of Jesse on the inside and a series of Old Testament patriarchs on the outer string.

INSIDE AMIENS CATHEDRAL

"A GREAT RESERVOIR OF air and light," in the phrase of Dany Sandron, Amiens is the largest of the Gothic cathedrals of the thirteenth century, and the highest. The internal structure is distinguished by the width of its transepts and the length of its chevet compared to that of the nave. The distance from the center of the transept crossing to the eastern end of the axial chapel is equal to that between the west entrance and the crossing. Seen from above, the cathedral is built more along the lines of a Greek cross, with arms of equal length, than the Latin cross of the Crucifixion, whose horizontal member divides the vertical in a proportion of two to one. Amiens is noted for the simplicity of its interior design according to a three-tier elevation—arcades, triforium, and clerestory. The triforium, which girdles without interruption nave, transepts, and choir, is particularly large, sixteen feet high, and an added source of light where the solid wall behind its columns and arches opens to stained glass windows around the central crossing and the choir. Through the triple broken arches of the triforium on either side of the nave, the traces of arches now filled in with stone indicate that the outer surface of the passageway around the interior of the cathedral was originally to be filled with glass.

To enter Amiens Cathedral by the deep recess of the north porch of the west facade is to pass into a great funnel of light unlike any other in the great Gothic churches. The massive buttresses which punctuate the porch support the lighter rectangular towers above, which means that you enter directly into the nave without passing, as elsewhere, between heavy tower supports which obscure the area between the nave and the doors. Not readily visible from the ground, two round windows behind the porch gables add to the immediate play of light upon entry. The flood of light throughout the cathedral is, however, another, and sad, story.

There is reason to believe that Amiens originally resonated with the same reverent blue hush experienced upon entering Chartres. Scholars have even speculated that, since the stained glass of Chartres was completed around the time that the construction of Amiens called for narrative and decorative stained glass windows, teams of glaziers, who were as itinerant as the masons who moved between building sites, might have migrated from the Beauce region to Picardy. The subsequent history of the glass of Amiens has, however, been one of loss of color in favor of clear glass which may let in more light, but which has progressively eroded the chromatic luminosity of the interior just as the fretting of paint on the outside has dulled the vivid polychromy of the exterior walls. The removal of original glass began in the fourteenth century with the installation at Amiens, as at Notre-Dame Paris, of side chapels which extended the covered space between the buttresses and pushed the windows, newly built, beyond the initial walls of the nave. An explosion at a nearby powder mill in the seventeenth century and storms in the course of both the seventeenth and eighteenth centuries damaged the stained glass of Amiens at a time when the prevailing esthetic of the Enlightenment, along with an aversion to the Gothic style, meant that, between 1760 and 1780, when broken windows were repaired, the old colored glass was replaced by transparent sheets of grisaille. Amiens, like Reims, was hit by bombs in World War I, and windows which had been removed in 1918 for restoration by the glass painter Edmond Socard were ruined in a workshop fire two years later, thus further depleting the stock of stained glass for reinstallation in the cathedral.

THE STAINED GLASS OF AMIENS

DESPITE ALL THE DAMAGE, Amiens is not completely devoid of interesting stained glass, a mix of windows from the thirteenth, nineteenth, and twentieth centuries. We know from records before the centuries of destruction that, from the mid 1250s to the 1500s, over forty windows were offered to the cathedral by the bishops and canons of the church as well as by city officials, including the guild of woad and textile workers and dealers, the mayor, the counts of Vermandois, and the inhabitants of towns within the diocese. A 1269 gift of Bishop Bernard d'Abbeville, the only intact high window of the choir, presents the bishop and the Virgin in four lancets, mirror images of each other, above an inscription acknowledging the donation. Some of what has survived has been shifted in discreet panels from its original to its current location. A fragment of an original panel depicting the story of Adam and Eve, once set in the nave, is now found in the north choir aisle. The piece must at the outset have been a gift of the carpenters' guild, as the image below the first couple shows three men wielding woodworking tools to put in place a frame of the type used in the construction of vaulted masonry to support the stonework while the mortar sets. Pieces of a Jesse Tree, once in the axial chapel, now sit in the Saint-Nicaise chapel at the southeast angle of the apse. Fragments of a window dedicated to saints Edward the Confessor and Edmund, witness to the closeness of Amiens to England, are now to be found on the west side of the north transept.

Much of the Amiens glass that remains intact is either from the late Middle Ages, verging on the Renaissance, or even later. The south rose window from around 1500, which replaced an original rose from the thirteenth century, sits atop a gallery of bishops. Its brightly colored glass may have been recuperated from the earlier window or even assembled from repurposed shards of glass removed from windows on the aisles to make side chapels. In the undulant tracery of this great whirligig of color, twenty-four angels enclosed in flamboyant petals of red, blue, and green spin around the central six-pointed rose which is as close as one comes in Gothic cathedrals to the secular Roman motif of the wheel of fortune. If you look closely, you can see that whoever planned the south rose of Amiens made sure to position the heads of the angels facing inward so that at the bottom of the wheel they are upright, while at the top they are plunged head-first downward. The natural cycle of rise and fall in the glass of the interior rose is reproduced on the outside around the upper radius of a giant wheel of life. If you take the trouble to step outside again and to compare the angels in glass with the humans in stone, you will appreciate the ways in which medieval artists rendered similar motifs in different media, and to different effect: while the whirling angels of the south rose window illustrate a cycle of eternal return embodied in a seamless circle, the humans on the outside participate in a course of rise and fall that, once run, does not begin anew. It is the difference between the eternal life beyond the empyrean realm and the circumscribed life of individuals, no matter how exalted. Beginning at nine o'clock on the wheel of life, a figure in a smock grabs the gear-like sprockets of a giant pulley and rides through seven successive positions, like the Seven Ages of Man, to the top of the world. There, scepter in hand, he sits in majesty on what looks like a throne, before being cast down, his smock lifted and genitals exposed, through seven positions until the last—a freefall to the ground.

The northern rose window of Amiens, which sits over a gallery of kings, is purely decorative, consisting as it does of an interweaving of jewel-like patterns radiating from a five-pointed star in the middle and terminating in elongated petals with trilobe and quatrelobe tracery around the outer edge of the circle. The western rose, designed to ratify visually the peace between Amiens and the kingdom of France after the Hundred Years' War, interlards images of ivy and gold fleurs-de-lys, the combination of the two serving as the coat of arms of the city until the present day.

A DISASTER IN THE MAKING

AMIENS HAS KNOWN its share of disasters in addition to the loss of original glass over the course of centuries. Though nothing like the collapse of significant masonry at Beauvais, a fire on the night of August 31, 1258, destroyed the roof structure of several of the radiating chapels on the east side of the church. Astonishingly, Amiens offers the rare opportunity to observe a disaster in the making. As early as 1497, a buckling of the piers around the central crossing and cracks in the masonry of the adjoining arcades alarmed those responsible for the "fabric," not only the construction, but the maintenance of the cathedral.

The last quarter of the fifteenth century was a period not only of peace but also of relative prosperity in Amiens due to the arrival of textile workers fleeing urban unrest in the city of Arras. It was, in other words, a good time to address looming structural catastrophe along with renewal of the three rose windows. On March 14, 1497, a team of master masons and carpenters assembled to examine and assess the situation and recommended to the dean and canons of the church that a chain of "Spanish iron of a good thickness" be installed around the cathedral at the level of the triforium and that it be "tensioned in such a way that they [the links] can resist and hold together without allowing the said masonry to stretch." To that end, eighty-four iron links, each thirteen feet long and an inch-and-a-half-by-three-inches thick, were joined with thick cotter pins and secured with vertical studs into the masonry of the floor of the open passageway all around the cathedral. As per the prescription of the inspection committee, holes were drilled in the piers to allow the belting bars to tie into the masonry adjoining the central crossing. Several years later the flying buttresses on the outside

Spanish Iron Chain Around Triforium (Stephen
Murray / Image courtesy of the Mapping Gothic
France Project, Media Center for Art History
© The Trustees of Columbia University)

of the cathedral were reinforced to address the lateral thrust of the ogival
vaults in the affected area.

The dramatic intervention to save the main vessel of Amiens between
1497 and 1503 has stood the test of time but has not proven definitive.
Recent examination of the pillars reveals that they continue to buckle.
Using laser technology that permits measurement within millimeters,
Stephen Murray and fellow art historian Andrew Talon discovered in
2015 that the distance between the pillars on the west side of the crossing
varied between 11.62 meters at the lowest level, about twenty feet above
ground, separating the crossing from the choir; 11.526 meters at the bottom of the triforium; and 11.709 meters at the top just under the vaults.
This difference, if diagrammed, would look like a top-heavy hourglass
which buckles inward at the middle, and shows a significant shift in the

plumb of the piers: ten centimeters from the lowest place of measurement to the midpoint, and a difference of twenty centimeters between the middle and the top. Coupled with the cracks still visible in the masonry of surrounding arcades, the shifting of stonework at Amiens calls for the convening of another committee of structural engineers and serves as a reminder that, though Gothic cathedrals have survived for over eight centuries, they nonetheless demand constant vigilance and care.

THE CHOIR STALLS OF AMIENS

THE EYE DOES NOT experience uniformly the space inside a great cathedral like Amiens. The vast nave, flanked by the private chapels of noble families and guilds, can be apprehended in a wide perspective without fixing closely upon particular patches of light or color. Other areas like the choir and ambulatory around it are, however, filled with works of such refinement of detail that they call for a closer look—especially the wooden choir stalls inside the choir and the *tableaux vivants* all around its outer wall.

The choir, which once was hidden behind a high masonry screen at the end abutting the transept, is now separated from the rest of the cathedral by an ornate metal grill. On the model of Solomon's temple with a Holy of Holies within the Tabernacle, the choir is the space reserved for the daily worship of the clergy and was not accessible to the public. Abbot Suger, writing in the middle of the twelfth century, noted that at Saint-Denis he had built wooden seats for the "choir of the brethren, which had previously been detrimental to their health because of the coldness of the marble and the copper." The two rows of highly decorated wooden choir stalls currently visible behind the grill at Amiens go far beyond health and comfort: they are among the most elaborate and delicate programs of wood sculpture to be found anywhere. Referring to the incomparably supple carvings on the wooden prayer stalls of Amiens, John Ruskin wrote in his classic late nineteenth-century *Bible of Amiens*, "Sweet and young-grained wood it is: oak, trained and chosen for such work, sound now as four hundred years since. Under the carver's hand it seems to cut like clay, to fold like silk, to grow like living branches, to leap like living flame."

Carved between 1508 and roughly 1520, the over four thousand figures among the 110 seats of the choir were the product of a collaboration between some eight artisans—woodworkers, cabinetmakers, fine carpenters—and the canons in charge of this multilayered sculptural program according to which each cleric with the privilege of praying in the choir was assigned his own seat: canons in the top row, chaplains, choirboys, musicians, and guests on the lower level. The proprietary claim over a particular seat is, in fact, at the root of the word "install," literally in + stallum, "to take one's place in the ecclesiastical hierarchy by seating in an official stall."

The carvings of the Amiens choir stalls decorate the handrests between seats, the railings between upper and lower levels, the side panels or reliefs at the ends of the rows of stalls, the pendentives that arc over the top seats, and the miséricords or "mercy seats" which, incised on the underside, fold up both to expose figures in low relief and to facilitate standing—by leaning—for long periods of prayer or chant. Decorative motifs appear between figurative carvings in much the way that medieval manuscripts are embellished with droleries and doodlings in the margins. Some images associated with Renaissance design—birds, dolphins and sirens, monkeys, salamanders, frogs, vases and horns of plenty—appear alongside an abundance of vegetation and flora—grapevines, hops, ivy, and oak leaves. A Green Man, like that in the northwest portal, is carved in a spandrel between two putti playing luth-like instruments in the panel on the side of the lower seats at the southwest side of the choir. The walls surrounding the stalls were originally covered in fleurs-de-lys which were removed by King Louis-Philippe who in 1831 ordered the ancient symbol of monarchy to be removed from "the interior and exterior of the cathedral of Amiens as well as from other public buildings"—a mid-nineteenth-century example of cancel culture. They have, however, been restored thanks to the 1931 legacy of the president of the Association of Antiquarians of Picardie and the painstaking work of a young sculptor, Léon Lamotte, who in 1953 finished reproducing and replacing two thousand fleurs-de-lys on the walls behind the prayer stalls of Amiens.

The carvings of the choir exhibit many of the motifs found elsewhere in the cathedral, with the exception of images of the saints, which are almost completely absent. On the south side, a pendentive, or low-hanging junction between two ribs of the decorative vaults that serve as canopies over the canons' seats, shows two men holding a plate with the head of John the Baptist, and a handrest between two lower seats on the north side displays a woman selling pilgrimage medals and candles. The liturgical labor of the stall figures is uneven to the extent that the miséricords exhibit scenes from the Hebrew Bible while the relief panels on flat surfaces either prefigure the life of the Virgin or narrate her life beginning with that of her parents, Anna and Joachim. Mary's childhood is captured in glimpses of her learning to read and her weaving, while the birth, infancy, and Passion of Christ are rendered by stagings of the Annunciation, Visitation, and Nativity along with the Massacre of the Innocents, Flight into Egypt, Wedding at Cana, Crucifixion, and Resurrection.

The Book of Genesis, beginning with Creation, is magnificently carved in scenes on the panel facing the stall reserved for the dean or head of the chapter in the upper row at the southwestern end of the choir. As on the base of the trumeau of the southwestern entrance to the cathedral, Adam is seen clutching his throat after eating the apple, and the Virgin is depicted above the tree of knowledge of good and evil in triumph over the serpent. Old Testament history from Noah and Abraham to Jacob picks up in the miséricords under the top row of seats on the south side, loops under the seats on the lower row through the stories of Joseph and Jacob, then jumps to the upper row on the north side with

Choir Stalls, Joseph with Grain (Stephen Murray / Image courtesy of the
Mapping Gothic France Project, Media Center for Art History
© The Trustees of Columbia University)

a continuation of Joseph's time in Egypt, before ending under the lower northern stalls with bas relief images from the lives of Job, David, Samson, and Moses.

As in all narrative sculpture built into a frieze, the artist must choose representative moments within the larger arc of a tale. In the case of the choir stalls, the story of Joseph occupies pride of place. The portrayal of the exiled youngest son of Jacob amid bursting storehouses of grain figures prominently on the ramp next to the seat on the northwest corner of the upper stalls reserved for the king or his representative. The visual message about Joseph's successful management of resources during the seven years of abundance followed by seven years of famine, from Genesis 41, is paired with a depiction of Herod and the Massacre of the Innocents in the relief on the other side of the king's seat. Juxtaposed, these iconic images of good and bad rule, like Ambrogio Lorenzetti's much earlier (1338 CE) allegory of good and bad government in Siena's Palazzo Publico, are aimed at reminding the monarch, only three decades after Amiens, which had been an independent city linked to the Crown, officially became annexed to France, of the importance of wise royal rule.

Like the Renaissance scenes of the birth of Jesus against the backdrop of an Italian hill town, the biblical choir carvings are all set in late medieval or early Renaissance Amiens. Both the city and its dwellings are depicted in great architectural and domestic detail. The city perimeters in the apocryphal and New Testament scenes of Anna and Joachim meeting at the Golden Gate or Jesus's entrance to Jerusalem are accurate in terms of contemporary defenses right down to the crenelations on top of the walls, the overhanging machicoulis above and portcullis behind the city gates, and the arrow slits all up and down the round towers. These, too, are a reminder of the alternative to good government in the aftermath of the Hundred Years' War. Peace in the last quarter of the fourteenth century led not only to needed repair and artistic flourishing in the cathedral of Amiens but also to the rebuilding of the city ramparts.

The choir stalls of Amiens are a social mirror of their time, an inventory of noble and bourgeois domestic habits and interior spaces, and a valuable source of information about daily life. Through them we are witness to the public, private, and spiritual lives of the citizens of Amiens, to how ordinary men and women worked, traveled, ate, bathed, slept, entertained themselves, dressed, arranged their hair, and, of course, prayed. As in the vernacular literature of the High Middle

Ages, the carvings take us into their homes with special focus upon decorative and necessary elements of finished design and furniture: moldings, bookcases, staircases, doors, railings, balustrades, and wainscoting alongside of tables, benches and workbenches, sideboards, chests, beds, dressers, prie-dieux, mirrors, and a clock. In keeping with the choir seats themselves, chairs are a special object of fascination and are represented with extraordinary variety, from the banquette on which Rebecca sits with Isaac, to the folding work stool on which Mary sits at her weaving, to the taborets under dining tables, to dining chairs, to the great chair with a high worked back and claw feet in which Jacob sits to bless Joseph before his death, to the throne with baldachin on which Pharaoh sits and dreams.

The carvings are a key to the trades of medieval Amiens. The hand-rests, in particular, show masons, money changers, butchers, bakers, shoemakers, clerics, an apothecary, town crier, beggar, wet nurse, water carrier, even the town executioner. One trade, however, is highlighted above all others—woodworking. Noah is shown on the relief panel to the left of the dean's seat hammering lapped planks in the construction of the ark; the miséricord of this seat depicts the ark floating in heavy seas that engulf the towers of a walled city not unlike Amiens. The stalls are punctuated with carpenters and cabinetmakers along with images of the products of their craft, the furniture and trappings with which the homes of Amiens were filled. Artisans working with wood appear in panel reliefs and several hand rests, a carpenter preparing the cross for

Choir Stalls, Woodworkers (Stephen Murray / Image courtesy of the
Mapping Gothic France Project, Media Center for Art History
© The Trustees of Columbia University)

the Crucifixion, another dressed in an artisan's apron with a plane in his hands, still another, a woodcarver whose name is inscribed on the outer curve of panel separating two stalls. Jean Turpin, a mallet in one hand and a chisel in the other, shapes the recognizable figure of a man that could be one of small sculptures among the myriad carvings of the prayer stalls.

HIGH RELIEF ON THE
AMIENS CHOIR WALL

WITH THE EXCEPTION OF the grill on its western flank and several lateral entrances, the choir is surrounded by a wall that serves both as a backing for the outer row of stalls and a platform for a series of intricately carved tableaux illustrating representative episodes from the lives of saints whose remains were either in or adjacent to the choir. As elsewhere in the cathedral, the art of fine carving is emphasized in the high relief, hyper-realistic, polychrome scenes, striking in their dense depiction of crowds. Created two decades before the choir stalls (1490–1500), they transmit the same Renaissance esthetics of plenitude, including an abundance—yea, an overflow—of artistic material to fill the space available; a wide variety of people and things synonymous with a festive fullness of the world; and a refinement in the working of the artistic medium to the point that flamboyance borders on decadence. So effusive are these banks of dramatic illustrations that they spill over the edges of their frames, projecting the illusion of scenic depth upon the walls at either end. The tableaux, limned by subtitles explaining their content, are arranged in groups of four, above funerary monuments, themselves surrounded either by painting or by enamel quatrefoils related to the scenes of central interest. Each of the groupings is framed on top by finely scalloped pendant frames whose pointed arches, covered in foliate crockets, blossom into an elaborate open work balustrade with miniature arches mirroring the design of the triforium and pinnacles jutting above the arches like those on the frontispiece of the cathedral.

The tableaux on the southern wall repeat and elaborate upon the life and afterlife of Saint Firmin whom we encountered on the outside of the church (see p. 219). The scene on the far left depicts the arrival of the first bishop of Amiens who is greeted by a crowd of men and women, including the Roman senator Faustinien, as he passes through the city gates. According to the inscription below, "On the tenth day of October Saint Firmin made his first entry [into] Amiens: At which Faustinien and his people rejoiced greatly." It is interesting to note that the painted diorama in the background features the defensive walls and towers surrounding the city and, in the far distance, a church which may be the Abbey of Saint Acheul, erected on the burial ground where the remains of Firmin were discovered, in what is a clear chronological error: Firmin arrived in Amiens in the third century, his relics were uncovered at the beginning of the seventh century, and the church of Saint Acheul was not built until the eleventh. The heraldic shields bearing fleurs-de-lys above and on either side of the city gate are the signs of Amiens' recent alliance with the Crown. They bear upon the gisant below of Bishop Ferry de Beauvoir (d. 1473), who had sided against King Louis XI in the Franco-Burgundian conflict of the 1460s and who, thanks to his nephew Dean Adrien de Hénencourt (d. 1530), the patron of the images around the choir, made posthumous peace with the Crown. In the second tableau, Firmin is shown preaching, again en plein air, as the city is visible in the background. In the third, he baptizes the people of Amiens. The accompanying inscription indicates that he may have converted a few too many: "[Firmin] baptized Faustinianus, the noble Atilla, wife of Agrippa, [their] family [and] children together with three thousand [others] in a single day, confessing the [Christian] faith." In the right tableau of the first bay, the proselytizing bishop is seized by the Roman authorities, and, in a representation of the city dungeon protruding from the adjoining wall, Firmin, hands joined in prayer, is beheaded by the city executioner.

The second bay of polychrome carvings along the south wall of the choir reproduces scenes from the north or Saint Firmin portal of the west facade. Over the gisant of Bishop Ferry's nephew Dean de Hénencourt, Saint Salvius, surrounded by parishioners, prays inside of a church for enlightenment concerning the tomb of Saint Firmin, which arrives in the second tableau as a ray of light piercing the tracery of a grisaille window painted in trompe l'oeil at the top of the fretted frame. In the third tableau, Firmin's remains are uncovered as a result of the spadework of an elegantly dressed priest surrounded by a gathering of townspeople, choirboys, clerics, and bishops "summoned by the sweet odor of the place to witness the discovery." And, finally, in the last scene, the newly invented relics are carried back to Amiens amid an emotional

outpouring of those seeking miraculous cures beneath the elevated cas-
ket and a mid-winter flowering of trees in the background between the
procession and the city gates. This last carved image is close to the carving in stone of the same event on the north portal of the west facade
and resembles as well the translation of the relics of Saint Honoré on the
southern entrance to the cathedral.

Rounding the apse, you will encounter three chapels restored by
Viollet-le-Duc in the middle of the nineteenth century. They are worthy of note because of the restorer's attempt to recreate the appearance of
thirteenth-century stained glass along with the polychromy of columns,
arches, and walls. The first bay on the northeast side of the axial chapel commemorates the third-century martyr Saint Theudosie, who was
born in Amiens, though she died in Rome. The gift of Napoleon III,
Napoleon Bonaparte's nephew and emperor of the French from 1852 to
1870, and his wife Eugénie, one of the windows, on the model of the relics window in the Sainte-Chapelle, recounts the life and the martyrdom
of the saint, the discovery of her body, and the negotiations surrounding the translation of her relics from Rome to Amiens in 1853, including images of the emperor and empress, the bishop of Amiens Antoine
de Salinis, and Pope Pius IX. To the right, the name of the axial chapel, *Notre-Dame-Drapière* ("Our Lady the Clothier"), attests to its local
origins among the cloth manufacturers and merchants of Amiens. This
extended radiating shrine once served as the parish church of the city
and is still worthy of note because of the elaborate retable behind the
altar, with its broken arches framing scenes of the Infancy of Jesus, along
with the Virgin and Child and a gilded miniature spire between the altar
and the windows, recreated in the mid-1800s, in the medieval mode.

Across the ambulatory aisle opposite the axial chapel a sculpted putto,
known as the "weeping angel," sits atop the mausoleum of canon Guil-
lain Lucas (d. 1636), the founder of an orphanage who is depicted kneeling before the Virgin and Child. The weeping angel rests his left hand
upon an hourglass and right elbow upon a human skull as a memento
mori, a reminder of death that was nonetheless a popular image on postcards sent by troops stationed on the Somme during World War I. In the
wake of a cholera epidemic which decimated Amiens in 1866, the chapel
to the right of the axial chapel was rededicated to the Sacred Heart of
Jesus, a conservative movement aimed at reversing the deleterious effects
of the French Revolution upon the Church of France. The restoration in

Weeping Angel (Stephen Murray / Image courtesy of the
Mapping Gothic France Project, Media Center for Art History
© The Trustees of Columbia University)

2009–10 of Viollet-le-Duc's nineteenth-century renovation gives some impression of the brilliance of the original colors of the columns, capital decorations, broken arches, and portraits of saints all around the curvilinear wall of the room.

The carved tableaux on the north side of the wall around the choir recount visually the life and death of Saint John the Baptist and are deployed in the same sequence—that is, from west to east—as the images of Saint Firmin on the other side. The first sequence shows John preaching in the desert, baptizing Jesus in the River Jordan, recognized as the forerunner, and, in turn, recognizing Christ—"Here is the very dear lamb of God." The second bay of tableaux focuses upon John's beheading at Herod's feast, which we encountered at the beginning of this chapter with the arrival of the head relic in Amiens (see p. 206).

Four of the five quatrefoils beneath the northern lateral screen recount the fate of the headless body of Saint John the Baptist, beginning, on the right under the scene of imprisonment, with burial by his followers at Sebaste near the current city of Nabulus. Moving to the left, his bones are exhumed, burned, and the ashes reburied, purportedly by the fourth-century Roman emperor Julian the Apostate (361–363).

Amiens is distinguished by the number of painted and sculpted images of the burial and unearthing of bodies, from Firmin on the north portal of the west facade, to Fuscien, Victoric, and Gentien on the tympanum of the Saint Honoré portal, and Firmin again on the south side of the wall around the choir; these in addition to Adam's spadework on the base of the trumeau of the Mother of God portal. The multiple portrayals of bodies taken from the earth summon the great representation in spectacular detail over the central portal of the cathedral of bodies emerging from their tombs for the Last Judgment at the end of human time. Together, the images of the martyrdom and the recuperation of the relics of saints, reminders of what will happen to each of us at the end of our lives and at the end of history as we know it, testify to the power of pictures and sculpture to transport us to other places and other times, even to project us into the future. If, standing in the choir of Amiens and looking up at the light from the stained glass windows and down the high nave by which you will leave the cathedral, you do not experience the most profound cathedral effect, a foretaste of paradise, you might at least have a spiritual experience of your own, or, you might simply, as I do every time I enter a cathedral, have an esthetic experience that takes me outside of myself to that mysterious zone where, beyond words, I feel the presence of something older, better, bigger, more beautiful and meaningful than I am.

REIMS
The Cathedral of France

NOTRE-DAME REIMS. PLACE DU CARDINAL LUÇON
AT THE END OF THE RUE ROCKEFELLER,
EIGHTY MILES NORTHEAST OF PARIS.

Access via rapid train (TGV) from Paris's Gare de l'Est and a fifteen-minute walk. Begun in 1211 CE, site of baptism of Clovis, first French king, coronation cathedrals of kings from the eleventh century to 1825, heavily damaged in World War I, rebuilt between 1918 and 1938, known for modern stained glass, including the champagne makers window and three panels by Marc Chagall, site of reconciliation between Germany and France beginning in the 1960s.

CLOVIS AND THE BIRTH OF FRANCE

THE GREAT ART HISTORIAN Émile Mâle declared at the end of the nineteenth century that "Reims is the national cathedral. The others are catholic, that is to say, universal, Reims alone is French." What he meant, of course, was not that other cathedrals are not situated within the geographic limits of France, that they are not part of national patrimony, or that they have not played an important role in the history of relations between church and state; rather, that Reims occupies a unique place in the consciousness of the nation.

France can arguably be said to have first come into being in the city of Durocortorum, Roman Reims, at the end of the fifth century CE. According to the tenth-century priest and historian Flodoard (d. 966), Reims was founded by soldiers loyal to Remus after his slaying by Romulus who went on to found the city of Rome. In the middle of the first century BCE, the Remès, a Gallic tribe which occupied the region of Champagne-Ardenne, sided with Julius Caesar against fellow Gauls and managed, like the inhabitants of Amiens—at a distance of only one hundred miles—to thrive along the trade routes of cereal, wine, and textiles linking northern and southern Europe. Also like Amiens, Reims was Christianized in the early centuries of the common era with the arrival of a first bishop dispatched by Pope Sixtus II (257–258) and the violent death of a first martyr, Saint Nicasius, in 407.

Bishop Nicasius is credited with founding the first cathedral of Reims, other sites of worship having existed outside the city walls. The move to town and the building of a church on the site of what had been a Roman bath, a natural setting for baptism, may have been motivated by the arrival in the area of invaders from the north during the period of the "great migration" (ca. 300–700 CE). Pressured by the Huns from the East, the Vandals, a Germanic tribe originally from southern Poland, moved westward, and, in 406 CE, crossed the Rhine into present-day France. Neither the city walls nor the church itself could protect Bishop Nicasius. When most of the inhabitants of the city fled to safety in the surrounding countryside, the brave bishop and a few followers stood at the entrance to the cathedral. There, Nicasius was beheaded along with his sister Eutropie, as, together, they became the stuff of legend. Like Saint Denis, who ambled headless from Montmartre to the place of his burial north of Paris, Nicasius picked up his severed head whose lips continued to recite a prayer—*Vivifica me, Domine, secundum verbum tuum* ("Let me live, O Lord, by thy word")—and placed it upon a nearby altar. Eutropie gouged the eyes of her brother's executioner before meeting her own death. The martyred brother and sister pair may not have been as successful as Saint Geneviève, who in 451 diverted the troops of Attila the Hun from Paris to Orleans, yet their courage is commemorated still both inside and outside the cathedral, and at the entrances, in symbolic homage to Nicasius's and Eutropie's defense of the first building's first threshold.

In the decades following Nicasius's and Eutropie's deaths, the Vandals crossed the Pyrenees into Spain and North Africa, attacking Rome in 455. But toward the end of the century, the steady course of attack on the part of the northern tribes, culminating in the deposition of the Roman emperor Romulus Augustulus by the Germanic leader Odoacer in 476, took a surprising twist. In the course of conflict between northern tribes, which not only sought to occupy the vestiges of the Roman Empire but also struggled for territory among themselves, the Merovingian king of the Salian Franks, Clovis, found himself hard pressed in battle against the Alammani or Swabians from the Upper Rhine River. Facing destruction in the midst of fierce fighting near the town of Zülpich between Aachen and Bonn, Clovis remembered the exhortations of his wife Clotilde, who had been raised as a Christian. In the account of the historian and bishop Gregory of Tours (d. 594), the Frankish leader "raised his eyes to heaven, and with remorse in his heart he burst into tears and cried: 'Jesus Christ, whom Clotilda asserts to be the son of the living God, who art said to give aid to those in distress, and to bestow victory on those who hope in thee, I beseech the glory of thy aid, with the vow that if thou wilt grant me victory over these enemies, . . . I will believe in thee and be baptized in thy name.'" Renouncing the pagan gods which had failed him, Clovis embraced the Christian God, whereupon "the Alamanni turned their backs, and began to disperse in flight."

Though scholars have long debated the actual date of the defeat of the Alamanni by the Salian Franks, there is little doubt that the conversion of Clovis to Christianity in the aftermath of the Battle of Tolbiac was one of the great moments of turning in the West. On Christmas Day, either in 496 (or in 508), the ferocious warlord from the North, guided by Archbishop Remi, stepped into the baptismal font at Reims and likely the very spot on which, almost a century earlier, Nicasius had been decapitated. Gregory of Tours renders the event as an exotic spectacle worthy of the Eastern emperor Constantine whose edict of tolerance for Christianity after the successful Battle of Milvian Bridge in 312 is evoked in the conversion of Clovis—"another Constantine advanced to the baptismal font": "The squares were shaded with tapestried canopies, the churches adorned with white curtains, the baptistery set in order, the aroma of incense spread, candles of fragrant odor burned brightly, and the whole shrine of the baptistery was filled with a divine fragrance. The Lord gave such grace to those who stood by that they

Baptism of Clovis, Grandes Chroniques de France
(Paris, BnF, Français 2813, f.12v.)

thought they were placed amid the odors of paradise." According to the
ninth-century archbishop Hincmar of Reims, the press of the crowd
was such that the holy oil required to anoint Clovis could not reach the
baptismal font, when Saint Remi, "raising his eyes and hands to the sky
began to pray in silence. All at once, a dove, whiter than snow, appeared
with a little vial of holy chrism in its beak." The account summons, of
course, the baptism of Christ who "came out of the water: and lo, the
heavens were opened to him: and he saw the Spirit of God descending as a dove, and coming upon him" (Matthew 3:16). The baptism of
Clovis tops that of Christ, however, combining as it does the holy dove
of the New Testament with the oil with which the kings of the Old
Testament—Saul, David, and Solomon—were anointed. As you visit
the interior of the cathedral, do not miss the plaque, placed in the floor
of the fifth bay of the nave in 2009 after an archeological investigation,
which marks the location of the original baptismal font: "ICI SAINT
REMI BAPTISA CLOVIS ROI DES FRANCS" ("Here Saint Remi
Baptized Clovis King of the Franks").

It took a miracle to end the clash of civilizations between the northern
invaders and the inhabitants of "Second Belgium," the term of Roman

administrative rule. The miracle of Clovis's conversion along with three thousand of his soldiers and "a great number of women" signaled a seismic shift of sovereignties and cultures with repercussions clear to the present day. Just as Constantine had prepared the way for Christianity to become the official religion of the Roman state in decline, the conversion of the Salian Franks laid the groundwork for the transformation of Roman Gallia into "Francia," the "land of the Franks," with Reims—"mother and mistress" church of the realm (Saint Bernard)—at its core. To this day, and with all the complications of an unabashed alliance between church and state, the conversion of Clovis signaled the beginning of France. Interviewed by the journalist David Schoenbrun in 1959, General Charles de Gaulle, just fifteen years after the conclusion of his own struggle against invading Germans, noted that, "For me, the history of France begins with Clovis, elected as king of France by the tribe of the Franks, who gave their name to France. Before Clovis, we have Gallo-Roman and Gaulish prehistory. The decisive element, for me, is that Clovis was the first king to have been baptized a Christian."

Late fifth-century Reims was the theater of decisive psychological, cultural, religious, and political events. The military conquest of a more or less settled population by raiders from the North culminated not in an act of war, but of inner turning, of reconciliation and adaptation. The conversion of the Franks brought an amalgamation of Germanic and Roman cultures, of Pagan and Catholic religions. It opened the way to settlement on the part of a nomadic peoples, to state formation on the model of imperial Rome, and to an integration of Classical learning, preserved by churchmen who still knew how to read and write, among those for whom the sword was mightier than the pen.

In the wake of Clovis's victory over the Alemanni at Tolbiac, he subdued other Frankish tribes and managed to bring the Amorican peninsula (Brittany) as well as the Visigothic kingdom of Toulouse under his rule. From Toulouse, as Gregory tells us, Clovis traveled to Tours, and, "leaving Tours, he went to Paris and there he established the seat of his kingdom." The establishment of a capital from which to administer the embryonic version of a realm, which included the codification of Salic Law, did not, however, signal the end of Clovis's conquests, even against his own kinsmen. "Having killed many other kings and his nearest relatives, of whom he was jealous lest they take the kingdom from him, he extended his rule over all the Gauls." At the time of his death in 511, Clovis, having recognized the strategic advantage of adopting the vestiges of Roman imperial administration still lodged in the Church, ruled a kingdom that included most of Roman Gaul as well as western Germany. He stood at the origin of the first of three dynasties—Merovingian, Carolingian, and Capetian—to rule France until the abolition of the monarchy in 1792, and, after the restoration of 1815, until the end of the July Monarchy in 1848.

REIMS AND ROYAL CORONATION

REIMS WAS THE first archbishopric in France. Like the other metropolitan seats of Roman provinces, it had jurisdiction at least in theory over the eleven bishoprics in the region, many of which had stunning cathedrals of their own: Soissons, Laon, Noyon, Beauvais, Châlons, Senlis, Thérouanne, Arras, Cambrai, Tournai, and Amiens. At the height of its administrative purview, Reims was responsible for 205 abbeys, 237 priories, and 68 schools. In his secular incarnation, the Archbishop of Reims, a direct vassal of the King of France, became a count in the eleventh century and a duke in the twelfth. More important, in the tradition of the baptism of Clovis, he had the power to anoint kings, many of whose legitimacy was contested, but whose claims to the throne were fortified by unction—royal *sacre* or anointing—in the sacred birthplace of monarchy itself. This had not always been the case. In the centuries before the advent of Louis VI as king of the Franks in 1108, coronation floated, in keeping with the mobile nature of royal authority which resided more in the person of the king than in a fixed seat of government, between Rome and a number of cities in northern France. Charlemagne's father Pepin the Short was anointed at Soissons in November 751, his two sons at Saint-Denis in 754. Charlemagne traveled to Rome where he was crowned in Saint Peter's Basilica on Christmas Day, 800 CE. Unhappy about having received the crown from the hands of Pope Leo III whom he had come to Rome to defend against rebellious members of the Roman aristocracy, Charlemagne insisted that Pope Stephen IV travel to Reims in 816 for the coronation of his son Louis the Pious, whose very name Hludovicus was rooted etymologically in that of Clodevecus, affirming the genealogical link between Louis and Clovis.

Louis could not hold the empire together after his father's death, and the quarrels between his two sons led to two coronations. Charles the

Bald received unction in 848 at Sens. His brother Louis the German tried to have himself ordained at Reims in 858, but Archbishop Hincmar was opposed; and when Charles seized the middle kingdom or Lotharingia in 869, Hincmar crowned him at Metz, which is when the story of the holy dove and oil first came into being. "The glorious Clovis, King of the Franks," Hincmar reveals, "was anointed with a chrism descended from heaven and that we still possess." Of the eleven sacred anointings which took place between 879 and 1017, nine were located in the metropolitan seat of Reims. Between 1027 and 1825, thirty out of thirty-two coronations were held in the cathedral itself.

The vial of holy oil was a real object first discovered in 852 when the tomb of Saint Remi, who had baptized Clovis, was opened and his relics were transferred to the Abbey of Saint Remi. It was kept in the abbey from which it was ceremoniously delivered to the cathedral for each and every unction and coronation, a distance of less than a mile. The legend of the white dove from heaven was a retrospective invention of Hincmar and a blending of the ceremony of baptism with that of coronation. Remi's relics were profaned during the Reign of Terror in 1793 when it was noted that the skin on the saint's cranium was still intact as were the hairs of his beard, leading to the conclusion that the oil was, in fact, leftover embalming fluid. On October 7, 1793, the vial was removed from the Abbey of Saint Remi and publicly destroyed to cries of *Vive la République!* by members of the National Convention, the first entirely non-monarchic government after the Revolution. The man in charge of the holy smashing, Citizen Rühl, noted in his report, "I broke the holy ampulla on the pedestal of Louis the Lazy ("Fainéant"), the fifteenth of that name. . . . The great and generous people will never again witness the insidious farce of the anointing of a happy bandit. . . . The holy vial no longer exists, this sacred bauble of fools." Such revolutionary delight was not, however, the end of the story. Alerted the previous night, a local priest removed a small amount of the dried-out remnants of the thousand-year-old elixir and transferred it to another vessel, yet not so much as to bring his clerical cleverness to the attention of the authorities. Like a relic, the myriad splinters of the True Cross, for example, the smallest quantity of the holy oil contains the essence and power of the whole. Thus, in preparation for the last sacred coronation at Reims, that of Charles X in 1825, the salvaged powder was mixed with fresh oil and placed in a replica of the destroyed vial. The holy ampulla was last opened in 1937 to reconsecrate the rebuilt altar of Reims after the damage suffered in World War I. It is still visible in the archbishop's palace, the Palais du Tau, adjoining the south side of the cathedral.

The anointing with holy oil was part of a highly coded ritual or *sacre* involving prayer vigils, processions, solemn oaths, confession, communion, dubbing, a binding of spurs, symbolic swordplay, undressing and dressing, and, finally, the archbishop's anointing of the kneeling king on the head, chest, back, shoulders, and hands. Once anointed, the new king assumed a status somewhere between the human and the divine. Proof of altered royal status lay in the king's "touch"—the power to heal those suffering from the "royal sickness," tuberculous cervical lymphadenitis or scrofula. The monk and chronicler Guibert de Nogent (d. 1124) claims that he saw a crowd of subjects suffering from swellings of the neck cured by Louis VI's "touching them with the sign of the cross." From the cure of scrofula, the supernatural royal power to heal, modeled on that of Christ and of the saints, was generalized to cover diseases more generally. With Saint Louis, it became a daily or weekly affair, one of the attributes of divine kingship bestowed at Reims and preserved intact until the end of the Ancien Régime. Louis XVI "touched" 2,400 assembled sick people in June 1775, periodically washing his hands in water mixed with vinegar, which certain of the suffering subjects carried away with them to drink during the nine days of a novena. "I would not have been surprised if several of these good people were cured," recounted a witness, the Duc de Croÿ.

FIRES, FINANCES, AND FIGHTING
IN MEDIEVAL REIMS

THE HISTORY OF THE CATHEDRAL of Reims, like that of all the great Gothic churches, is one of the building and rebuilding of increasingly large and elaborate structures which cover or incorporate preexisting ones. The Merovingian church where Saint Nicasius was beheaded stood on the site of Roman baths and an early Christian baptistery. It was replaced at the end of the tenth century by a Carolingian basilica, which was, in turn, enlarged in the middle of the twelfth century by the enterprising Archbishop Samson de Mauvoisin (d. 1161) who, having attended the dedication ceremony at the Abbey of Saint-Denis in the 1140s, imagined something similar for Reims. Saint-Denis and Reims were royal rivals, one the site of the burial of kings, the other the site of coronation, though paraphernalia for the *sacre* was kept at Saint-Denis and brought to Reims each and every time a new king was crowned, just as the holy oil was delivered ceremoniously from the nearby Abbey of Saint-Remi. Archbishop Mauvoisin's cathedral, with its radiating chapels and towers on the west facade, was a perfectly adequate structure, yet, within a period of some fifty years, it no longer compared to the Gothic buildings going up all around, a situation resolved, once again, by fire. Chartres had burned in 1194, Évreux in 1195, Rouen in 1200, Nevers in 1211, Amiens in 1218, Beauvais in 1225, and Châlons in 1230, all followed by ambitious building campaigns in the new Gothic mode.

Annals for the year 1210 note a catastrophic blaze in the cathedral of Reims. Just one year later, however, "walls were erected on the extremely deep foundations on the side of the archbishop's palace." The timing was suspicious. Preparations for a building project on the scale of Reims Cathedral required financial negotiations between the canons and the archbishop, the location of a skilled architect and the fixing of plans, the clearing of debris from the fire, the digging and reinforcement of suitable foundations, the location, cutting, and transportation of stones from the quarry. Further, dendrological analysis of wood from one of the tie beams of a pillar on the north side of the nave and wood stuck in the holes where scaffolding was inserted for the erection of the south arm of the transept indicate that the trees from which they came were felled in 1211, either before or at the time of the fire. Thus, plans for rebuilding Samson's cathedral may have been in place before it was actually destroyed to make way for the Gothic building that came into being over the extraordinarily short period of the next seventy years.

Reims at the beginning of the thirteenth century, a city of some 12,000 to 15,000 inhabitants, was one of the largest in France. Like Amiens, the local economy of shopkeepers, combined with grain, wine textile, and woad production in the surrounding countryside, the work of shepherds, shearers, dyers, carders, and fullers, also made it one of the richest. To the north, long-range trade routes connected Reims to markets in towns belonging to the Flemish Hanse League of London. To the south, the textiles of Reims—wool and linen, rugs and serge— were sold at the fairs of Champagne, and reached, via Italian merchants, markets as far away as Syria, Persia, and Egypt. Yet, despite their wealth, the bourgeois inhabitants of Reims did not pay, at least not at the outset, for the new church in the Gothic style. Nor did the archbishop participate significantly in the initial funding of the cathedral. The canons of the chapter, those responsible for the maintenance of the liturgy and for what was termed the "fabric" of cathedral building, were unusually wealthy. Their income from taxes in the city and the surrounding countryside, from agricultural estates, from fulling mills that supplied the burgeoning textile industry, went to pay for the initial phases of the construction. In addition, the canons organized relic quests of the type also practiced at Amiens (see p. 214).

The relics of medieval Reims were considerable, including at their high point a fragment of the crown of thorns, a piece of the cross and of the tunic that Jesus wore, clothing of the Virgin, and bodily parts of Saints Peter, Paul, Stephen, Denis, and Nicasius—all paraded throughout the region. Reims' status as the metropolitan church of the district afforded a precedence and a freedom to roam without restraint in the collection of pious donations in exchange for the cures of body and of soul that relics provided. The translation of the cranium of Saint Nicasius to another shrine in 1213 was a source of contributions to the fabric of the cathedral. In 1221 Pope Honorius III granted an indulgence to all who donated to the "distinguished and extremely costly structure." We know about this in part because the Bishop of Laon complained to the pope that the relic questors of Reims had intruded upon their own fundraising territory.

The financing of cathedral building was not a uniform or a uniformly peaceful process. The need for money in the initial phase of the plotting and laying of foundations was less than that involved in the erection of scaffolding and the hoisting of heavy materials to the upper parts of the structure. So, when, in 1233, the chapter turned to the citizens of Reims to fund the increasing costs of construction, they revolted, built barricades in front of the archbishop's palace with stones designated for the walls of the church, and forced the canons to flee. Eventually, King Louis IX intervened. Ruling against the urban insurgents, the king imposed sanctions upon the townspeople, which combined public penance, an appearance barefoot before the canons at the Porte de Mars, the main gate of the city, and fines to repair the damage caused by their revolt. Louis's ruling permitted the canons and the archbishop to return to town and for work on the cathedral, which had been suspended for a period of three years, to resume. Using stones cut to measure, which was an efficiency in the building process, the apse and choir were completed by 1241, the west facade by 1260, and the nave and rose windows by the end of the century. This left only the gallery of kings, essential to the place of coronation of kings, which was completed by the middle of the fifteenth century. And, as we shall see (p. 293), the interior decoration of Reims Cathedral continued throughout the 1400s along with upper galleries of the nave, which crowned the cathedral at the beginning of the 1500s.

REIMS IN THE WORLD WARS

THE SOLIDITY OF THE bond between Notre-Dame Reims and France itself contributed to the vulnerability of the cathedral throughout World War I.

German troops captured Reims at the outbreak of the war. Having moved through Belgium where the university library at Louvain with its medieval manuscripts had burned to the ground, the Kaiser's army entered the city on September 4, 1914, camping in the open space in front of the cathedral whose floor was strewn with straw to accommodate German wounded. The unexpected victory of the Allies, British and French, at the First Battle of the Marne (September 6–12, 1914),

Bombing in World War I, April 19, 1917 (HIP / Art Resource, NY)

however, stopped the German advance to Paris and caused the withdrawal of the invading army from Reims to surrounding forts which had, in fact, been built to defend the city in the aftermath of the Franco-Prussian War of 1870–71. From there the Germans began to shell the town. On September 17, three bombs struck the cathedral, the next day, thirteen. Then, on September 19 at around three o'clock in the afternoon, a bomb struck the wooden scaffolding erected for the purpose of making repairs to the north tower of the west facade, setting it on fire, which quickly spread to the roof structure of the entire cathedral. The upper parts of Notre-Dame Reims burned in much the same manner as the roof of Notre-Dame Paris in April 2019.

Molten lead which ran down the top of flying buttresses designed to receive rain from above coagulated in the mouths of the gargoyles like twisted tongues that would cry in outrage if they could. Some are still on exhibit in the Palais du Tau adjoining the cathedral on the south side. Fires caused by shelling elsewhere in the city severely limited efforts to extinguish that of the cathedral from which as many of the three thousand German wounded as possible were evacuated along with liturgical objects and articles of value rescued from the treasury. This was only the beginning of the destruction at Reims, as a total of 287 shells struck the cathedral between this first assault and the armistice of 1918, some piercing the vaults that had been exposed with the loss of a roof cover. The

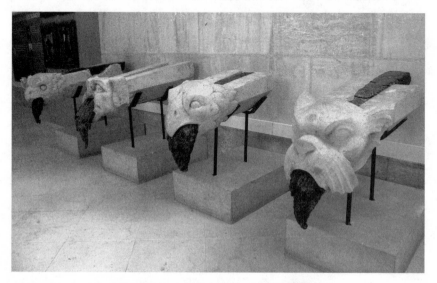

Lead-Spewing Gargoyles, Palace of Tau

damage to the masonry, including exterior sculpture that was calcified in the flames, was severe. But the destruction of medieval windows was irrecuperable, as myriad shards of colored glass lay scattered on the floor which at the beginning of the war had been strewn with straw.

The question of what happened at Reims is a matter of dispute. Those who shelled the town and seem to have made little effort to avoid the cathedral claim that its towers were being used as observation posts from which to detect enemy troop movement; this in violation of the Hague Conventions of 1907 which prohibited public monuments and churches from being used for military purposes. Inhabitants of the town denied this allegation, maintaining that a white flag posted on the ramparts of the church, along with its status as a Red Cross shelter for the wounded, should have protected it from shelling. In response, the German Ministry of War blamed the French for the fire because of having "incomprehensibly neglected" to dismantle the scaffolding around the north tower or taken sufficient action to extinguish the flames. The lodging of German soldiers under the protection of the Red Cross flag was, the Ministry maintained, "a diabolical plan, whose perfidy and baseness were exceeded only by the manner in which it was carried out." Anxious to rebuild even a temporary roof structure to prevent damage to the open vaults exposed to the elements, yet afraid that workmen on the upper parts of the cathedral would again be taken for military observers, the French turned to Pope Benedict XV who wrote to the Kaiser requesting that he give the Apostolic See assurances that "the German Imperial Army will not initiate any further shelling of the cathedral during the intended work." The Kaiser replied by reaffirming his commitment "to protecting venerable religious sites and artistic monuments . . . from the horrors of war," which has not always been successful. "I have especially lamented this," he concluded, "because of Reims Cathedral, . . . which suffered damage as a result of the military measures undertaken by our enemies."

The shelling of Notre-Dame Reims led to a campaign of propaganda that struck to the heart of national identity on both sides and that eventually affected the outcome of the war. It was, on one level, a reprise of the wars of religion of the sixteenth century. Pitting Protestants against Catholics, the targeting of Notre-Dame Reims held, in the phrase of Maurice Landrieux, a curé of the cathedral who meticulously documented the damage, "some furor of Lutheranism, that old rancor of the

Reformation against the Church and the Holy Virgin." The spirit of anti-Catholicism from the North was not without some basis in fact. "I hate this religion that you have embraced," the Kaiser wrote to his maternal first cousin Princess Elisabeth of Hesse-Darmstadt, who had converted to Russian Orthodoxy in 1884 and entered a nunnery after the Socialist Revolutionary Party had assassinated her husband in 1905, "for you have acceded to this Roman superstition, the destruction of which I consider one of the goals of my life." There is some evidence, too, that German military authorities sent regiments composed primarily of Protestant soldiers against Catholic Belgium and France, and Catholic troops against the Roman Orthodox to the East.

For their part, the French, citing examples reaching all the way back to classical sources, summoned ancient haunting images of the barbarous Huns and Vandals cutting a path of ruin wherever they went, simply for the pleasure of destruction. The French Ministry of Culture published a volume entitled "The Germans, Destroyers of Cathedrals and of Treasures of the Past" signed by important cultural and political figures, among whom the journalist, who would in 1917 become Prime Minister, Georges Clémenceau, novelist Anatole France, artists Claude Monet, Pierre Bonnard, Henri Matisse, and Auguste Rodin, composers Camille Saint-Saëns and Claude Débussy. The thrust of their claim was that Germans were not only the enemies of France but also the enemies of civilization, which is synonymous with art, and of which the cathedral, "the most beautiful and the fullest of our family homes," in the phrase of the journalist Maurice Barrès, is the highest and fullest expression.

In response to accusations of barbarism, the Germans founded the Kunstschutz (art protection) propaganda unit which both embraced the charge of barbarism and transformed it into a virtue. "We welcome the feeling that we are the barbarians who smash a rotten political world," wrote the art historian Paul Clemens, head of the Kunstschutz. "We are the nation that has . . . earned the status of greatest youth in the family of central European nations, and thus has the right to the most secure and lasting future." German Major General Wolfgang von Ditfurth was quoted to the effect that for Germany the ends of war justified the means, even when it meant the destruction of Reims Cathedral: "If all the glorious monuments ever created be destroyed, it is of no consequence, so long as by their destruction we promote German victory.

The humblest gravestone of a German grenadier is more beautiful than all the cathedrals of Europe."

The theorist of war Carl von Clausewitz famously remarked that "war is the continuation of politics by other means." The propaganda struggle between the Germans and the French over the shelling of Reims Cathedral was a continuation of war by cultural means, and so much rhetorical posturing next to the effects of the images of the devastated cathedral, "the great skeleton of medieval France," in the words of Auguste Rodin. Photographic and hand-drawn images in newspapers and pamphlets, on posters and postcards, circulated widely all over the world in the aftermath of the initial assault of September 1914, and the vilification of the Germans in terms of barbarian destroyers of art and all that is precious to Western civilization, indeed, of civilization itself, elicited global sympathy for the French. A persuasive claim has been made, in fact, that pictures of Reims in ruins, along with the sinking of the *Lusitania* in May 1915, had something to do with the eventual entry of the United States into World War I. They had much to do with the restoration of the cathedral after the war.

Reims was liberated on October 5, 1918. The armistice ending the Great War was signed a little over a month later. Throughout the bombings that had destroyed much of the city, France's national cathedral still stood, and an assessment of the damage began almost immediately alongside discussions about whether to rebuild or to leave the devastated structure, like the Parthenon after the Persian destruction of Athens in 480 BCE, as a monument to the past—a lasting architectural reproach to the Germans. The roof had been completely destroyed in the fire at the outset of hostilities, and rain and freezing had in the meantime further damaged the high ceilings, the masonry, and the plaster of the walls. The vaults had been pierced in nine places by the direct hit of bombs that exploded within the structure. Of the twenty-two flying buttresses, seven had been severely damaged, while fifteen were affected to a lesser degree. The sculpture of the west facade had been severely mutilated. Of the thirty-five jamb statues around the three entry porches, only eleven remained unharmed. Half of the fifty-six figures that made up the gallery of kings were lost. The large figures of angels all around the top of the cathedral were disfigured alongside the gargoyles whose protrusion beneath their "angelic neighbors," in the phrase of art historian André Michel, made them especially vulnerable. On the inside, some

3,480 square feet of stained glass were irremediably lost, according to Henri Deneux, the architect who supervised rebuilding. The main altar from the eighteenth century had been destroyed along with more than nine hundred liturgical objects that had not been rescued at the time of the fire.

The rebuilding of Reims Cathedral suffered in the beginning from a lack of manpower, raw materials, and money. Those who might have begun the actual work of reconstruction were still mobilized after the armistice. The general devastation of much of northeastern France led to a lack of building supplies, wood in particular, along with a rise in the price of primary materials. Once the decision to rebuild had been made, however, it was a lack of funds, more than men and timber, which threatened to bring the project to a halt. Allocations of public money were insufficient as were the contributions that trickled in from various sources—the Society of the Friends of the Cathedral of Reims, proceeds from stamp sales in Denmark, and the Reims Cathedral Restoration Fund of England and the British Empire. A few private individuals donated as well, still wealthy aristocrats and newly wealthy industrialists. The widow of Napoleon III, the Empress Eugénie, who died in July 1920, was reported to have been so moved by the courage of those who remained in the cathedral throughout the war that she bequeathed one hundred thousand francs to the Committee for the Rebuilding of Reims.

The largest contribution to the repair of Reims came from the United States. President Woodrow Wilson had visited Reims while in France for the Versailles Peace Conference of 1919, publicly denouncing "German barbarism" amid the ruins of the cathedral. John D. Rockefeller Jr. followed suit in 1923, and, after some hesitation over appearing to interfere in the internal affairs of France, wrote to the President of the Republic Raymond Poincaré on May 3, 1924: "Returning to France last summer after an interval of seventeen years, I was impressed anew with the beauty of her art, the magnificence of her architecture, and the splendor of her parks and gardens. Many examples of these are not only national but international treasures, for which France is trustee; their influence on the art of the world will always be full of inspiration." Rockefeller had witnessed firsthand the damage at Reims. He recognized how long the process of repair might take and added, "In the meantime, I should count it a privilege to be allowed to help toward that end, and shall be happy to contribute One million dollars." The sum, earmarked for the repair of the roof of Reims as well as deferred maintenance on the Palaces of Fontainebleau and Versailles, was enormous, the equivalent of 18,500,000 francs at a time when the allocation of the French government was only between 2,000,000 and 3,000,000 francs. In 1927 Rockefeller earmarked another 9,200,000 francs for Reims. This was the same year that construction began on Riverside Church in the Gothic style, also financed by Rockefeller, on New York City's Upper West Side.

As in the current reconstruction of Notre-Dame Paris, the first stages of the rebuilding of Reims consisted of securing the basic structure and erection of a temporary roof, which took more than two years. Over the course of the next couple of years, the towers, walls, vaults, and flying buttresses were reinforced. When a permanent roof framing was finally built, beginning in 1922, the old wooden substructure, in place since the original medieval struts perished in a fire at the end of the fifteenth century, was replaced by a system of preformed reinforced cement beams attached by wooden pegs. The shortage of wood for beams conditioned this choice, which was not completely unprecedented, as the roof structure of Chartres had been replaced by cast iron framing in the 1830s (see p. 106). The 1930s saw the repair of the flying buttresses, the grill of the choir, the north rose and other stained glass windows, the altars, floor tiles, the carillon, organs, and amenities like lights and heat. In all, the work of Reims took two decades. John D. Rockefeller Jr. visited on July 4, 1936, to see the fruits of his munificence, at which time the pedestrian mall leading to the parvis was renamed the rue Rockefeller. The cathedral was reconsecrated in October 1937 and inaugurated over a three-day period in July 1938 before a crowd of one hundred thousand spectators, including the President of the Republic Albert Lebrun and the great hero of World War I, Marshal Philippe Pétain.

Though the period of respite between the completion of the restoration in 1938 and the invasion of France by German troops in May and June 1940 was less than two years, precautions were taken to remove stained glass windows and to protect the restored sculpture of the lower parts of the church by a wall of sandbags. The damage inflicted upon the cathedral in World War II was relatively minor, the Germans possibly having learned that the destruction of cathedrals incurred a large moral cost with little visible military advantage.

APPROACHING THE NORTH FACADE

Reims is unique in that many of the features found on the west facade of other churches are situated on the north side of the cathedral of kings. It has even been argued that the north transept portals of Reims were, in fact, originally part of the west facade of Samson's twelfth-century building and that they were moved to their current position only when the Gothic church of the thirteenth century was expanded. The north side of the church is fascinating, however, not only for the elements it contains and that can be found elsewhere but also for the uniqueness of the urban legend around the base of the trumeau of the Judgment of God portal.

Standing at the base of the trumeau, you come face-to-face with one of the most intimately stunning sculptures on any cathedral in northern France, which also may be connected to the civil unrest in Reims

The Dishonest Draper, Trumeau North Transept Entrance

in the 1230s. Under a statue of the *Beau Dieu*, not unlike that found on the west facades of Amiens and Notre-Dame Paris, a narrative frieze showing several scenes of commercial exchange wraps around the five-faceted section between an undecorated pedestal at ground level and the classically draped feet of Christ. As you walk around it, observe in the leftmost facet men and women who discuss an object lying on the table between them. The men, who are missing their heads, are nonetheless recognizable by their dress. The women, better preserved for having been carved in lower relief, wear the wimples of middle-class ladies. Tellingly, the woman at the center of this first tableau fondles with her right hand the clasp around her neck, an indication that the scene depicted may have to do with the purchase of jewels. The mutilated object on the table resembles nothing so much as a pouch which may contain precious stones for purchase.

You may find the central scene of this sculptural tableaux both more intriguing and less ambiguous. Here a cloth merchant displays his wares, surrounded, again, by men and women who examine and touch the cloth spread upon the table before them. To the right a figure holds a sample in one hand, while a bundle of folded goods lies upon a stool, either having been purchased and bundled to go or waiting to be unfurled for display. Two features of the scene, however, mark it as unusual, perhaps unique in all the universe of Gothic sculpture: it seems to show a criminal captured in the act. A boy or small adult sits beneath the table, while a large figure draped in a mantle places his hands upon the merchant's shoulders. The lower form, hidden from the view of potential buyers by the draped goods spread across the table, attempts to cheat them, an account supported by the gesture of the standing figure whose strong arms apprehend the dishonest draper. The arrest is confirmed by the tableau to the right in which a large man firmly grasps the dry goods merchant by the arm. In the final scene of the multifaceted frieze, the draper, surrounded by several men in ecclesiastical headdress, kneels barefoot before a statue of the Virgin and Child on a throne in a posture of repentance.

The drama of the dishonest draper reveals much about urban life in thirteenth-century Reims. First, it offers a glimpse into the role of the church in maintaining the integrity of economic transactions. The bishop played a part in assuring the safety of those traveling to and from medieval trade fairs and was responsible for the fairness of business conducted there. In many cathedral towns merchant stalls filled the space between the buttresses just on the other side of the aisle chapels, rendering spatially the close proximity of religious worship and commerce. But Reims was special, and it is entirely possible that the apprehension of the deceitful seller of dry goods in such a center of textile manufacture and trade refers not to an individual merchant, but to an entire class of workers who were brought to heel by Archbishop Henri Braine after the urban revolt of 1233–36. The dates for the erection of the Judgment of God portal of the north transept, which range between 1220 and 1240, are not so firmly established as to make such a reading more than speculation, enriched, however, by one extenuating piece of circumstantial evidence. Surprisingly, given its role in the making of monarchy, Reims Cathedral remained relatively untouched by the ravages inflicted upon religious buildings in the aftermath of the French Revolution. With this exception: the figures in the frieze at the base of the *Beau Dieu* trumeau were singularly mutilated by the hammers of destructive revolutionaries, perhaps in reaction to the distant memory of the archbishop of Reims' subjugation of their medieval ancestors.

THE NORTH TRANSEPT PORTALS

THE JUDGMENT OF GOD or left portal of the north transept is unusual in that the motif of the Resurrection of Souls is more commonly placed within the topography of Gothic design on the west facade, or, as in the also exceptional case of Chartres whose sculptural programs influenced those of Reims, on the south side. Standing in front of the Last Judgment portal, you may notice that the figure of Christ as *Beau Dieu*, holding the globe of the world in his one remaining hand, is surrounded on the left by jamb statues of Saint Bartholomew, holding the knife with which he was flayed, Andrew with a Latin cross, Peter with a particularly frizzy beard; and, on the right, Saint Peter, holding a book and sword, James the Major with a pilgrim's bag with shells, and the young apostle John, the only beardless figure, who bears a lavishly bejeweled book. The depiction of resurrected souls in the trumeau above Christ's head inverts the usual narrative sequence, as the top two registers display bodies emerging from sarcophagi and urns, while the lowest rung contains, on our left (Christ's right), souls brought by angels to the bosom of Abraham who presses them in a cloth to his chest, and, on our right, men and women of all stations—an archbishop, a king, a moneylender, and a knight—enveloped in a chain by which the devil on the far right drags them into a boiling pot. Between the separation of the saved and the damned and the resurrection of bodies, the middle register displays a celestial court with king, queen, and angels, presided by a bishop. On the other side, a conclave of devils whose naked bodies were mutilated not by ardent revolutionaries, but by canons who, in the eighteenth century, dealt with their embarrassment at the devilish nudity by hacking at them such that only the outlines of their bodies remain. At the very top, Christ in majesty shows His wounds, surrounded by Mary on one side and Saint John the Baptist on the other with angels bearing the instruments of the Passion. The three rows of voussoirs depict churchmen reading books in a middle row, wise and foolish virgins on the inside, and angels bearing trumpets and crowns on the outer edge.

LOCAL SAINTS ON
THE NORTHERN FACADE

THE MIDDLE PORTAL or portal of the saints of the north transept features in the trumeau a statue of Pope Calixtus (d. 222) wearing a conical papal tiara on his head and a priestly pectoral or breastplate studded with twelve jewels, like that of Aaron in the *Book of Exodus*, around his neck. Calixtus is flanked on his right by a jamb statue of Saint Nicasius holding his head, between his sister Eutropie and a censing angel. On his left, Saint Remi is accompanied by an angel and an unidentified figure nearest the door. The disposition of the jamb figures is reproduced in the lintel. On the lower lintel, to the left of Calixtus's tiara, Saint Nicasius bows his head, while his sister pokes her fingers in the eye of a Roman soldier holding a sword in his hands. On the far left, Nicasius places his head, still wearing the bishop's miter, on the altar not far from where the very act is purported to have taken place in 407 CE. An angel hovers beneath a church-like gable, ready to exchange the crown of a martyr for the earthly headdress. To the right of Calixtus's tiara, the scene of Clovis's baptism stretches to the edge of the lintel. Bishop Remi officiates, while Clovis's wife Clotilde, having lost her head, stands on the other side of the baptismal font with a king's crown in her hands. Photographs from before 1914 show in low relief the dove descending over Remi's shoulder, the miraculous descent from heaven of the holy

Portal of the Saints, North Transept

oil now just a smudge on the wall behind the myriad figures of the first lintel of the portal of the saints.

If you look up at the three registers of the tympanum above the lintel, you will see a mysterious mixture of miracles from the life of Saint Remi and the Book of Job. On the lower level, as in the Annunciation of Gabriel to Mary, an angel announces to the monk Saint Montan, living as a hermit, that Celine, mother of the saint Bishop Remi, would conceive a son. The center of the second lintel depicts Remi's exorcism of a young woman in Toulouse, the devil, which has been partially effaced, leaving via her mouth. The third register offers a summary narrative account of the sufferings of Job, with scenes from left to right of a messenger announcing the loss of Job's flock and all his children, the murmuring of his friends, his wife's despair, and Job stretched out on the dung heap as the devil seizes him. The fourth level of the tympanum of the portal of the saints picks up, on the left, where the story of Remi's resuscitation of the young girl of Toulouse left off. She has subsequently died and is raised from her sarcophagus by the saint.

The right portal of the north transept, which once served as an entrance to the church from the west wing of the cloister, is only minimally decorated. Lacking a trumeau, jamb statues, a narrative tympanum, or layered voussoirs, the "Roman" portal features a simple and beautiful Virgin and Child seated within the architectural frame of a city with domed roofs and crenelated towers, yet reduced to the more intimate scale of a room with curtains draped from the wall in the background and looped around columns with capitals on either side. Because it is so deeply set within a relatively narrow space, the Byzantine Mary in majesty still shows traces of blue paint on the columns and on her dress, which is dappled with stars. The skin on her hands and face retains a pinkish flesh tone, while the gold of her crown still glows with its original metallic color, probably applied as part of a nineteenth-century restoration. Elaborate spiraliform and scroll-and-vine patterns surround the Virgin and Child who are protected from above by a ring of angels in the rounded Romanesque—and not broken Gothic—arch. Curious carvings on either side depict two scenes of clerical life, as this was the door by which the canons entered the church. On the left a cleric dips his sprinkler into a basin of holy water, and, on the right, his colleague holds a book from which the bishop reads prayers for the dead.

Before leaving the north transept of Reims, you should raise your eyes above the portals to take in the bigger-than-life figures of Adam and Eve, who holds in her hand a reptilian creature, more like a large lizard than a serpent. The first couple look at each other from either side of the large rose window. The rose windows of Reims are distinct in that they are capped by tympanum-like glass spandrels, which make for a broken arch on the outside of the church. If you follow the narrative sequence of the sculpture around the glazing, you will see episodes from Genesis—the birth of Eve, the eating of the forbidden fruit, expulsion from paradise, the sacrifices of Cain and Abel, Cain's killing of his brother, Adam working the earth while Eve spins—all mixed with scenes from the everyday life of medieval Reims: a peasant beating wheat, a baker kneading bread, another putting it in the oven. At the summit of the four buttresses of the north tower, shrines sustained by four columns each and pignon or gabled roofs house the figures of crowned kings with scepters in their hands. The watchful presence of royalty atop the coronation cathedral of France is sustained by a gallery of kings above the rose window and angels interlaced with fleurs-de-lys on the gable at the very top of the north transept tower.

THE MASKS OF REIMS

If you look closely at the small sculptures around the top of the cathedral, you will notice the unruly faces that protrude at regular intervals from the edges of the moldings between the protective shrines and the gabled roofs of the enclosed kings whose dignity and power they seem to undercut. Spread all around the upper reaches of the cathedral, a myriad of masks, striking because of the expressivity of their faces, are unique to Reims. Some grimace, others scream with open mouths and bulging eyes; some pucker their lips, while others bear their teeth; some are racially marked with large lips and a broad nose; at least one features a hooked nose and wears the hat associated with the figure of

Masks (© Jason Hong)

the Wandering Jew, as among the chimera of the western balustrade of Notre-Dame Paris (see pp. 94–98); some are barely human with devilish features, and a few belong outright to the animal kingdom—an ox, a lion, an owl. Again, like the doodlings in the margins of medieval man-uscripts, these human gargoyles without the function of carrying rain from the roof speak to the underbelly of cathedral construction and may be the not completely subdued signs of the social unrest that plagued Reims at the commencement of the construction of its upper parts. The grimacing, shrieking, distorted faces just above and all around the heads of kings, a chorus of common and underrepresented souls, may shout deep anger at the repression of the rebellion of 1233–36—a last word until, of course, the Revolution of 1789 when the anger of the repressed will manifest in the hammers of the masses.

JOAN OF ARC

STANDING IN FRONT OF the cathedral, look to the left. There, to one side of the entrance to the Palace of Justice, which combines a Roman arch with Greek columns and pediment, you will see a life-size statue of Joan of Arc mounted on her war horse, feet fixed in the stirrups, her torso erect and in full body armor. Reims was the site of the baptism of Clovis and of the consecration of royalty from the twelfth through the nineteenth centuries, but the cathedral lodged even deeper in the national consciousness during the Hundred Years' War when Joan of Arc convinced the dauphin Charles VII that a coronation at Reims, which was in the hands of the Anglo-Burgundian alliance, rather than in Orlé-ans, which was more securely under French control, would have much more meaning. The victorious campaign from Orléans to his anointing with holy oil in the City of Kings on July 17, 1429, was declared a mir-acle by Joan herself: "Noble King, now is executed the pleasure of God who wished I lift the siege of Orléans, and I bring you into this city of Reims to receive your holy coronation to show you are the true king, and the one to whom the kingdom of France must belong." The *sacre* had, in fact, played a role, if only in jest, in the century and a quarter of hostilities (1337–1453) between the English and the French, who main-tained that, while their kings were anointed with holy chrism brought from heaven, the kings of England were daubed with oil purchased at the local pharmacy.

In recognition of the place of Joan at the root core of French civic memory, on July 14, 1896, fifteen hundred years after the baptism of Clovis and on the very date of the arrival of Charles and Joan in Reims, President of the Republic Félix Faure dedicated a statue of France's most important national saint. With her left hand she grasps firmly the reins of her horse, while, with the right, she raises her sword defiantly in the air. What is most remarkable about the Reims Joan of Arc, however, is the intensity of her upward look whose meaning is not entirely clear. Is she is looking at the cathedral or at the sky? Has the sculptor, Paul Dubois, captured the otherworldly certainty of a visionary? Or, with all we know about Reims in the aftermath of the Franco Prussian War of 1870–71 and in anticipation of World War I, is it doubt and fear for the future written on her face, between her eyes and pursed lips which together continue to implore the aid of the almighty?

THE WEST FACADE OF REIMS

REIMS, LIKE AMIENS, is a sculptural wonderland, with 211 large statues nine-and-a-half-to-thirteen-feet high, 126 statues of medium height, and 936 small carvings, of which 788 are animals. Inside, the collection of 191 medium-size statues and fifty animals makes a total of 2,303 figures in the sculptural programs of the cathedral whose west facade contains a great abundance of sculpture all up and down its deeply recessed porticos, mid-level rose section, gallery of kings, and soaring towers. One feature, however, makes for the particular density of figures along the frontispiece of Reims. The three porticos feature stained glass—quatrefoils under trefoils on the north and south sides, a rose and spandrel in the center—where normally a carved stone tympanum is to be found. As a result, the darkest area of most Gothic cathedrals, the narthex or entryway, is flooded with light, but the sculpture that would have filled the tympana over the doors is displaced to the lintels, the archivolts, and the lateral buttresses.

Subjects ordinarily found in the tympana are projected to the top of the broken arches and below the gables atop each portico. The left portico or portal of the Passion features in the gable a Crucifixion, with Mary and John furthest from Christ and Longinus pointing his lance in Christ's direction, while the figure to our right extends a sponge with vinegar on the tip of his lance. The sculptural relief on the northern-

West Facade

most or left buttress is framed as a broken arch or tympanum, and, as it is the same size as the stone tympanum that would have filled the space over the northern door, it creates the illusion that stone has merely been pushed to the side by glass. The images carved there—now barely recognizable because of the bombings and fire of 1914, but known more clearly via prewar photographs—show, in the triangular drum, scenes of Emperor Constantine's mother Helena's discovery of the True Cross, as in the relics window of the Sainte-Chapelle (see p. 161). The damaged figures below depict the temptations of Christ. The devil on the left challenges Him to turn a rock into bread (Matthew 4:1–4), while that on the right, facing away from the center, encourages Christ to jump from the pinnacle of the temple, as the images on the buttress spill over to the outer edge of the voussoirs where Christ sits atop a miniature representation of the temple roof. The other rings of the voussoirs in the broken arches around the stained glass depict various episodes in the Passion and Resurrection of Christ, in keeping with the Crucifixion in the gable above.

Atlantide and Water Bearer, West Facade (© Jason Hong)

Between the devil who tempts Christ to jump off the roof of the temple and Christ sitting on the site of his temptation, the small statue of a man in a loosely draped tunic holding a jug is matched on the extended edge between the voussoirs of the northern and central portals by a similar figure who empties its contents. The motif of pouring water is repeated symmetrically on the side of the voussoirs of the central portal and between the southern porch and the adjoining lateral buttress, in a horizontal tying together of the portals of the west facade via the representation of what has been taken for symbols of the four principal rivers of France. Above each of the water carriers, the figure of a man in lay garments, his shoulders bent under the weight of the gargoyle above him, reproduces the classical motif of Atlas shouldering the weight of the world in Greek myth. Again, human beasts of burden between the water carriers and the gargoyles contribute to the visual unity of the west facade, but they also signal something more serious, which links them to the masked faces of anguish and protest on the cathedral's upper parts.

Thirty bent figures or "Atlantides"—from Atlas—are found all around the exterior upper parts of the nave and choir between the cornice of the roof and the top of the flying buttresses. Like the grimacing masks, they are extremely expressive in their body language and are also highly individualized. One carries a heavy sack on his back in addition to the weight of the corbel or bracket on his shoulders, another uses his hands and arms to help support the load, while still another places his hands upon his thighs, and another upon his brow in a gesture of weariness, and yet still another balances the upper part of his body with a cane, another with a crutch, still another leans on his fuller's stick. All are united by the onerous effects of the burden on their backs. The Atlantides around the nave and choir, with the exception of a knight resting on his sword, wear the tunics, belts, and leggings of peasants, artisans, and laborers. Several, in fact, have shed their smock to the waist to avoid oppressive heat or have raised their tunics to the waist to prevent soiling them in the muck of work. The universal expressions of woe upon their faces reinforce the marginality of such figures, the bearers of burdens concretized by the act of literally carrying the concrete weight of the cathedral on their shoulders. In the phrase of Jacques Le Goff, they are an expression of "the other Middle Ages," distinguished even from the classically dressed bent figures on the west facade, projections of what noble and middle-class inhabitants of Reims might have worn. Could it be, as this was the entrance by which the king and nobles entered and departed from the ceremony of *sacre*, that such images of oppression were reserved for the other facets of the coronation cathedral?

The lintels over the lateral doors of the west facade recount a single event, the conversion of Saint Paul on the road to Damascus. Over the left door, Paul, surrounded by his companions, falls to the ground, stunned by a flash of light, before the walls of Damascus: "And as he went on his journey, it came to pass that he drew nigh to Damascus. And suddenly a light from heaven shined round about him. And falling on the ground, he heard a voice saying to him: Saul, Saul, why persecutest thou me?" (Acts 9:3–4). Saul/Paul has been blinded by the light, which is where the lintel over the right door picks up as a single tableau with four episodes. Two men guide Paul into Damascus where his sight is restored in the house of Judas by "a certain disciple at Damascus, named Ananias" (Acts 9:10). Led in procession by a figure holding a cross, he dips into the baptismal font, in yet another allusion to the baptism of Clovis: "And immediately there fell from his eyes as it were scales: and he received his sight. And rising up, he was baptized" (Acts 9:18).

THE REIMS JAMBS

THE INDIVIDUAL JAMB STATUES, each approximately nine feet high, arrayed all along the west facade of Reims have been moved around sufficiently over time so that any original thematic relationship between them is difficult to recover. They are, in addition, crafted in different styles, some in a classical mode, others under the influence of the jamb statues of Chartres, still others in an original style identified specifically as that of Reims, characterized by heads with almond-shaped eyes and faces with a merry—mischievous, even—expression. Despite the dislocations of position and of appearance to the trained eye, the Reims jamb figures dwell harmoniously with each other above the carved base of drapery and below the floral frieze that runs the breadth of the west facade. Indeed, the jamb figures enjoy cordial relations. The left jambs of the south portal are arranged in pairs, with two apostles nearest the door and a pope wearing a tiara and breastplate, like Calixtus on the northern side of the church, alongside another apostle on the outside. The members of each couple seem engaged in conversation with each other. To the right of the door, Simeon and Isaiah are turned inward toward John the Baptist holding a plate with the Lamb of God, Isaiah having prophesied the birth of a redeeming child, John having foretold it, and Simeon holding Jesus in his arms. The pair on the outside, consisting of Moses holding a tablet of the Law in one hand and the pillar with the bronze serpent in the other, and Abraham grasping his son Isaac by the hair, looks vaguely upward, with Samuel, in the position of the lonely bishop, staring into the distance. The four figures in the left jambs of the central portal are a single gathering, with Mary handing the infant Jesus to Simeon in the center, while Joseph watches from the outer edge and a servant stands by in the position nearest the door. The right side displays two communicative couplings we have seen elsewhere as part of the Infancy of Christ cycle in sculpture or stained glass, the Annunciation of the angel Gabriel to Mary alongside the Visitation of Mary and her cousin Elizabeth.

Among the congenial jamb figures of the west facade of Reims, one stands out as the most expressive and iconic figure of the entire cathedral: the so-called "smiling angel" just to the left of the north door. Angels are by nature gender fluid. Yet, this figure, with its slim curvilinear body, form-fitted gown tucked at the waist, rounded shoulders,

The Smiling Angel

and graceful hand gesture, is remarkably feminine, especially when compared to the angel on the other side of the headless saint—Denis or Nicasius, with its robust body, square shoulders, columnar neck, and square chin. But what about the face itself? And what about the smile? Rounded, mildly microcephalic, graced with almond-shaped eyes, delicate features, a pointed nose and chin, the cocked head of the smiling angel exudes mystery. In keeping with her ambiguous gender, her body hovers between that of an insubstantial angel and the hip-shot carriage of a Gothic Madonna, her hand gesture, between the act of blessing, giving, welcoming, and warning. Slightly malicious, somewhat bantering, nonetheless vulnerable and reticent, shy even, she seems to know something that we do not know. As in the case of the ambiguous facial expression of Leonardo da Vinci's *Mona Lisa*, we are bewildered, forced to read ourselves into the enigmatic smile of the Reims angel, which is, of course, part of the powerful appeal of such works of art for those who accept the psychological gambit. I, for one, cannot resist remembering that the smiling angel of Reims lost half her face in the bombing of the cathedral in 1914 and that she recovered it thanks to reconstructive cosmetic surgery based on a plaster mold taken of the statue in the nineteenth century by archeologists anxious to preserve France's medieval past. And, so, for me, the angel's intriguing expression is less of a smile than a smirk at having survived and triumphed over the deleterious effects of war on art.

THE SOUTH PORTAL

LESS DAMAGED IN THE disastrous fire which originated in the scaffolding of the north tower, the south portal of the west facade is devoted to the Revelation of Saint John, and is unique among Gothic sculpture, though an ample version of the images of John's vision is to be found in the west rose window of the Sainte-Chapelle (see pp. 196–98). Christ in majesty sits in the gable, displaced, again, above the broken arches of the archivolts, which themselves display scenes from the Book of the Apocalypse, spilling over to the sculptural tympanum on the far right buttress of the frontispiece of the cathedral. In the square lower section, an angel escorts John to the place—Patmos—where he will be shown a terrible vision. On the lower register of the triangle of images, the Lamb is shown opening the seven seals (Apocalypse 5:1–12). The middle register depicts the unleashing of horsemen that accompanies the opening of the fourth seal: "And behold a pale horse: and he that sat upon him, his name was Death. And hell followed him" (Apocalypse 6:8).

QUEEN OF THE ROYAL COURT

THE REIMS CENTRAL PORTAL is capped by the Virgin in the gable, queen of the royal court, her hands joined in prayer, her head bowed to receive the crown placed on her head by her son, and surrounded by angels. This dramatic scene is separated from the archivolt by a thick band of wavy masonry curls, marking the difference between the earthly and the heavenly realms, while the space between the frilly peak of the upper gable, a linked lacework of miniature arches, is left open to reveal the rose window which dominates the middle level of the west facade. The voussoirs, reworked at the beginning of the seventeenth century and again in the eighteenth, feature a rendering of the Tree of Jesse motif along with various scenes from the life of Mary amid an array of angels and musicians. The inscription on the non-figural lintel reads: "DEO OPTIMO MAXIMO, SUB INVOCATIONE BEATAE MARIAE VIRGINIS DEI PARAE, TEMPLUM SAECULO XIII° REAEDIFI-CATUM" ("This temple was reconstructed in the eighteenth century in honor of great and good God at the behest of the blessed Virgin Mary, Mother of God"). The Virgin in the Reims trumeau has little of the grace or charm found in the tilted body language and facial expression of the Golden Virgin of Amiens, or even of her colleague to the north, the smiling angel.

KINGS AND ANGELS ATOP REIMS

THE FRONTISPIECE OF Reims Cathedral is divided into four horizontal zones—that of the portals, the great rose window, the gallery of kings, and the towers. The exterior of the rose, which, again, consists of the distinctive Remois round window topped by a triangular spandrel, is flanked on either side by large figures in columned shrines, or aedicules, under decorated pignons. All are connected to Christ after the resurrection—Mary Magdalene and Saint Peter on the right, and

Christ disguised as a pilgrim on the way to Emmaus along with one of the apostles, on the left. The archivolt above the rose window displays scenes from the life of kings David and Solomon, including, on the right, David carrying the head of Goliath to Saul and, on the left, the judgment of Solomon. The large figures atop the broken arch of the rose depict in two tableaux David's slaying of Goliath. On the right, the young shepherd David is pictured among his flock, and, on the left, he launches a stone at the giant.

The depiction of David and Solomon on the west facade is significant, as these are the two Old Testament kings associated not only with force and wisdom, but with the origins of anointing as the essential element of divine kingship. The kings of France passed under the images of David and Solomon on their way to the *sacre* that linked them to the kings who, according to the vision of Jesse, preceded Christ's kingship. The prayer recited by the archbishop as part of the ceremony of consecration or *ordo* for the coronation of Philip Augustus in 1179 exhorted the new king to imitate the virtues of Abraham, Moses, and Joshua, while bringing to the fore the deeds of David and Solomon.

Kingship and coronation dominate the gallery of kings that runs the breadth of the west facade above the rose. In the middle, Clovis, hands joined in prayer, stands up to his waist in a baptismal font decorated on the front with the blind broken arches of a Gothic cathedral. To his left, Saint Remi, holding the bishop's crozier in one hand, blesses the domesticated king of the Franks with the other. Clotilde, wearing the crown of the queen of France, hands her newly baptized husband his own crown, both part of the regalia of royalty bearing the fleurs-de-lys retrospectively associated with the crowning of Clovis. The kings on either side of the sculptural portrayal of monarchy's founding moment bear swords and scepters as they stand guard on pedestals resembling miniature radiating chapels and under trilobe broken arches that terminate in the pointed gables limning the upper edge of the gallery of kings like the teeth of a giant saw. The king who entered Reims Cathedral for consecration was no doubt informed by accompanying clerics about the inspiring presence of David and Solomon, but the phalanx of bigger-than-life kings of France, surpassing in size those of any other cathedral, looked down at the new monarch as a stern visual reminder of the length of tradition and the weight of office.

The kings of the west facade take in the monarch as he arrives for coronation and as he departs to the west for the Abbey of Corbeny to test the curative royal touch (see p. 263), and then to Paris. They are joined, however, by monumental kings in daises on top of the buttresses of the transepts and who stand at attention above and all around the inner perimeter of the crossing where the ceremony of *sacre* takes place. The high kings of the transepts are surrounded by a chorus of angels at the same level atop the buttresses of the nave and choir. The angels, standing on decorated pedestals under protective canopies, bear various liturgical objects, books, reliquaries, scrolls, an aspergillum, a processional cross, a floral baton, a censer, a bowl, and a crown. The angelic figures around the choir of Reims, that is, to the east of the transept, have been compared to those guarding the holy city of Jerusalem in the Revelation of Saint John: "And it had a wall great and high, having twelve gates, and in the gates twelve angels" (Apocalypse 21:12). Yet, there are only eleven. The series is broken by the figure of Christ who, at the center and above the axial chapel, appears to lead the angels around the top of the choir in a procession that may, in fact, reproduce the relationship between the archbishop and the eleven bishoprics dependent upon the metropolitan church of Reims. Together, the angels and kings atop the buttresses, like the pointed fleurs-de-lys of the royal tiara, give the coronation cathedral the appearance of a giant crown.

INSIDE REIMS

Stepping inside Reims, you will understand how the raison d'être of France's coronation cathedral shaped its interior dimensions and altered the feelings produced by the proportions of this unique religious and royal space. The nave is longer, ten bays instead of the eight at Chartres or the seven at Amiens. The width of the transept is reduced relative to the nave, though the transept arms are wider. The five radiating chapels of the choir, again, make it shorter than at Chartres or Amiens. This combination of a longer nave, shallow choir, and enlarged transept crossing reflects the uses to which the cathedral was put. Reims is less a pilgrimage church meant to accommodate visitors circulating around the perimeter of the sanctuary without interrupting the divine service than a gathering place of large numbers of high church officials, nobles, and functionaries of the realm. In fact, the nave itself was double, with both public and private spaces. The first part of the ceremony of *sacre*, an exclusive affair involving ritual interaction between king and clerics, took place between the altar situated in the transept crossing and the prayer screen set almost four bays to the west. Once this semiprivate phase of the *sacre* concluded, the king mounted the prayer screen, erected for each coronation until 1416 and a permanent structure until its removal in the 1740s, and followed the coronation mass. Like a theater which maximizes the size of the stage without sacrificing that of the orchestra, Reims was built for dramatic courtly spectacle.

THE REVERSE WEST WALL

THE UNIQUENESS OF REIMS is written all over the interior west wall where a series of sculptural niches are carved into the masonry around the doors and lower roses. The ensemble of small statues, like chess pieces in "the game of kings and the king of games," are impressive in number—fifty two around the central portal and sixteen around each of the lateral doors—and in the detail with which each summons a story from the Hebrew or Christian Bible or the apocrypha. Some continue motifs on the exterior side of the wall, some introduce new material, but all relate to the themes of kingship or coronation. The lowest register to the right of the central door and just above the sculpted curtain that runs along the base of the reverse wall, as it does on the outside, shows the priest and king Melchizedek offering bread and wine to Abraham dressed as a medieval knight, while a third knight, still bearing his shield, looks on, indicating that they have just returned from battle. In the second row, Saint John the Baptist, between the figures of two apostles, is shown with an axe planted in the trunk of a tree at his feet, as per Matthew 3:10: "For now the axe is laid to the root of the trees. Every tree, therefore, that doth not yield good fruit shall be cut down and cast into the fire." John's executioners, Herod and Herodias, stand in the niches above the Baptist, who triumphs at the center of the fourth rung, between two apostles, holding the Lamb of God. In the sixth register John baptizes Christ, which, as the prototype of all baptisms, ties the reverse interior wall to the outside by summoning Clovis's immersion and anointing in the lintel of the north exterior portal as well as in the gallery of kings.

The effects of disastrous kingship, embodied by Herod, continue in

Inner West Wall

the top three rungs of the left set of reverse niches where he is depicted in the fifth register from the bottom ordering the Massacre of the Innocents, carried out in the sixth set of reverse statues below the Flight into Egypt of Jesus, Mary, and Joseph at the top. The lintel above the door and below the rose is concerned with the afterlife of John the Baptist, portraying as it does the burial of his body along with the disinterment and burning of his bones, images also found along the north side of the wall around the choir at Amiens. Standing in the middle of the lintel above the trumeau which serves as a tall thin pedestal, the figure of headless Saint Nicasius ties the saint and first bishop of Reims to the beheaded Baptist. The association is reinforced by statues, at the level of the lintel, of vandals, Nicasius's executioners, who are themselves flanked by angels, suspended on either side of the thick wall around the doorway and rose window.

Physically, the reverse wall of the west facade presents as a chess-board, a beehive, a pigeon coop, a bookshelf. Each of the figures is small, and the thematic groupings are not obvious to the uninitiated observer who may nonetheless be seduced, as by the serried ranks of the clay warriors of Xi'an or the multiples of Andy Warhol, by their beauty and number alongside the play of similitude and difference between them. But you may wonder how they were used. What role could such small and difficult-to-recognize statues have played in the consecration of kings? I invite you to imagine that, in the time before the actual rite of *sacre* at the altar, the king and his retinue were escorted by clerics in the know, stopping before the statues lodged in the reverse wall to explain the good uses and abuses of kingship. In this respect it functions as a memory palace and a storehouse of wisdom, like the "mirrors of princes," literary and political works addressed to rulers, about good government. The famous examples of wise and wicked rulers were seen by the king before he was anointed and, again, as he exited the central portal of the cathedral as through a triumphal arch which marked him, like a Roman emperor, as divine.

THE GLASS OF REIMS

IT IS HARD NOT TO BE struck by the bright interior of Reims Cathedral. Some of the light which floods the western end is a function of the glass in the tympana of the portals which elsewhere are made of stone. The brilliant effects of the cathedral are also a function of the lack of side chapels whose lower roofs in other churches attenuate light from the outside. Renovations carried out during the "centuries of light" contributed to the luminosity of the interior. Beginning in 1742, the clôtures or walls separating the inner part of the choir from the surrounding ambulatory were replaced by iron grills affording an unimpeded view from the nave through to the chapels radiating off the apse. The *jubé* or screen separating the choir from the nave, actually located three bays west of the crossing, was removed at the same time. Most of all, beginning in the second quarter of the eighteenth century, the canons of the church replaced the medieval stained glass windows in the lower parts of the nave, the transepts, and chapels with lightly patterned grisaille in what seems in retrospect an astonishingly unenlightened attempt to capture the spirit of the Enlightenment. The upper parts of the nave, miraculously intact through the fire that destroyed the roof, were destroyed in the bombings of 1917 which left only lattices of lead. Even so, a heroic effort was made to rescue the shards of glass strewn among the fallen masonry debris. Jacques Simon, whose family had been the guardians of Reims glass since 1640, organized a team of soldiers and firemen to remove vestiges of the windows and to bring the fragments to safety in Paris, which resulted in the rescue of hundreds of square meters of glazing. Once upon a time, the experience of the interior of Reims was like that of Chartres whose rich tenebrous colors transmit an aura of reverence that no longer hovers in the striking blankness and brightness of the cathedral of kings.

Above the reverse statues of the west wall and the small rose in the tympanum, nine lancet arches and windows make what appears to be a gallery of kings and archbishops, joined by two women. The identity of this series of lay and ecclesiastical figures remains a mystery, though the uncrowned king at the center, dressed in a blue robe with gold fleurs-de-lys and standing next to an archbishop, links the series to the rite of *sacre*. The upward-turned sword in the king's right hand is a further clue. Coronation at Reims involved an elaborate "ballet" of the sword in which the archbishop girded and then ungirded the king, unsheathed his sword, bestowed it upon the monarch who passed it to the seneschal or chief administrative officer of the realm, who was obliged to hold the royal sword point in the air until the end of the ceremony. The figures in the glass gallery at the level of the triforium are arranged in symmetrically layered rings.

Moving outward, the king in the middle is flanked by archbishops, who are circled by women, then bishops, and, on the outer edges, kings with long scepters capped by fleurs-de-lys in their hands. Is this a rendering of the coronation of Clovis in the presence of his wife Clotilde, as in the gallery of kings on the outside? That of Charles VII accompanied by Joan of Arc, or of Saint Louis, as suggested by two small castles of Castile of the type that abounds in the Sainte-Chapelle over his head? That there is no way to know with certainty who is being crowned in the glass gallery of the west wall. It attests, nonetheless, to a certain repetitive generic quality of the windows of Reims, which are, with a few exceptions, less wrapped in the identity of particular saints, apostles, popes, patrons, bishops, archbishops, and heroes and heroines of biblical narrative than in the institutional trappings and transfer of royal power in the place where such transfers occur.

Of the windows in the nave, two thirds lack color, and only the four bays nearest the transept crossing contain stained glass figures, which are so highly stylized as to be interchangeable. Each double lancet of the bays on the north and south side of the nave displays a bishop or archbishop beneath a seated king. Each wears and holds the attributes of office, crowns and scepters for royalty, maniples, miters, pectorals, and croziers for those of high ecclesiastical berth. These are windows that were shattered in 1917 and reconstructed after the war on the basis of tracings made by the Simon family beginning in the nineteenth century. The only king identified by name is KAROLUS, in the fourth bay west of the crossing, with no way of telling whether this reference is to Charlemagne or to Charles the Simple who was anointed at Reims in 893. The visually hierarchical relationship of kings on top of archbishops is ambiguous: while physical position signifies superiority, the king could not rule without the unction administered by the archbishop over whom he sits, like the evangelists in the lancets of the south rose of Chartres posed on the shoulders of Old Testament prophets—"pygmies on the shoulders of giants," in the phrase of Bernard of Chartres.

Though the rose windows of Reims managed to escape the attention of the light-seeking canons of the eighteenth century, they have not fared well over the almost nine hundred years since the completion of the north rose in 1241, when the clergy took possession of the choir. The great western rose was badly damaged as the result of a hailstorm in 1886. Restored by Paul Simon at the beginning of the twentieth century, it was shattered in the bombing and fire of 1914, only to be rebuilt by Paul's son Jacques after World War I. This lacy network of stone with twelve radiating petals is focused upon the dormition and the assumption of the Virgin who draws her last breath in the central oculus, surrounded by the twelve apostles in the medallions of the inner ring. The angel musicians of the middle circle accompany Mary to heaven in consonance with the sculptured frieze in the gable of the central portal of the west facade, just on the other side and a little below the rose, which shows Mary crowned in heaven by her son. One is never very far from coronation in the glass and sculptural programs of Reims. The quatrelobe tracery around the outer edge of the western rose is rimmed by angels at the top, prophets cascading down the upper slopes, and crowned kings with fleur-de-lys–tipped scepters all around the lower half.

The rose window in the north arm of the transept was destroyed by storms in 1580 and 1739, at which time certain of the pieces of colored glass removed from the lower parts of the nave were used in its repair. The window was reworked in the nineteenth century, only to be destroyed by a bomb in 1915, rebuilt after the war, and then completely reworked in the 1970s. The theme of the north rose, like the sculptural figures around the opening of the window on the outside, is that of creation. God occupies the central oculus, surrounded by the sun, the moon, angels, and stars. The interior ring of circular medallions features the story of Adam and Eve, whose full-length statues flank the northern rose on the exterior wall of the north tower. The sequence of the stained glass scenes follows only loosely the order of the Genesis story. The Creation of Adam occupies the noon position, while, moving clockwise, the window displays images of Adam and Eve in paradise, Eve spinning while Adam works the land, Eve suckling an infant, and God cursing Cain, who murders Abel at the bottom of the circle. Moving up the left side, we see the successful offering of Abel, the expulsion from paradise, God warning Adam, the eating of the forbidden fruit, and Adam and Eve beneath the tree of the knowledge of good and evil after the Fall. The outer ring of the north rose is filled with angels and the animals of Creation, while the spandrel on top shows the Virgin nursing Jesus. The rose of the south transept, redone in 1934, shows Christ, arms outstretched, at the center, surrounded by the tetramorph, winged symbols of the four evangelists; in the oculus, angels in prayer in the second ring, and apostles identified by name around the outer edge.

The Christological contents of the three roses of Reims are an exception to the general theme and tenor of earthly—ecclesiastical and royal—power expressed elsewhere in the glazings of the cathedral. If kings dominate the gallery between the two west roses, and archbishops and kings the high lancets of the nave, an archbishop and bishops are strategically arrayed in the high windows of the choir so as to affirm the authority of the metropolitan church, the seat of the archbishop, over the dependent churches of the region. The center or axial chapel, facing due east, features in the left lancet an image of the Virgin and Child in the upper half over a schematic representation of Reims. On the left, a monumental Crucifixion sits atop a full-length portrait of Archbishop

Henri de Braine, who is identified by name. Gold fleurs-de-lys on a blue background, the symbol of French royalty, run up both sides and meet at the top of the lancet. Henri was the great-grandson of King Louis VI, and it was Louis's great-great-grandson Saint Louis who rescued him from the civil unrest of 1233–36.

You may remember (see p. 275) that Henri de Braine served as archbishop during the period of intense urban unrest (1233–36), and he was the likely donor of the window, under pressure to contribute to the fabric of the cathedral alongside the canons and the bourgeois he brought to heel in their rebellion against his authority. Henri's contribution was not, however, without benefit. Not only was his hold over Reims legitimized by his commanding portrait under Christ, but he is allied with the cathedral of Reims under Mary. The five pairs of lancet windows on either side of the portraits of Christ, Mary, Henri de Braine, and the cathedral each reproduces the defining layout of the central panels, with an apostle on top of each lancet, in turn, above a bishop next to his church. To the south, Paul and James are seen above the bishop and cathedral of Laon, Thomas and Philip, above the bishop and cathedral of Châlons; to the south, Peter and Andrew sit above the bishop and church of Soissons, John and James the Less over the Bishop of Beauvais and his church. The proportions visually plotted by the high windows of the choir hold that Christ stands in relation to the apostles, his followers, as Henri de Braine, the archbishop, stands in relation to the bishops, his followers. The bishops, moreover, as the avatars of the apostles under whom they are pictured, make Henri the heir to Christ under whom his portrait, the only one identified by a name and not a function, looks out at the eleven members of the high ecclesiastical court assembled around him like the eleven angels and Christ in the pinnacles of the roof above their heads.

THE MODERN WINDOWS OF REIMS

OUTSIDE OF THE REALM OF royal or ecclesiastical power, a number of windows installed at Reims after the Great War, modern by any standard, are the most interesting of the cathedral. The lancets below the southern rose were devoid of stained glass until 1954 when the Corporation of Wine Growers of Champagne commissioned Jacques Simon to create three panels depicting grape growing and winemaking. The

The Champagne Makers Windows

winemakers windows, executed in a deliberately retro-medieval style, display an astonishing mix of biblical references to the fruit of the vine, wine as part of the sacrament of the Eucharist, and the tools and techniques of wine production in the region of Champagne. In each of the panels, marginal decoration surrounds illustrations of viticulture entwined in a grapevine winding up the center. The plant stock at the bottom stands in clear reference to the shoot protruding from the belly of the sleeping Jesse in the Tree of Jesse windows found in almost every Gothic cathedral, including a nineteenth-century reproduction now in the southern part of the ambulatory of Reims.

Under the watchful eye of Saint Vincent, patron saint of winemakers, the figures of the left panel plant and plow the soil, trim and tend the vines, as per Isaiah 5:7: "For the vineyard of the Lord of hosts is the house of Israel: and the man of Juda, his pleasant plant." In the top panel two men dressed in costumes from the ancient world, a comet and a palm tree in the background, carry an enormous cluster of grapes suspended between them on a pole, an illustration of the scene in the Book of Numbers in which Moses, still in the desert, sends spies to view the land of Canaan: "As forward as far as the torrent of the cluster of grapes, they cut off a branch with its cluster of grapes, which two men carried upon a lever" (Numbers 13:24). Canaan is, as the spies chosen from the twelve tribes of Israel recognize, the symbol of the prosperity of the promised land—"which in the very deed floweth with milk and honey and may be known by these fruits" (Numbers 13:28)—and that is directly related to the prosperity of the vintners of Champagne. Like the platonic ideal of a wine list from the finest of French restaurants, square panels on each side of the core depictions of wine growing, display the names, along with an image of the village church, of eleven vineyards of regional wine production. This framing motif, which draws the villages in the orbit of Reims into the visual program of the cathedral, may seem like shameless self-promotion. It belongs, nonetheless, to a tradition reaching back to the Middle Ages of relations, including economic exchange, between the mother church and the surrounding countryside.

The central panel, meant to be read from the bottom up, begins with a written inscription—"Homage of the Corporation of Champagne and its Allied Industries"—and features barrel makers, the harvesting, transportation, sorting, and pressing of grapes, and, at the top, two angels turning the "mystical press," an allegory of the blood of Christ from Isaiah 63:3: "I have trodden the winepress alone." The borders feature a display, as if at a local agricultural fair, of the winegrowers' tools—rakes, hoes, shovels, watering cans, shears, funnels, baskets, and barrels.

At the bottom of the right panel of the winemakers window a lavish table replete with a variety of foods shows a bottle of champagne surrounded by six champagne flutes, like stars around a radiant sun. Moving up the core, John the Baptist, patron saint of those who work in wine cellars, stands beneath a man turning champagne bottles in a cellar rack, part of the process of producing sparkling white wine. The central image of the panel is that of Dom Pérignon, the famous cellar master of the Benedictine Abbey of Hautvillers, who perfected a number of wine making techniques at the end of the seventeenth century and whose name is practically synonymous with champagne. The top of the right panel of the winemakers window depicts the miraculous transformation of water into wine performed by Christ at the Wedding at Cana. The names of the wine-producing villages and their local churches in the margins bring the total to forty-four, in addition to the coats of arms and names of Epernay at the bottom of the left panel and Reims on the right, labels associated with champagne.

While the winemakers windows at Reims look back to the medieval tradition of narrative and figural glazing, several of the newer windows are more firmly rooted in the abstract, and even minimalist, art of the middle of the twentieth century. Between 1961 and 1981, Jacques Simon's daughter Brigitte Simon-Marq designed a total of seven windows in the minimalist style, grisaille-worthy of the etymological root in *gris* or "grey." The beige, pale green, faint grey, and traces of blue of this complex web of splintery segments, possibly evoking the shattering of glass in World War I, was titled by its makers *The Water of Life*, referring both to the restoration of that which has been broken and to its position beneath the baptismal font in the south arm of the transept. It is interesting to note that *The Water of Life* is the only work at Reims in any medium that can be assigned with certainty to a woman.

THE CHAGALL WINDOWS

In 1970 the Simon stained glass studio began to work with the artist Marc Chagall (d. 1985) on a set of windows now in the axial chapel. The commission was not without controversy, as Chagall was Jewish and had neither hidden the memory of traditional Jewish life in the shtetl of Vitebsk, where he grew up, nor had he shied away from core Christian themes in his paintings after emigrating to Paris before World War I. He was known, in fact, for combining material from the Hebrew and Christian Bibles. A 1938 painting, *The White Crucifixion*, portrays Christ, His head covered in the Jewish mode and wearing a tallit or traditional Jewish prayer shawl as a loincloth. Images of torment hover menacingly all around the Crucifixion—burning villages turned upside down as Cossacks arrive with drawn swords, fleeing Jews grasping a Torah or their belongings, refugees aboard an overcrowded boat—in a clear visual analogy between Christ as a suffering Jew and the pogroms and persecutions of the first half of the twentieth century. In a work completed shortly after his own flight from France to New York in 1941, *The Descent from the Cross*, Chagall sounds the depths of his own identification with Christ by substituting for the traditional "I.N.R.I." at the top of the cross the letters "MARC CH." An angel floating in the air

The Chagall Windows

brings the gift of brushes and a palette to the crucified painter, the title of another work which shows him on the cross, brushes and palette in hand. A work of 1943, *The Yellow Crucifixion*, depicts Christ on the cross with phylacteries on His head, His right arm extended to touch a Torah, while, in the foreground, a mother, father, and child escape on a donkey in clear allusion to Mary, Joseph, and Jesus's Flight into Egypt and the Massacre of the Innocents. In combining Jewish and Christian motifs, Chagall famously confessed that, "For me, Christ has always represented the prime example of the Jewish martyr. . . . But he is only one, with his Jewish mother, surrounded by our Jewish prophets."

There was every reason to believe that Chagall, in the commission for the axial windows of Reims, would continue in the line of blended traditions, especially since the window the artist designed for the cathedral of Metz (1958–64) mixes images of the sacrifice of Isaac with that of

Jesus. And, yet, of Chagall's work, the Reims windows are those which make the least connection between Judaism and Christianity. The two lancets on the north side of the axial chapel offer a modern version of the Tree of Jesse. The rendering is, in fact, so free-form that the traditional function of the Jesse Tree, to establish a direct genealogical affiliation between the dreaming Jesse and the royal ancestors of Christ, is attenuated. Only Saul, Jesse's son David, and David's son Solomon are recognizable with the top branches of the tree swept into whorls of color—blues and greens, patches of brown and turquoise, and dots of red—that render time synchronous and lineage moot.

The central panel of the Chagall windows features, in the left lancet, scenes of Abraham's sacrifice of Isaac, a climbing of Mount Moriah, the father's pinning, knife raised, his son upon a pyre of logs, and the immolation of a lamb in Isaac's place. The crucified Christ, by far the largest and most recognizable figure of the Chagall windows, dominates the right central lancet above the traditional motifs of Deposition and Resurrection. The south lancets display, in vivid reds, purples, oranges, and greens, scenes linked directly to the history of the cathedral of Reims and France. The Baptism of Clovis occupies the lower left quadrant with the thirteenth-century cathedral in the background. Above Clovis, Saint Louis, arms outstretched like those of Christ, sits under a tent dispensing the justice for which he was famous to the crowd assembled before him. Several images from the Parable of the Good Samaritan—the tending of the wounded traveler and his transport to safety on a horse—float above Saint Louis. The parable of human generosity to strangers from the Book of Luke figures elsewhere in Chagall's stained glass oeuvre, notably in the Good Samaritan window of the Rockefeller Union Church in Pocantico Hills, New York, where it had special meaning for the artist who was saved from certain death in Europe through the generosity of David Rockefeller whose father had in the 1920s rescued the cathedral of Reims. The right lancet of the Chagall windows of Reims features at the bottom the entrance of Joan of Arc into Reims in 1429 below the *sacre* of Charles VII of France (see p. 280).

Chagall's windows are considered great artistic works of reconciliation between Christians and Jews after the Holocaust, and there is something to it. After their completion in 1974, Archbishop Ménager, who apparently had urged the artist to minimize the Jewish elements of his creation, declared that he was pleased with the artist's faithfulness to

Christian tradition. Chagall himself was convinced that the mélange of religious cultures could only contribute to mutual recognition of their intimate links. Windows on either side of the Chagall axial bay of Reims were designed by German artist Imi Knoebel to express the spirit of reconciliation between Germany and France. The primary colors of these glazings—four shades of blue, three of red, two of yellow, and white—take the art of the glassmaker beyond the modernist esthetic of Chagall, for whom shapes and figures are still recognizable, beyond the abstract design of Brigitte Simon-Marq's benevolent *Water of Life*, to a level of abstract expressionism that blurs the boundary between reconciliation and aggression.

Leaving the cathedral of Reims, it is worth stopping for a moment before a tombstone affixed to the wall of the north arm of the transept, that of Hugues Libergier. The names of the architects or master masons

Hugues Libergier Tombstone

of Reims Cathedral are known because they were written on four corners of an octagonal labyrinth set in the floor between the third and fourth bays of the nave, until the canons, apparently annoyed at children playing in its enticing maze, removed it in the eighteenth century. Libergier's tomb, however, displays a unique example of the formal portrait of a cathedral builder holding in his left hand one of the tools of his trade, a full-length rod for plotting ratios, and, at his feet, a compass and square for the mapping of the finer components of cathedral design. Hugues is framed by columns decorated with floral capitals and a trilobe arch under a gable capped by crockets running up both slopes of the roof. In his left hand, the master mason holds a model of a church, identified by the inscription that runs around the four edges of the tombstone: "HERE LIES MASTER HUGUES LIBERGIER WHO BEGAN THIS CHURCH IN THE YEAR OF THE INCARNATION TWELVE HUNDRED AND TWENTY NINE THE TUESDAY OF EASTER AND DIED IN THE YEAR OF THE INCARNATION TWELVE SIXTY THREE THE SATURDAY AFTER EASTER." The church that Hugues Libergier built, the abbey church of Saint Nicaise of Reims, was destroyed by revolutionary vandals in 1798, while the cathedral of Reims survived the Revolution, the Franco-Prussian War of 1870–71, and two world wars in the last century.

Vestiges of the last war are visible as you leave the cathedral, not in the form of damaged stone or glass, but as words set in the pavement in front of the church. So, before leaving Reims for a glass of champagne in the heart of champagne country or a visit to one of the nearby battlefields, be sure to take in the plaque in German and French, addressed in Charles de Gaulle's voice to the archbishop of the cathedral. It commemorates a mass of peace celebrated by the leaders of the former warring countries: "EXCELLENCE, THE CHANCELLOR ADENAUER AND I COME INTO YOUR CATHEDRAL TO SEAL THE RECONCILIATION OF FRANCE AND GERMANY. CHARLES DE GAULLE, SUNDAY, JULY 8, 1962 11:02 A.M." The precision of the hour and minute is symbolic: the President of the French Republic meant to draw attention to the hour—11:00 a.m.—that the armistice between Germany and France was declared on November 11, 1918—the eleventh hour of the eleventh day of the eleventh month. Reims had become a significant site of rapprochement between the former enemies, and the symbolic two minutes after the formal end of hostilities projects both caution and hope for the future, which has been ratified in subsequent meetings. On July 5, 1987, Chancellor Helmut Kohl met President Jacques Chirac, and on July 8, 2012, Angela Merkel met François Hollande to reaffirm at a distance of twenty-five and fifty years, respectively, and on the same sacred spot the historic meeting between Adenauer and de Gaulle. The cathedral survives not only as a durable monument to those who built and repaired it over the centuries but also as a witness to an investment beyond national identity in the spirit of a building that is more than wood, glass, metal, and stone.

EPILOGUE

Each of the cathedrals we have visited via *Paris and Her Cathedrals* occupies a particular place in the constellation of churches in and around the Île de France: Saint-Denis as the place of royal burial; Notre-Dame as the center of Paris and eventually all of France; Chartres as an immense gallery of original stained glass and a catalyst to crusade; the Sainte-Chapelle as the private chapel of Saint Louis, the repository of the relics of the Passion, and a new Jerusalem on the Seine; Amiens as the largest and most perfect; Reims as the site of the coronation of kings and, after World War I, a wound upon the body politic only healed in the 1960s. Each revels in its own traditions, history, and style, in its celebration of local as well as universal saints, its especially valuable relics, its contributions to commerce, and, like today's universities, hospitals, cultural centers, and museums, its honoring of particularly generous patrons. And yet, the cathedrals of Paris are remarkably alike in structure. With the exception of the Sainte-Chapelle, each is in the shape of a cross with nave, choir, transept arms, a three-portal west facade, a system of external buttresses to support high walls and wide vaults, and tall windows that reach, like the tall trees once considered to have inspired them, toward the light.

As you move among the cathedrals of Paris, you also encounter much that is familiar in the decorative arts around their entrances, atop their towers and spires, on the walls separating ambulatory from choir, and all up and down the stained glass windows that have survived from the Middle Ages or that have been restored. The Creation and the Fall, Moses holding the tablets of the Law, Abraham's sacrifice of Isaac, the Tree of Jesse, cycles of the Infancy of Jesus, including the Annunciation, Visitation, Birth, Massacre of the Innocents, and Flight into Egypt, choruses of angels and patriarchs, life-size sculptures of Mary with the infant Jesus on her hip and the Dormition of the Virgin, the Last Judgment and the redemption of souls at the end of time are but a few of the motifs from both the Hebrew and Christian Bibles that we have seen repeatedly in our journey around the cathedrals of northern France. The general nature of certain images, events, and themes attests to common beliefs on the part of the churchmen who built the cathedrals, an important component of an overall cathedral effect. In the High Middle Ages, pilgrims encountered familiar visual cues as proof of the omnipresence of the core message of Christianity wherever they might travel.

The repetition of similar motifs throughout the cathedrals draws attention to the popularity of some themes and figures but not others. The Bible of the poor is an abridged anthology of extracts, like a medieval florilegium or a collection of quotations from classical authors or Church Fathers. And what may seem like a full rendering of the holy text is, in fact, an amalgam of relatively few stories from among the vast array of material from both testaments and the apocrypha. Guided by the canons responsible for the fabric of the church, medieval sculptors and glassmakers made choices, and the events, scenes, figures and stories not adopted far outnumber those that were.

Choices made at the outset were repeated in the buildings erected throughout the Age of Cathedrals, though they were reproduced in different media, in different locations, and in different styles. The Tree of Jesse, originally at Saint-Denis, was copied both in glass and in the voussoirs around the northern portal at Chartres, in glass at the Sainte-Chapelle, in sculptural relief on the south portal of the west facade of Amiens, and on the royal or central portal of Reims. Scenes from the Infancy narrative are to be found in the stained glass of the choir of Saint-Denis, relief sculpture in the tympanum of the south portal of the west facade of Notre-Dame Paris, the glass of the west wall of Chartres as well as the choir of the Sainte-Chapelle, and in the retable of the axis chapel of Amiens. In this habit of reiteration, the sculptors and glass painters who circulated among the cathedrals of the Parisian basin did what artists have done in every age, whether Roman sculptors inspired by Greek forbears, Dutch genre painters of the seventeenth century imitating one another, or cubist painters whose endless bottles, violins, and newspaper clippings sometimes make it hard to distinguish between them. Artists learn from each other. With little direct knowledge of the biblical text, medieval sculptors and glassmakers copied what they had seen. In the absence of books, this is one of the ways the Gothic cathedral served as a teaching tool for craftsmen who were themselves most likely illiterate.

Artists who decorated Gothic cathedrals were less like theologians who taught there or clerics who prayed there and more like those later Renaissance artists, who may have painted religious subjects, but for whom art was its own religion. This step in the direction of art for art's sake, only fully realized in the late 1800s, accounts for our experience of their work not solely as a revelation of the precepts of Christianity, but also as objects of great beauty, reminders of an underlying mystery—call it faith, inspiration, vision, talent, creativity, or genius—that fosters the frisson of a spirit in the artful shaping of otherwise inert—and even secular—matter.

One of the pleasures of writing a volume like this is that one's perspective changes in the process of writing. To wit: I came to realize in looking more closely at the cathedrals that I have visited frequently over the years the extent to which they belong to more than one tradition. Not only do they hark back to the legacy of Judaism as well as Christianity, to the great reservoir of culture of Byzantium as well as the Latin West; they also combine both sacred and profane elements of their surroundings. The religious iconography on their walls is mixed with images from the secular world around them. The very term "secular," arising from the Latin *saeculum*, means "generation," "lifetime," "century," "spirit of the age," "fashion," and refers to worldly as opposed to religious things.

Powerful knights and political figures, including Charlemagne, stand tall in the high glass windows of Chartres whose southern jambs, along with the glass of the Sainte-Chapelle, built on the eve of the seventh crusade, are imbued with crusaders doing the Lord's work via military means. They may be the equivalents of today's entrepreneurs and industrialists whose names and portraits adorn the walls of our universities, showing their reverence for the institution's mission of education and research, while having pursued other professional paths. The Works of the Months and the signs of the zodiac, inherited from pagan culture, appear in sculpture and glass at Saint-Denis, Notre-Dame Paris, Chartres, and Amiens. Building trades and local merchants dominate the donor windows at Chartres. Woad producers figure in glass and external sculpture at Amiens. The dishonest draper greets us as we enter by the north transept portal at Reims, while the laborers who contributed to the construction of the cathedral look down at us from grimacing masks and heavily burdened Atlantides. They are the cousins of the fantastical chimera and gargoyles, including the strix, the birds of prey, and Ahasver the Wandering Jew, atop Notre-Dame Paris.

Cathedral-building was an enormous engine of economic growth, a source of immense employment over decades and even centuries, a conduit of exchange extending via roads and rivers into the quarries and forests of the region, and in some cases throughout the Parisian basin. The Age of Cathedrals coincided with a first phase of what Max Weber calls the "capitalist spirit," associated with the Renaissance of the sixteenth century but nonetheless present in that of the twelfth and thirteenth centuries. This was a period of immense growth in the size and shape of cities, the revival of long-range trade routes, and the return of a money economy, all commerce conducted in an urban environment with such high churches at its center. Cathedrals concentrated capital among the canons and bishop with landholdings in the surrounding countryside, and generated income for local businesses from sufferers drawn to town for miracle cures and pilgrims seeking salvation for their souls. The bishop guaranteed the safety of roads necessary for trade along with the honesty of exchange at the commercial fairs under his jurisdiction and in the market stalls that often abutted the church itself.

A large element of the secularization of the High Middle Ages was linguistic. This is the period that welcomed the return of writing in almost every area of human endeavor, and the rise of literature in the vernacular tongues as against Church Latin. The first epics in Old French along with the love lyrics written in Provençal, the language of southern France, were aimed at increasingly literate lay audiences and were accompanied by comic tales, the fabliaux, detailing the everyday habits and deceitful dealings of merchants, artisans, clerics, and peasants. Written to entertain the bourgeois inhabitants of towns in the orbit of cathedrals, these earthy and often ribald stories were initial seeds of European literary realism, best known to Italian readers through the *Decameron* of Boccaccio and to the English-speaking world through *The Canterbury Tales* of Geoffrey Chaucer. The love lyrics which emigrated from the South to northern France in the mid-1100s were the first examples of Western romantic love, a cult legitimizing adoration of noble ladies alongside worship of the Virgin Mary. Beginning in the twelfth century, men of distinction were required to love a woman of flesh and blood; the more they loved, the more they suffered; and the more they suffered, the more noble they seemed. From the medieval version of secular love, it is a straight shot to the Romantic poets and novelists of the nineteenth century and a certain kind of trouble for lovers ever since.

The university just to the south of Notre-Dame in Paris's Latin Quarter spawned the secularization of religion, the growth of philosophy out of theology. Peter Abelard (d. 1141) sought to introduce reason into faith, and he was not alone. The recapture of the liberal arts from their pagan past is depicted at Chartres around the tympanum of the south portal of the west facade. And in Paris, the logical writings of ancient philosophers, Aristotle in particular, bear witness to the return of dialectic and debate, seen in the dados on the south side of the nave of Notre-Dame. These were teaching tools capable of producing truth in the first instance in distinction to mere citation of the early Church Fathers or blind belief. Abelard's ecclesiastical enemies forced him to toss into a fire with his own hand the book in which he tried to make logical sense of how the one of the Trinity could be three, or the three one—still a tall order without philosophy as the handmaiden of unexamined trust.

How is it that the construction of such monumental religious buildings coincided with a secularization of culture and of the everyday practices—manufacturing and transporting goods to market, buying and selling, working for wages, calculating cost, profit, and interest according to the bourgeois time of clocks?

The temporal turn that is no less a feature of the Age of Cathedrals than the buildings themselves suggests that the churches in the orbit of Paris were both an expression of religious fervor and a bulwark against the incursion of worldly pursuits and ideas. The more traditional modes of religious belief came into question, the higher and larger and more elaborate the cathedral became as a monument to faith, also understood as a compensation for loss of faith. In this, the Gothic moment was, again, a first step in the direction of the Renaissance of the sixteenth century, when, according to the tenets of the Reformation, an individual might read the Bible on his own in the vernacular and relate directly to God in the absence of clergy. Thus, a displacement of the reverence once reserved for God toward man, as in Shakespeare's "what a piece of work is man" and the philosopher Michel de Montaigne's (d. 1592) exploration of the inner self as an essential component of the human condition. The loss of faith that made the cathedrals possible in the first place will culminate in the Enlightenment by a transformation of reason into a religion. Cathedrals were, after all, rebaptized as "temples of reason" after the Revolution of 1789 which brought the divestment of the clergy, the partial destruction of churches, and the scattering of their relics along with the enormous treasure accumulated over the course of half a millennium.

In the wake of the democratic revolutions of the eighteenth century, the cathedrals of northern France summon a spectrum of current meanings. For the casual tourist they are reliable sites of wonder which, in the phrase of the famous Michelin Guide, are "worth the trip." For the historian they are a rich source of information about the relationship between power, money, and piety throughout the Middle Ages, and for the art historian, a repository of valuable images and artifacts. Inhabitants of cities defined by their medieval cathedrals may well be proud of them, may even profit from the visitors drawn to town because of them, though they never step foot inside or even look up to take in their full measure. The average French person living far from the capital may not even be aware of her cathedrals, until, of course, one of them is menaced, as was the case during the 2019 fire at Notre-Dame which became a national catastrophe. For believing Roman Catholics, the cathedrals still resonate with religious feeling, proof of the enduring truth of a religion that has survived the vicissitudes of modernity. The reader of this book, now an informed visitor to one or more of the cathedrals in and around Paris, will, I hope, experience some of the delight along with the spiritual power that flows from any strong work of art and that connects us—via beauty beheld—to something older, bigger, better, and more mysteriously meaningful than ourselves.

ACKNOWLEDGMENTS

I am indebted to my students at Yale and to my medievalist colleagues, chief among them Paul Freedman and Jacqueline Jung with whom the chance to teach as a team has deepened my understandings of medieval art and history. I am also appreciative of what I have learned from the writings of Stephen Murray and for his generosity, along with that of Painton Cowen, in sharing their collections of images of Gothic cathedrals while I have been pinned close to home waiting for the pestilence to pass. This book could never have seen the light of day without Bob Weil, whose readerly wisdom and editorial eye of the lynx are without peer.

GLOSSARY

Many of the terms are basic and can be found at:
https://www.pitt.edu/~medart/menuglossary/index.htm.

AEDICULE—A small shrine, or, in classical architecture, a niche.

AMBULATORY—A semicircular or polygonal aisle around the east end of the choir, reserved for canons or clergy, and chapels radiating from the apse.

APSE—A vaulted extension or projection from the choir at the east end of the church, containing the altar, and generally circular or polygonal in shape.

ARCADE—A series of arches supported by columns or piers between the nave and side aisles to the west of the transept crossing.

ARCHIVOLT—Bands or moldings surrounding an arched opening.

BARREL VAULT—A vault forming a half-cylinder.

BAS RELIEF—A sculpture, carving, or molding in low relief from a flat background.

CANON—A permanent member of the clergy of a cathedral, responsible for the maintenance of the divine office, daily prayer, as well as the "fabric": construction and upkeep of the building.

CAPITAL—A decorative element that divides a column or pier from the masonry it supports.

CHAPTER—The union of the canons of a cathedral, who meet in the chapter house.

CHOIR—The area of the church between the transept and main apse. It is the area where the service is sung, and the main or high altar is located.

CLERESTORY—An upper story of a building with windows above the tribune level and adjacent roofs.

CORBEL—A piece of stone jutting from a wall to carry a superincumbent weight.

CRYPT—An underground chamber for relics or tombs.

GISANT—a reclining tomb statue.

GRISAILLE—Monochromal painting on glass, in distinction to saturated colored glass in many hues.

JAMB—A vertical element of a doorway or window frame.

JAMB STATUE—Statues carved on the jambs of a doorway or window. Jamb statues were often human religious figures.

LANCET—A slender, pointed window.

LINTEL—A flat horizontal beam which spans the space between two supports, also one of the horizontal bands of carving at the bottom of a tympanum.

MANDORLA—An almond-shaped motif in which Christ or the Virgin sits.

MULLION—The vertical element that separates the lancets of a window.

NARTHEX—A low projection at the western end of a church, like a porch.

NAVE—The central longitudinal space of a cathedral, usually flanked on its long sides by aisles which are separated from the nave by columns or piers.

OCULUS—A round or eye-like window.

OGIVAL VAULT—An arch with a pointed apex.

PORTAL—Any doorway or entrance but especially one that is large and imposing.

PIER—An upright support within the interior of the cathedral.

PIGNON—A gable.

PINNACLE—The pointed termination of a spire, buttress, or other extremity of a building.

PRAYER SCREEN—Also known as a choir screen, a rood screen, or a *jubé*. A partition between the nave and the choir, often heavily decorated, which separates the area in which the public prays from the area reserved for the prayer of canons and clerics.

QUATREFOIL OR QUATRELOBE—An ornamental form which has four lobes or foils.

RELIQUARY—A container for relics, often in the shape of a church or of the body part which it houses.

RIB, RIBBED VAULT—An arch of masonry, often molded, which forms part of the framework on which a vault rests.

ROSE WINDOW—A circular window composed of patterned tracery arranged in petal-like formation.

SHIELD BOSS—A keystone used in vaulting to provide a junction for intersecting ribs.

SPANDREL—The roughly triangular wall space between two adjacent arches.

SPIRE—An elongated, pointed structure which rises from a tower, turret, or roof.

TRANSEPT—A rectangular area which cuts across the main axis of a basilica-type building and projects beyond it. The transept gives a basilica the shape of a cross and usually serves to separate the main area of the building from the apse at the east end.

TRANSEPT CROSSING—The area of a church where the nave, choir, and transepts intersect.

TREFOIL—An ornamental shape that has three foils or lobes.

TRIBUNE—An upper story over the aisle which opens onto the nave or choir. The tribune corresponds in length and width to the dimensions of the aisle below it.

TRIFORIUM—A narrow passage in the thickness of the wall with arches opening onto the nave at the level of the clerestory windows or below the clerestory.

TRUMEAU—Vertical architectural member at the center of the portal that supports the lintel and tympanum.

TYMPANUM—The semicircular area enclosed by the arch above the lintel of an arched entryway and surrounded by the rings of the archivolt.

VOUSSOIR—One of the rounded- or wedge-shaped rings that make up an arch above the tympanum.

SUGGESTIONS FOR
FURTHER READING

Branner, Robert, ed. *Chartres Cathedral.* Norton Critical Studies in Art History. New York: W. W. Norton, 1969.

Cohen, Meredith. *The Sainte-Chapelle and the Construction of Sacral Monarchy. Royal Architecture in Thirteenth-Century Paris.* New York: Cambridge University Press, 2015.

Crosby, Sumner McKnight. *The Royal Abbey of Saint-Denis from Its Beginnings to the Death of Suger, 475–1151.* Edited and completed by Pamela Z. Blum. Yale Publications in the History of Art. New Haven: Yale University Press, 1987.

Favier, Jean. *The World of Chartres.* New York: Harry N. Abrams, 1990.

Fitchen, John. *The Construction of Gothic Cathedrals. A Study of Medieval Vault Erection.* Chicago: University of Chicago Press, 1961.

Focillon, Henri. *The Art of the West in the Middle Ages.* Vol. II. *Gothic Art.* Ithaca, New York: Cornell University Press, 1980.

Frankl, Paul. *Gothic Architecture.* New Haven: Yale University Press, 2000.

Gerson, Paula Lieber, ed. *Abbot Suger and Saint-Denis. A Symposium.* New York: The Metropolitan Museum of Art, 1986.

Hahn, Cynthia. *The Reliquary Effect: Enshrining the Sacred Object.* London: Reaktion Books Ltd., 2017.

Jordan, Alyce A. *Visualizing Kingship in the Windows of the Sainte-Chapelle.* Turnhout, Belgium: Brepols, 2002.

Jung, Jacqueline. *Eloquent Bodies. Movement, Expression, and the Human Figure in Gothic Sculpture.* New Haven: Yale University Press, 2020.

Mâle, Emile. *The Gothic Image. Religious Art in France of the Thirteenth Century.* New York: Harper Torchbook, 1958.

Murray, Stephen. *Notre-Dame of Amiens. Life of the Gothic Cathedral.* New York: Columbia University Press, 2021.

———. *Plotting Gothic.* Chicago: University of Chicago Press, 2014.

Panofsky, Erwin. *Gothic Architecture and Scholasticism: An Inquiry into the Anal-*

ogy of the Arts, Philosophy, and Religion in the Middle Ages. New York: Meridian Books, 1957.

Sandron, Dany and Andrew Tallon. *Notre Dame Cathedral: Nine Centuries of History*. University Park: Pennsylvania State University Press, 2020.

Scott, Robert A. *The Gothic Enterprise. A Guide to Understanding the Medieval Cathedral*. Berkeley: University of California Press, 2003.

Simson, Otto von. *The Gothic Cathedral: Origins of Gothic Architecture and the Medieval Concept of Order*. New York: Harper Torchbook, 1962.

Viollet-le-Duc, Eugène Emmanuel. *Lectures on Architecture*. 2 vols. New York: Dover Publications, 1987.

Williams, Jane Welch. *Bread, Wine, & Money. The Windows of the Trades at Chartres Cathedral*. Chicago: University of Chicago Press, 1993.

Williamson, Paul. *Gothic Sculpture 1140–1300*. New Haven: Yale University Press, 1995.

Wilson, Christopher. *The Gothic Cathedral: The Architecture of the Great Church*. London: Thames & Hudson, 1990.

WEBSITES FOR FURTHER
EXPLORATION OF IMAGES

MAPPING GOTHIC

A wonderful collection of images from all over France and England, with pictures and panoramas, maintained by Columbia University Media Center for History of Art: https://mcid.mcah.columbia.edu/art-atlas/mapping-gothic/map

Saint-Denis:
https://mcid.mcah.columbia.edu/art-atlas/mapping-gothic/saint-denis
-basilique

Notre-Dame Paris:
https://mcid.mcah.columbia.edu/art-atlas/mapping-gothic/paris
-cath%C3%A9drale-notre-dame

Chartres:
https://mcid.mcah.columbia.edu/art-atlas/mapping-gothic/chartres
-cath%C3%A9drale-notre-dame

Sainte-Chapelle:
https://mcid.mcah.columbia.edu/art-atlas/mapping-gothic/paris-sainte
-chapelle
https://play.google.com/store/apps/details?id=com.cmn.vitrauxsaintechapelle
&hl=fr&gl=US

Amiens:
https://mcid.mcah.columbia.edu/art-atlas/mapping-gothic/amiens
-cath%C3%A9drale-notre-dame

Reims:
https://mcid.mcah.columbia.edu/art-atlas/mapping-gothic/reims
 -cath%C3%A9drale-notre-dame

THE ONLINE STAINED GLASS PHOTOGRAPHIC ARCHIVE

An extremely rich collection of English and French Stained Glass and some
sculpture: https://www.therosewindow.com/pilot/index.htm

LIFE OF A CATHEDRAL: NOTRE-DAME OF AMIENS

A wonderfully interactive site for Amiens, complete with virtual tours:
http://projects.mcah.columbia.edu/amiens-arthum/content/home-page

IMAGES OF MEDIEVAL ART AND ARCHITECTURE

http://www.medart.pitt.edu/image/France/mainfran.html

Especially rich for Chartres:
http://www.medart.pitt.edu/image/France/Chartres/Chartres-Cathedral/
 chartres-main.html

INDEX

Note: Page numbers in *italics* refer to illustrations.

ABOUT THE AUTHOR

R. Howard Bloch is Sterling Professor of French and Humanities at Yale University. He attended Amherst College and Stanford University and has taught at the State University of New York at Buffalo, the University of California, Berkeley, and Columbia University. Author of numerous works on medieval and modern French literature and culture, he is a fellow of the American Academy of Arts and Sciences, the American Philosophical Society, and is an officer in the French Order of Arts and Letters.